Christ
LIBERATION OF THE WORLD TODAY
CHARLES MASSABKI
Translated by Sr. Eloise Thérèse Mescall

CHRIST: LIBERATION OF THE WORLD TODAY

By the same author:

Le Sacrement de l'amour.
            (The Sacrament of Love)
Le Christ, rencontre de deux amours.
            (Christ, Encounter of Two Loves)
Le péché originel, peut-on y croire encore?
            (Can one still believe in original sin?)

LIBERATION OF THE WORLD TODAY

CHARLES MASSABKI
Translated by Sr. Eloise Therese Mescall

ALBA · HOUSE   NEW · YORK

SOCIETY OF ST. PAUL, 2187 VICTORY BLVD., STATEN ISLAND, NEW YORK 10314

Library of Congress Cataloging in Publication Data

Massabki, Ch
  Christ, liberation of the world today.

  Translation of Le Christ, libération du monde aujourd'hui
  Includes bibliographical references.
  1. Jesus Christ—Person and offices. 2. Salvation.
  3. Spiritual life—Catholic authors. I. Title.
  BT202.M37713   232   78-12998
  ISBN: 0-8189-0374-0

Nihil Obstat:

James T. O'Connor, S.T.D.
Censor Librorum

Imprimatur:

Joseph T. O'Keefe
Vicar General, Archdiocese of New York
August 26, 1978

Designed, printed and bound in the United States of
America by the Fathers and Brothers of the
Society of St. Paul, 2187 Victory Boulevard,
Staten Island, New York, 10314, as part of their
communications apostolate.

1 2 3 4 5 6 7 8 9 (Current Printing: first digit).

PREFACE

Christ brought liberation to the world, and He continues to do so in today's world by the power of His Spirit. This liberation will never be entirely and definitively accomplished. Men will never be absolutely free as long as they are human beings. They will always have to allow the Holy Spirit to free and to expand their entire being, by making them like Christ, by making them participate more in Christ's life, and in Him, in the life of the Blessed Trinity. He who would think that the Holy Spirit has definitively triumphed in him over the old man, to the point of making him unbeatable, would prepare himself for the worst disappointments. However, he who would, also, repeat constantly that he does not advance, that he always has so many faults, would lack supernatural realism, and would forget the universal survival, until their death, of the carnal man in spiritual men. So do not be discouraged. The struggle for liberation is the normal state of man here below.

However, in Jesus Christ, we are certain of total and definitive liberation. Furthermore, this liberation is already acquired for us by the blood of the Cross and by the triumph of Easter. Our struggle sanctions and makes ours today a liberation that Christ accomplished in the past once for all. We can only struggle because we are brought to life again. For that reason, our struggle ought to be marked, whatever its bitterness and whatever the humiliating deceptions that can cloud it, with the sign of the triumphant paschal joy. Our faith in Christ's Resurrection invites us unceasingly to allow the Holy Spirit to make us become what we are: free human beings. It invites us to believe in our liberation, a liberation that will not be our work, but that of the Spirit of love in us. It is, indeed, through the Holy Spirit that, from ascent to ascent, we will let ourselves be transformed into the image of Christ, the free man par excellence. "All of us," says St. Paul, "who, with face uncovered, reflect as in a mirror the Lord's glory — that is, Christ, for 'the glory of God, says the same Apostle further on, 'is on Christ's face'(2 Cor 4:6) — are transformed into the constantly more glorious image by the action of the Spirit of the Lord," (2 Cor 3:18) and we become freer and freer, as St. Paul again expresses it, with the freedom by which Christ has liberated us" (Gal 5:1).

Paris, April 14, 1974
The feast of Easter

CONTENTS

INTRODUCTION

In the sixteenth chapter of the Acts of the Apostles, it is told that, at the time of his second trip to Asia Minor, St. Paul changed plans on his apostolic journey by the spirit of Christ. Thus, feeling himself directed toward the West, he arrived in Troy, the most progressive port, and entrance to that West still unknown to him.

There, as the account goes, "during the night, he had a vision: a Macedonian came to him and begged him: 'Come to Macedonia and help us!' " (Ac 16:7-9). "Help us!" This call is the same cry that humanity utters unceasingly, consciously or unconsciously, since its very beginning.

What help did the man from Macedonia, or rather, humanity need? Humanity needed to be liberated from the state of decay which was his from the beginning. This decay, as Christian faith teaches us, was the result of a fault committed by the first human beings; it was called original sin. I have spoken about it in detail elsewhere.[1]

Indeed, this sin had subjected man to a spiritual death, and thus, impaired mankind's dignity, submitting his intelligence to ignorance and error, his liberty to evil, his love to corruption, his body to wicked inclinations, suffering and death, temporal values to profanation, and earthly activities to worldliness.

However, directly after the first fall, because God is love and because He had not ceased to be love and to want to make man His very own son, He came to the assistance of His unhappy creature. In mysterious terms, He promised him a liberator: "And God said to the serpent: 'I will put an enmity between you and the woman, between your descendants and hers; she will crush your head, and you will crush her heel'" (Gn 3:15).

This prophetic announcement is the first biblical passage that designates the Messiah. By the woman's descendants must be understood Christ and all God's children who will be united to Him. This prophecy is clear if it is joined to the following text of St. Paul: "In the fullness of time, God sent His Son, born of a woman in order to confer upon us filial adoption" (Gal 4:4-5).

The promised liberator is, then, Jesus Christ. He came almost twenty centuries ago, and, by His death on the cross and by His resurrection followed by His ascension, He liberated the world effectively from all the servitudes to which it had been subjected.

However, this liberation which Christ accomplished two-thousand years ago is not a simple historical event nor only a single historical fact. It is a universal and eternal act which does not attain immediately its full effect. Inaugurated by Christ since His incarnation, accomplished in fact by His sacrifice, it profits humanity in the present, as well as in the past and in the future. The liberating activity of the risen Christ is, then, ceaseless and ever present. Christ continues to exercise it in and by His Church, thanks to "the Spirit Whom He sent from His Father, and Who continues His work in the world."[2] Relevant to this point is this text of the epistle to the Hebrews: "Jesus Christ is the same yesterday, today and He will be so forever" (Heb 13:8). That is the reason for the title of this work: *Christ: Liberation of the World Today.*

Jesus Christ can say to the men of today just as He did to the men of His time: "Today is fulfilled this scriptural passage: 'The Spirit of the Lord is upon me because He has consecrated me with His anointing. He has sent me to bring the good news to the poor, to announce to the captives their deliverance, to restore sight to the blind, to give liberty to the oppressed, and to proclaim the Lord's year of grace' '' (Lk 4:18-22).

1. In a work entitled, *Le Christ, Rencontre de Deux Amours* (Christ, Encounter of Two Loves) Edition la Source, Paris, 1956, I have devoted several chapters to this dogma. I discussed it again partially in another: *Le peche originel, peut-on y croire encore?* (Can One Still Believe in Original Sin?) Edition la Source, Paris, 1972, in order to finalize certain points in the work previously quoted.

2. cf. The fourth eucharistic prayer.

Chapter 1

THE MODERN WORLD IS A WORLD IN PROGRESS

The world of today is a world in progress. I will first state what is meant by the present world, and outline its basic characteristics. Then I shall underline its positive values, and, finally, I will show in what esteem the Church holds these values, as well as the open and receptive attitude she asks her children to adopt.

Characteristics of the Modern World

What must be understood by "modern world" or "world of today?" What does the word "world" mean here? In biblical language, especially in St. John's works, it has several meanings. "The world was made by him," (Jn 1:10) referring to the Word of God. "I am the light of the world" (Jn 9:5), says Jesus. Also, "I left the Father and I came into the world, and now I leave the world and return to the Father" (Jn 16:28). "My kingdom is not of this world" (Jn 18:36). "So that the world may believe that you have sent me" (Jn 17:21). "God so loved the world that He gave His only Son" (Jn 3:16). "I have not come to judge the world, but to save it" (Jn 12:47). "I give you my peace not as the world gives it" (Jn 14:27). "You are of this world; I am not of this world" (Jn 8:23). "Because you are not of the world since I have taken you from the world, the world hates you'' (Jn 15:19). ''I do not pray for the world'' (Jn 17:9). ''I do not ask you to leave the world, but to protect it from Evil'' (Jn 17:15). ''We know that you belong to God — it is St. John speaking — while the entire world is under the power of Evil'' (Jn 5:19). ''Do not love the world nor anything that is in the world. If someone loves the world, the Father's love is not in him. For everything that is in the world — the lust of the flesh, the lust of the eyes and the pride of life — does not come from the Father but from the world'' (1Jn 2:15).

The meaning of ''world'' varies according to the context in which it is found. Several can be given to it. According to Pope Paul VI in one of his general Wednesday audiences, the word ''world'' can mean creation, the cosmos, the immense universe of creation which we will continue to know and to discover endlessly, and which can be for us a ''ladder leading to the discovery of God'' (cf. Ac 17:27). Men of today, formed by the school of science, have been invited to a new search for God, to a new religious spirit — not to atheism — precisely by this way which, if we follow it faithfully, will cause us to know natural and spiritual wonders, The world is a large, marvelous, mysterious word of God.

The word ''world'' can mean humanity. The Council[1] understood it thus — the theater of human drama devastated by sin, but loved and virtually saved by God and Christ: ''God has so loved the world that He gave His only Son so that every man who believes in Him will not perish but will possess eternal life'' (Jn 3:16). This is the human domain in which the history of salvation unfolds.

There is a third meaning to the word ''world,'' which is pejorative and hostile. World taken in this sense is still mankind, but humanity having become slave of the mystery of evil. It is the negation of God's Kingdom, the rebellion against Him, the union of false virtues, rendered powerful, unfortunately, by their emancipation from their supreme end. It is, in practice, a conception of life deliberately blind to its true destiny, and deaf to the call of an encounter with God. It is an egocentric spirit drugged by pleasure and self-satisfaction, and incapable of true love. It is "the witchery of evil" (Ws 4:12), the seduction of ephemeral values, and is incapable of responding to man's profound and essential aspirations. It is a situation we encounter at every step of our earthly experience, which can be fatal for us.[2]

Which world is Vatican II talking about when it speaks about the world today? The Council, itself, has answered our question, as Paul VI has just told us. In the pastoral Constitution on "The Church in the World Today," Vatican II has, indeed, delineated and outlined what is meant by this world. In its own words it gives: "some of the basic traits of the present world," of the world in which we live.

"The world which the Council has in mind, as we read in the preface of the above-mentioned Constitution, is that of men, the entire human family with the universe at the heart of which it lives, works and struggles. It is the theater where is enacted the story of mankind, the world marked by man's efforts, defeats and victories. For the faith of Christians, this world has been founded and remains preserved by the love of the Creator; it has fallen under the slavery of sin, but Christ, by the Cross and Resurrection, has broken the power of the Evil One, and has liberated it so that it is transformed according to God's design and succeeds in its fulfillment."[3]

However, this world is in perpetual evolution. It changes, rapidly with each generation and with each age. Presently, it is in the midst of a crisis of growth and change. Thus, we have to ask ourselves what are the characteristics of the world of today. The Council answered this question thus: "The human race lives today a new age in its history, characterized by profound and rapid changes which are extending little by little to the entire world. Brought about by man, by his intelligence and creative activity, they react on man himself, on his judgments, his thinking and acting, with regard to things as well as to his fellow creatures, to such a degree that one can already talk about a truly social and cultural transformation whose effects are felt even in religious life.[4]

This transformation is the result of a "general change

which leads to the predominance, in the formation of the mind, of mathematical, natural or human sciences, and, in action, to the predominance of the technical, the handmaid of the sciences. The scientific spirit which has shaped, in a way different from the past, the cultural state and modes of thinking[5] has given man, thanks to technical advances, the power to "transform the face of the earth and, already to embark on the conquest of space." It has, likewise, given him the possiblity of extending his dominion over time: "for the past by his historical knowlege; for the future, by prospecting and planning."[6] Finally, it has given him, thanks to the advances of human sciences — psychology, psychoanalysis, sociology, statistics, linguistics — the power to know himself better and to explain human activity in depth.

"At the same time," continues the Council, "it produces from day to day more important changes in the local traditional communities (patriarchal families, clans, tribes, villages), in different groups and social relations. An industrial society is developing little by little, bringing certain countries to an economy of opulence, and transforming radically the ideas and secular conditions of life in society. In the same way urban life and the attraction it offers, are intensified, through the growth of cities and population, or through the expansion of the style of urban life into rural life . . . actually, this evolution manifests itself above all in nations that already are benefiting from economic and technical progress. Yet, it is also in operation among those peoples in the process of developing, who are eager to procure for their countries the benefits of industrialization and urbanization. These peoples, especially if they are attached to older traditions, experience at the same time the need to exercise their liberty in a more adult and more personal way."[7]

These changes result in the constant multiplication of man's relationships with his fellowmen, thanks especially to this modern phenomenon called "socialization." "Among the principal aspects of today's world," the Council affirms, "one must count the multiplication of relationships among men, to which development today's technical advances contribute largely."[8] Further on: "From now on, under the influence of diverse factors, mutual relationships and interdependences will continue increasing: from whence various associations and institutions, of public and private right."[9] These lines from the Constitution *Gaudium et Spes*, summarize a passage from the encyclical *Mater et Magistra* on this subject: "One of the characteristic traits of our times," writes John XXIII, "is, without a doubt, socialization: these interdependencies, more numerous each day, which are entrenched in the life and action of men in numerous forms of social ties, generally recognized in public and private law. To them can be attributed the origin of a certain number of factors peculiar to our time: scientific and technical progress, the growth of productivity, the progress of civilization.

"These developments of social life are at the same time an index and cause of the State's increasing intervention which penetrates more and more into important and delicate matters touching the innermost part of one's being: preservation of health, formation and education of youth, professional orientation, reeducation and rehabilitation of the physically or mentally handicapped. However this evolution results, also, in a natural and almost incoercible tendency, which causes men to associate with one another spontaneously, in order to attain goods for each other, desirable but out of the reach of isolated individuals. As a result of this tendency, especially of late, there have sprung up everywhere on the national or international scene, groups, societies and institutions of an economic, social, cultural, recreational, athletic, professional or political character."

A phenomenon related to that of socialization, and just as modern, is the progressive unification of all mankind. The conciliar Constitution, *Gaudium et Spes,* speaks of it in many ways: "By his work and talent, man strives always to give broad development to his life. Yet, today, aided above all by science and technology, he has extended, and continues to extend, his dominion over almost all of nature. Thanks, especially, to the multiplication of means of exchange of all types among nations, the human family recognizes itself and constitutes itself little by little as a community united to the heart of the universe."[10] In another paragraph, it says: "In these very years, when the sorrow and anguish of sometimes devastating and menacing wars still weigh so heavily upon us, the entire human family is arriving at a decisive moment in its evolution. Little by little gathered together, already more conscious of its unity everywhere, it ought to undertake a work which can only lead to good by the renewed conversion of all toward a true peace: to build a world which is more human for all and in all places."[11]

The Council has just alluded to peace. In this domain, likewise, the felicitous effect of the progress of science and of its technical applications makes its presence felt by the change which these have effected in men's minds today. Such is the thought of Louis Armand who stated in his excellent work, *Plaidoyer Pour l'avenir* (Plea for the Future): "Denis de Rougemont, wrote on the eve of Hiroshima: 'The bomb is not at all dangerous. It is an object. What is horribly dangerous is man.' Thus, it is he who must improve. Now technology has justly brought about considerable progress in this area, that of a collective crisis of conscience, of reflection, of a positive anxiety. The appearance of atomic power has in some way forced information, from whence the favorable results recorded in many countries where research on how to undertake world disarmament has begun .... The balance of terror in which we are is worth finally more than the quarrelsome will of the pre-atomic era. The Welsh general recalls in his book on strategy in the nuclear age that, if the politic of dissuasion continues to be applied, and, if conflicts remain localized, such a condition will represent a serious step forward."[12]

It is not only from the social, but also from a cultural point of view that the profound transformations which characterize today's world affect the conditions of modern man's life. They involve the universal thrust of culture.

Included in culture, according to the Council, is — "all that by which man improves and develops the multiple capacities of his mind and body; he endeavors to dominate the universe by his knowledge and work; he humanizes social, and family life as well as all civil life, thanks to the progress of mores and institutions; he translates, communicates and preserves ultimately in his works, in the course of time, great spiritual experiences and man's major aspirations so that they are used for the development of a large number, even for all mankind."[13]

These changes open "new ways to perfect and to extend culture. These ways have been prepared by a considerable impetus from the natural, human, and also, the social sciences, by the development of technology and by the progress and better means of permitting men to communicate with each other. Modern culture can then be characterized thus: sciences called "exact" develop to the maximum a critical sense; the most recent research in psychology explains in depth human activity; historical disciplines push hard to confront things under their changing and evolving aspect; customs and ways of life are tending to become more and more uniform; industrialization, urbanization and other causes that favor collective life create new forms of culture (mass culture), from which result new ways of feeling, acting and using leisure. At the same time, the increase of exchanges among different nations and social groups reveals more widely all the riches of diverse cultures, and thus is formed, little by little, a kind of more universal civilization which results in the growing unity of mankind, and causes it to express itself to the extent that it respects better the individuality of each culture."[14]

The institution of marriage and the family has been affected, also, by the profound changes in contemporary society. "These changes," says the Constitution, *Gaudium et Spes*, "very often cause the true nature of this institution to appear and in diverse ways."[15]

In short, it is not only the Christians' life of faith that has felt the repercussions of the effects of the world's social and cultural metamorphosis: "The change of mentalities and of structures," affirms the Council, "often leads to a questioning of values received, especially among the young. (. . . These) new conditions affect . . . religious life itself . . . The impetus of a critical spirit demands a more and more personal and active adherence to faith; many, then, arrive at a more living sense of God."[16]

Values of the Modern World

Now let us ask the following questions: Is man's mastery of creation, which facilitates economic advancement and the struggle against misery, causing an improvement in living conditions, notably by freeing him from a number of maladies, of countless annoying or painful tasks, of certain thankless or difficult professions, an evil? Is a more profound knowledge of mankind an evil? Is a more complete development of the human person an evil? Are these evils: the unification of all mankind, an increase of chances for peace, a new drive toward culture, a better knowledge of the nature of the institution of marriage and the family, a more personal and more adult faith in a truer and more living God? Are all these developments to be despised and condemned as being, as some believe, decided and realized under the influence of evil spirits led by Satan? The Council does not think so. While underlining and recognizing the insufficiencies, the inconveniences and, even, the dangers which these different improvements include and which I will discuss, the Constitution, *Gaudium et Spes*, not only has underscored the undeniably good aspects, but, also, has affirmed explicitly many times that they are willed by God, that they are in conformity with the Creator's eternal plan concerning His creation.

With regard to man's increasing mastery of the universe, the Council declares that, thanks to "this immense undertaking which already is involving the entire human race," "man is procuring for himself from now on and by means of his own efforts, countless goods that formerly he received from superior forces."[17] Then the Council adds: "For believers, one thing is certain: considered in itself, individual and collective human activity, this gigantic effort by which men, down through the centuries, work to better their conditions in life, corresponds to God's plan. Man, created in God's image has, in reality, received the mission to control the earth and all that is in it, to govern the cosmos in sanctity and justice (Gn 1:26-17; 9:2-3; Ws 9:2-3), and while recognizing God as the Creator of all things, to refer his being as well as that of the universe to Him, so that, everything being subject to man, God's very name is glorified by all the earth (Ps 8:7,10). This teaching has value, also, for the most ordinary daily activities. Because these men and women, while earning a living and providing for their family, conduct their activities in a manner that serves society well, they are justified in seeing in their work a continuation of the Creator's work, a service to their fellow men, a personal contribution to the realization of the plan of providence in history.[18] Far from opposing the conquests of genius and of man's courage by God's power and of considering the rational creature as a sort of rival of the Creator, Christians are, on the contrary, strongly persuaded that the triumphs of humanity are a sign of the divine grandeur and a consequence of His ineffable design."[19]

As for the human sciences whose success is truly so remarkable and causes us to discover further certain aspects of what man is, the Council recognizes all the importance and all the profit that faith and morals can derive from them. These sciences can "contribute to an expansion of thought of believers, and to a more critical and more accurate knowledge of the sources and structures of faith."[20] "The advances of biological, psychological and social sciences not only allow man to know himself better, but also furnish him with the means to exercise a direct influence on the life of societies by the use of appropriate techniques."[21]

Concerning the development of social relations or "socialization," the Council states that "it involves numerous advantages which allow the qualities of a person to strengthen and grow, and to guarantee his rights."[22] Furthermore, this total development of the human person, thanks to socialization, is in conformity with God's plan and will. Indeed, "man's social character is made to look as if there is an interdependence between the development of the person and that of society itself. In reality, mankind who by his very nature has total need of a social life,[23] is and must be, the principle, the subject and the end of all institutions. Social life for man, then, is not something added: likewise, it is by the exchange with another, by reciprocal services, by dialogue with his fellow men, that man grows according to his capacities and can respond to his vocation."[24]

In what concerns humanity's unification, the Council points out the benefits for individuals as well as for nations. It "recognizes what is good in the social dynamism of today, especially the movement toward unity."[25] It affirms, moreover, that this unification of the world is in conformity with the divine plan. It states: "In reality, to promote unity is in harmony with the Church's profound mission since the latter is 'in Christ as a sacrament, that is, both the sign and the means of intimate union with God, and of the unity of the entire human race.'[26] The Church's proper reality manifests to the world that a true, social, visible union flows from the union of spirits and of hearts, namely from this faith and charity upon which, in the Holy Spirit, her unity is indissolubly established. The energy that the Church is capable of sharing with contemporary society is to be found in this faith and in this charity effectively lived, and does not depend upon an exterior dominion which would be exercised by purely human means. Furthermore, just as by her nature and mission, the Church is not linked to any particular form of culture, nor to any political, economic or social system, by this very universality, the Church can be a very close link between different communities and nations."[27] A little earlier, the Pope had said: "God who watches like a Father over all, has willed that all men form one single family and treat each other as brothers."[28] "For that reason, the love of God and of neighbor is the first and the greatest commandment. Holy Scripture, for its part, teaches that the love of God is inseparable from the love of neighbor: ' . . . Every other commandment is contained in this word: you will love your neighbor as yourself . . . Charity, then, is the law in all its plentitude' (Rm 13:9-10; 1Jn 4:20). It is quite evident that this fact is of extreme importance for those men more and more dependent upon one another, and in a constantly more unified world."[29]

As for the help brought to safeguard peace by the development of science and of its technical applications, which characterizes the modern world, the Council recognizes it expressly, even though with very great reservations. "Scientific arms," it says, "have not been accumulated with the sole intent of being used in war. In reality, just as one considers that the defensive power of each side depends on the terrifying capacity for exercising reprisals, this accumulation of arms which worsens from year to year, serves as a paradoxical means of deterring possible adversaries. Many think that it is the most efficacious means capable of assuring a certain peace today among nations."[30]

A propos of the spread of culture, the Council, after having recalled that "it is man's right to reach truly and completely humanity only by culture, that is, by improving the good things of the earth and the values of nature,"[31] speaks of "the birth of a new humanism" whose advantages it recognizes. Advantages of a moral order: "In whatever group or nation to which they belong," declares the Council, "the number of men and women who are aware of being agents and promoters of the culture of their community is growing constantly. In the entire world the sense of autonomy, as well as responsiblity, increases more and more; without any doubt, it is of the greatest importance for the spiritual and moral maturity of mankind. It is even more noticeable, if one does not lose sight of the unification of the universe and the mission which is imparted to us to construct a better world in truth and justice."[32] Advantages of the spiritual order: "By studying various disciplines, philosophy, history, mathematics, natural sciences, and by cultivating the arts, man can contribute greatly to awakening the human family to the most noble values of the true, the good and the beautiful, and to a view of things having universal value. Thus, he receives some new lights into this admirable wisdom (Pr 8:30-31) which has been forever God's, who arranges all things for him, is present on earth, finding his delight among the children of men."[33] Advantages even for faith: "By the very fact that the human spirit, less a slave of things, can more easily lift himself to the adoration and contemplation of the Creator. Furthermore, he is prepared to recognize, under the impulse of grace, the Word of God Who, before becoming man in order to save all and to gather all to himself, "was already in the world as the true light which enlightens every man" (Jn 1:9-10). A little further, the Council returns to all those advantages which it calls "positive values." It says, "among these latter, it is appropriate to signal out: the preference for sciences and the unfailing fidelity to truth in scientific research; the need to work as a team in specialized groups; the sense of international solidarity; the ever-clearer responsibility which intellectuals have to help and even to protect men; the will to procure for all the most favorable living conditions, especially for those who are deprived of responsibilities or who suffer from cultural indigence. In all these values, the evangelical message will be able to find a kind of preparation, and the divine charity of Him Who came to save the world will cause it to succeed."[34]

However, while recognizing completely "that between the message of salvation and culture, there are multiple links," the Council has taken care to reaffirm the independence of faith with regard to whatever the culture. According to the Council, "God, while revealing Himself to His people even to His total manifestation in His Incarnate Son, has spoken according to the kinds of culture proper to each age. In the same way, the Church who has recognized in the course of time diversified conditions of existence, has used the resources of different cultures in order to extend and to reveal by her preaching Christ's message to all nations, in order to reveal it better and to go more deeply into it, in order to express it more perfectly in the liturgical celebration, as well as in the many-faceted life of the community of the faithful. Yet, at the same time, the Church, sent to all peoples of all times and places, is not linked in an exclusive and indivisible way to one race or nation, to any kind of specific life, to any old or new custom. Constantly faithful to her own traditions and, at the same time, conscious of the universality of her mission, she can enter into fellowship with diverse civilizations: the result is an enrichment for her and for the different cultures."[35]

With regard to the fact that the changes of contemporary society have allowed a better understanding of the nature of the institution of marriage and of the family, the Council sees there — these are its own words — "a fact that shows us very well the vigor and solidity" of this institution.[36] It invites "Christians, in union with all those who think very highly of this community, to rejoice sincerely in the different supports which cause the esteem of this community of love and the respect of life to grow among men, and which assist married couples and parents in their eminent mission."[37] Likewise, this progress, because it helps to make apparent the true nature of marriage, coincides with God's thought of it, and disposes Christians, as well as all those who are forced to preserve and to promote the original dignity and the holy and privileged value of marriage," to understand and to welcome the teaching that the Council, "strong in the light of the Gospel and of human experience," gives to them on this subject.[38]

Finally, alluding to the problems that can make more difficult the realization of "the harmony between culture and Christianity,"[39] the Council affirms that "these difficulties do not necessarily bring a prejudice to the vitality of faith; they can even bring about a more exact and profound knowledge of it. In fact, the most recent research and discoveries in science, as well as in history and philosophy, pose new questions which bear consequences for life itself, and demand new research on the part of theologians themselves. Since then, while completely respecting the methods and rules proper to theological sciences, they are invited to look unceasingly for the most effective way to communicate the doctrine to men of their times; one thing is the deposit itself of the truths of faith, another is the way that these truths are explained, on the condition, however, of preserving its meaning and significance.[40] In the pastoral area, one must have sufficient knowledge not only of the principles of theology, but also of secular scientific discoveries, especially in psychology and sociology, and they must use them. In this way, the faithful, in turn, will be led to a very great purity and maturity in their life of faith."[41]

Attitude of the Church Towards the Modern World

Such are the principal values of the modern world, which allows us to affirm that this world is in progress. It is understood, then that the Council has recognized the help that the Church has received from mankind in general, and especially from mankind today. It is not surprising that the Council has suggested to Christians a welcome and open attitude toward the world today. It says, "the Church is not unaware of all that she has received from the history of the evolution of the human race. The experience of past centuries, the progress of sciences, the wealth contained in diverse cultures, which permit a better understanding of man himself, and which open new ways to truth, are equally useful to the Church. In fact, from the beginning of her history, she has learned to express Christ's message, while using the concepts and the languages of different people and, furthermore, she has done her best to enrich it by the wisdom of the philosophers with a view to adapting the Gospel, within acceptable limits, both to the understanding of all and the demands of the learned. Truly, this appropriate way to proclaim the revealed word ought to remain law for all evangelization. In this manner, actually, one can arouse in every nation the possibility of expressing the Christian message in a way appropriate to it, and, at the same time, one promotes a viable exchange between the Church and diverse cultures."[42] In order to grow from such exchanges, the Church, above all today when things move so quickly, and where the ways of thinking are extremely varied, needs especially the support of those living in the world, who know its diverse institutions, its different disciplines, and who take up its mental formulas, be they believers or non-believers. It falls back on all the people of God, especially pastors and theologians, with the help of the Holy Spirit, to scrutinize, to discern and to interpret the multiple languages of our times and to judge them in the light of the divine word, in order that revealed truth can be constantly better perceived, better understood and presented in a more adaptable form. Since she possesses a visible social structure, a sign of her unity in Christ, the Church can and is also enriched effectively by the development of social life: not as if there were something lacking in the constitution that Christ gave her, but in order to deepen her to explain her better and to adapt her more felicitously to our times. The Church admits with gratitude that she receives from men of every rank and condition a variety of help which profits the community she forms, as well as each of her children. Indeed, all those who contribute to the development of the human community on the familial, cultural, economic, social, political (national as well as international) level, offer by that very fact, and in conformity to God's plan, a substantial help to the ecclesiastical community, in as much as the latter relies on the exterior world. Furthermore, the Church recognizes that from the very opposition offered by her adversaries and persecutors, she has derived great benefits, and she can continue to do so.[43]

This attitude that Vatican II wishes the Church to adopt with regard to today's world, more so and better than she had done with regard to the world in the past, is an attitude which does not consist of being in the presence of the world, nor along side of it, nor at the same time being it, but with it. (The Council says, "the Church walks with all mankind and shares the earthly lot of the world"[44]). This attitude of comprehension, of being open, of sincere reception, even of admiration, will surprise some. One question can, indeed, come to mind: On what basis does the Council ask the Church to assume such an attitude, especially of accepting the fruits of the intelligence of both non-Christians and non-believers? The answer must be that the Council relies on the following truth to which it returns at times. If it is true that, as the Council recalls in referring to Vatican I, "there exists two distinct orders of knowledge, that of faith and that of reason,"[45] and that there are, consequently, two kinds of knowledge, that which proceeds from faith and that which proceeds from reason, it is no less true that it is the same God who is the author of reason as well as of faith. Both are a gift from God. Created in God's image, man participates truly in the light of divine intelligence. In short, then, it can be said that the Council relies on the dignity of the human person, stemming from man's having been created in God's image. Knowledge which is dependent on human intelligence inasmuch as it expresses truths or produces authentic values, is then, according to the actual words of the Constitution *Gaudium et Spes*, "extremely good."[46] Consequently, the Church can accept them all the more as the human spirit, even that which reflects without the help of the light of Christian faith, is no less helped by the light of "God's Word" Who, before becoming man in order to save and to gather all to Himself, "was already in the world," as "the true light which enlightens every man," (Jn 1:9-10) and thus He always remains. Consequently, this declaration of the Council is understood: "The methodic research, in all levels of knowledge, if it is directed in a truly scientific manner, and, if it follows the norms of morality, will never be really opposed to faith: secular and religious realities find their origins in the same God. Furthermore, he who strives perseveringly and with humility, to penetrate the secrets of things, even if he is not conscious of it, is led, so to speak, by the hand of God Who supports all creatures and makes them what they are."[47]

Thus, by welcoming into her patrimony the worthwhile acquisitions of the human mind, the Church intends to assimilate them in order to change, to christianize, to enrich and to offer them to God by consecrating them to Him. So "all those who, in any situation in which they find themselves, work under the action of grace to do something good and worthwhile, something which represents a human value in the true sense of the work, these persons work, in reality, for the Church, without knowing it." (de Montcheuil)

If it is so, if today's world offers advantages and benefits some of the more important of which we have cited, and which the Council recognizes and emphasizes forcefully, if the world is not a fixed and static one, but a world on the move, a dynamic world,[48] in change, in progress, if this world is "a world which is developing itself, which is in the act of developing itself," conformably to the divine will, realizing then God's plan for it, if this world, thanks to science and technology, is evolving towards a new world and, if as the Council affirms, "the Spirit of God Who, by an admirable providence, leads the course of time and renews the face of the earth, is present in this evolution,"[49] that world cannot be, and is not the world that Christ condemned and cursed. It is not the world in the sense of evil that is found and operative there, the world of which Sts. Peter, John and Paul speak when they say: "We have been snatched from the corruption prevalent in the world because of lust" (2P 1:4); the second: "do not love the world nor those in the world. If anyone loves the world, the Father's love is not in him because all that is in the world: the lust of the flesh, the lust of the eyes and the pride of life, is not of the Father, but of the world" (1 Jn 2:15); the third: "Do not model yourselves on the present world" (Rm 12:2).[50]

The world of which the Council speaks and to which it addresses itself, is then, indeed, as it has been defined in the passage which I have already quoted, "the entire human family with the universe at the heart of which it lives, works and struggles . . . the world fallen into the slavery of sin, but which Christ liberated so that it might be transformed according to God's design, and that it might attain its fulfillment." It is the world that Paul VI had in mind in this unforgettable passage from his talk of September 29, 1963, at the opening of the second session of Vatican II: "Love fills our soul and that of the Church assembled in Council. We look at our times and at its diverse and contrasting manifestations with a very great sympathy and a tremendous desire to give to men of today the message of love and of salvation: 'God did not send His Son into the world to condemn the world, but so that the world might be saved by Him' (Jn 3:17). Let the world know: the Church looks at it with profound understanding, with sincere admiration, sincerely ready not to dominate it but to serve it; not to depreciate it, but to value it; not to condemn it but to support and to save it . . . . The Church observes the craftsmen of human culture, scholars, scientists and artists. In their regard, also, the Church professes high esteem and a very ardent desire to entertain their hopes, to strengthen their thinking and to preserve their liberty . . . . The Church regards workers, their dignity as people, and the dignity of their work; she is interested in their lawful aspirations; their need for social promotion and inner elevation. . . ."

If such is the meaning of the world today, it is not surprising to hear the Council affirm that Christians have, not only the right, but the obligation to collaborate with all men, with all their energies, in the construction of this world. The Council invites them to do it, "willingly and with a generous heart,"[51] with all their brothers, without exception: "The Church, rejecting absolutely and totally atheism, proclaims, nevertheless, without any ulterior motive, that all men, believers and unbelievers, ought to strive for the just construction of this world in which they live together."[52] Likewise it notes further on: "the Christian message does not deter men from the construction of the world, and does not incite them to be indifferent to the fate of their equals: on the contrary, it gives them a more urgent obligation."[53] It is an obligation of justice and charity: "The profusion and rapidity of changes urgently demanded that no one, through lack of attention to the evolution of things or through inertia, is content with an individual ethic. While each one, contributing to the common good according to his proper capacities and taking into account the needs of others, is also effectively preoccupied with the growth of public or private institutions which serve to better conditions of human lives, then each fulfills more and more his obligation of justice and charity. Yet there are people, who while professing great and generous ideas, continue to live in practice as if they had no concern for social responsibilities. Moreover, in certain countries, many pay little attention to social laws and prescriptions. Many are not afraid of avoiding, by various and fraudulent subterfuges, legitimate taxes and other aspects of social debts. Some neglect certain rules of social life, such as those which are concerned with the preservation of health or driving, without even realizing that, by such indifference, they place in danger their own and another's life. Let all take very much to heart to consider social solidarities among man's principal obligations today and to respect them. In reality, the more that the world becomes united the more obvious it is that man's obligations go beyond individual groups, extending little by little to the entire universe. The result is that individuals and groups cannot help but cultivate among themselves moral and social values and share them with others. Then, with the necessary help of divine grace, there will rise up men truly new, artisans of a new humanity."[54]

To this collaboration of Christians with all men, the Council returns with greater insistence in another passage: "The Council exhorts Christians, citizens of whatever country, to fulfill with zeal and fidelity their earthly tasks, letting themselves be led by the spirit of the gospel. Those separate themselves from the truth, who, knowing that here we do not have a lasting city, but that we march toward a future city, believe they can neglect their human tasks, without realizing that their very faith, taking into account each one's vocation, gives them a very demanding duty."[55]

The same invitation is given with regard to the development of culture: "Let believers live, then, in a very close union with other men of their times, and let them make every effort to understand basically their ways of thinking and of feeling, expressed by their culture. Let them unite their knowledge of science and new theories, such as the most recent discoveries, with the traditions and the teaching of Christian doctrine so that religious sense and moral rectitude complement scientific knowledge and constant technical progress. Thus, they will be able to appreciate and to interpret everything with an authentically Christian feeling.

Those who apply themselves to theological disciplines in seminaries and universities will want to collaborate with men versed in other sciences, combining their energies and viewpoints. Theological research, at the same time it plumbs the depths of revealed truth, ought not to lose contact with its times, in order to facilitate a better knowledge of the faith of men educated in different branches of knowledge. This excellent agreement will render great service in the formation of sacred ministers: they will be able to present the Church's doctrine concerning God, man and the world in a manner more adapted to our contemporaries who will accept their words all the more willingly."[56]

However, if the Council urges Christians to collaborate with all men in the development of the world today, in order to better the conditions of earthly, even material existence, it is definitely, with a view to the moral and religious life of the kingdom of God.

Good living conditions in the temporal order can be favorable to the growth of the spiritual life, while inhuman conditions created by misery, promiscuity, and social disorder, risk, in the long run, a turning away from God and morality because a minimum of well-being is necessary for the practice of virtue and religion. "How can mysticism," Bergson used to say, "grow in a humanity absorbed by the fear of being hungry? Man will not lift himself above temporal unless a powerful tool furnishes him with a fulcrum. In other words, the mystic calls for a mechanic."

Furthermore, this world on the move is not without a tie with the future world, the "Kingdom of God": it is the preparation for it and it marches toward it, as Vatican II has strongly emphasized: "We do not know the time for the end of the world and of humanity (Ac 1:7); we do not know the manner of transforming the cosmos. Certainly it changes the face of this world disfigured by sin (1Cor 7:31).[57] However, we have learned that God is preparing for us a new dwelling and a new earth, where justice (2Cor 5:1) will reign and whose blessedness will fill and surpass all the desires for peace in man's heart (2Cor 5:1, 2P 3:13) . . . .Yet, the expectation of the new earth, far from weakening in us the concern for cultivating this earth, ought rather to vivify it: the body of the new human family is growing in it, offering already a rough draft of the world to come."[58]

Footnotes

1. Cf. The pastoral Constitution *Gaudium et Spes*, on "The Church in Today's World," *Doc. Cath.*, 1967, no. 1 464, col. 195, no. 2.
2. General audience, April 5, 1967, *Cath. Doc.*, 1967, no. 1 493, col. 784-785.
3. Const. *Gaudium et Spes*, *Cath. Doc.*, no. 2, par. 2.
4. *Ibid.*, no. 4, par. 2.
5. *Ibid.*, no. 5, par. 1.
6. *Ibid.*, no. 5, par. 2.
7. *Ibid.*, no. 6, par. 1-6.
8. *Ibid.*, no. 23, par. 1.
9. *Ibid.*, no. 25, par. 2.
10. *Gaudium et Spes*, no. 33, par. 1.
11. *Ibid.*, no. 77, par. 1.
12. Louis Armand, *Plaidoyer pour l'avenir*, Calman-Lévy, Paris, 1961, p. 145.
13. *Gaudium et Spes*, no. 53, par. 2 *Doc. Cath.*
14. *Ibid.*, no. 54.
15. *Ibid.*, no. 47, par. 2.
16. *Ibid.*, no. 7, par. 1 and 3.
17. *Ibid.*, no. 33, par. 1.

18. John XXIII, *Pacem in Terris*, p. 297.
19. *Ibid.*, no. 34, par. 1, 2, and 3; Cf. no. 57, par. 2.
20. Rev. Paul Joseph Schmitt, *Jesus-Christ, Sauveur et esperance des hommes, aujourd'hui*, Ed. Centurion, Paris, 1969, p. 117.
21. *Gaudium et Spes*, no. 5, par. 2.
22. *Ibid.*, no. 25, par. 2.
23. St. Thomas, 1 Ethic., lect. 1.
24. *Gaudium et Spes*, no. 25, par. 1.
25. *Ibid.*, no. 42, par. 2.
26. *Lumen gentium*, ch. 1, no. 1, p. 5.
27. *Gaudium et Spes*, no. 42, par. 3 and 4.
28. *Ibid.*, no. 24, par. 51.
29. *Ibid.*, no. 24, par. 2.
30. *Ibid.*, no. 81, par. 1.
31. *Ibid.*, no. 53, par. 1.
32. *Ibid.*, no. 55.
33. *Ibid.*, no. 57, par. 3.
34. *Ibid.*, no. 57, par. 6.
35. *Ibid.*, no. 58.
36. *Ibid.*, no. 47, par. 2.
37. *Ibid.*, no. 47, par. 1.
38. *Ibid.*, no. 46, par. 1.
39. *Ibid.*, no. 62, par. 1.
40. John XXIII, Speech delivered Oct. 11, 1962 at the opening of the Council: A.A.S., LIV (1962), p. 792.
41. *Gaudium et Spes*, no. 62, par. 2.
42. *Lumen gentium, Doc. Cath.*, ch. II, no. 13, p. 17.
43. St. Justin, *Dialogue with Tryphon*, ch. CX: P.G., VI, 729, ed. Otto, 1897, pp. 391-393.
44. *Gaudium et Spes*, no. 40, par. 2.
45. *Ibid.*, no. 59, par. 3.
46. *Ibid.*, no. 11, par. 2.
47. *Ibid.*, no. 36, par. 2.
48. Cf. Const. *Gaudium et Spes*, no. 5, par. 3.
49. *Gaudium et Spes*, no. 26, par. 4.
50. Cf. Const. *Gaudium et Spes*, no. 37, par. 3.
51. *Gaudium et Spes*, no. 88, par. 1.
52. *Ibid.*, no. 21, par. 6.
53. *Ibid.*, no. 34, par. 3.
54. *Ibid.*, no. 30, par. 1 and 2.
55. *Ibid.*, no. 43, par. 1.
56. *Ibid.*, no. 62, par. 6 and 7.
57. Cf. St. Ireneaus, *Adversus haereses*, V, 36, P.G., VIII, 1221.
58. *Gaudium et Spes*, no. 38, par 1; no 39, par. 1 and 2.

CHAPTER 2

THE MODERN WORLD IS A WORLD IN REGRESSION

In the preceding chapter, when speaking of today's world, of the fundamental traits that characterize it, of its positive values, of the welcome which Christians ought to give its riches, of their collaboration with all men in its construction, without a doubt, I have given the impression that the Council had a too optimistic view of this world. The reader will probably think that, for the Fathers of Vatican Council II, for others and, for the author of these pages, the world of today is the best of worlds where all is for the best, and that the Kingdom of God is in the process of being established like everything, naturally, thanks to man's progress, realized by the continuous development of science and technology.

Not at all. With the Fathers of the Council, I think that man's progress is ambiguous, and that, if the present evolution of the world brings with it "joys and hopes," it engenders at the same time, "sorrows and anxieties."[1] We read in the Constitution *Gaudium et Spes*: "As in all crises of growth, this transformation of humanity does not occur without serious difficulties. While man extends his power so much, it does not always happen that he is in control. Forcing himself to penetrate more deeply the innermost secrets of his being, he seems more uncertain of himself. He discovers little by little, and more clearly, the laws of social life, but he hesitates about the directions that he must give it.

Never has mankind been surrounded by so many riches, so many possibilities, and so much economic power; yet, a considerable part of the world's inhabitants are still tormented by hunger and misery, and countless human beings do not know how to read or write. Never have men had such a vibrant sense of liberty as today, but, at the same time, new forms of social and psychological slavery are born. While the world takes strong cognizance of its unity, of the reciprocal dependence of all in a necessary solidarity, it is violently torn apart by opposing forces that battle each other: political, social, economical, racial, and ideological dissensions still exist, and the danger remains of a war capable of total destruction. The exchange of ideas is growing, but the very words used to express extremely important ideas, are invested with very different meanings, according to the diversity of ideologies. In a word, we search carefully for a more perfect temporal organization without this progress being accompanied by an equally spiritual growth. A great number of our contemporaries have great difficulty in discerning permanent values, marked by so complex a situation; at the same time, they do not know how to harmonize them with recent discoveries. An uneasiness grips them, and with a mixture of hope and anxiety, they question the present evolution of the world."[2]

Actually, if the progress, realized by sciences and current technology in many human domains, is, as we have seen, indisputable and uncontested by the Council, these same developments can result in bringing with them, at the same time, inconveniences and dangers which the Council itself does not fail to point out forcefully and clearly. I will group them under two headings which I will designate by—may I be forgiven for using words not found in the dictionary—"atheization" and "dehumanization."

It is easy to guess what I mean by the first of these two neologisms: "atheization." Today's world is atheizing itself; it is letting itself be won over more and more by atheism which is, according to Paul VI's expression, "the most serious phenomenon of our time;" it has, also, been spoken of as "an unprecedented historical event" (Jacques Maritain).

Those who deny God, in theory or in practice, grow daily in number. They are to be found everywhere, in all countries, in all levels of society, among the young as well as the old. This widespread atheism has ended up by influencing the faithful of great monotheistic religions: Jews, Moslems and even Christians. In his pastoral letter of 1948 on the meaning of God, Cardinal Suhard was already writing about the last mentioned: "By dint of breathing this atmosphere, they end up by being imbued with it. Through all their senses, they take in the subtle poison whose greatest danger is that it does not cause one to die, but it immunizes its victims against its very self. It is also not necessary to search far for these 'Godless Ones.' They are found at every step. Many baptized, without being true atheists, act practically like them." As for Vatican II, it states sadly: "A constantly growing number of people is giving up the practice of religion. To reject God or religion, not to be concerned about it, is no longer, as formerly, an exceptioanl fact, the choice of just some individuals: today, in fact, such conduct is presented willingly as a demand of scientific progress or of some normal humanism. In many areas this negation or indifference, is expressed not only on a philosophical level; it, likewise, affects literature, art, the interpretation of human sciences, history and law itself."[3]

Atheism is cloaked in many ways, according to the diversity of its causes. The same Council describes briefly some: "Certain very diverse phenomena are described under the name of atheism. In fact, while certain atheists expressly deny God, others think that man cannot affirm absolutely anything about Him. Still others treat the problem of God in such a way that it seems devoid of meaning. Many go unduly beyond the limits of positive sciences. Either, they pretend only scientific reason explains everything; or, on the contrary, they do not recognize any truth as absolutely definitive. Certain ones make such a case of man that faith in God is found to be debilitating; they are absorbed, it seems in affirming man rather than in denying God. Others represent

God in such a light that, by rejecting Him, they reject a God Who, in no way, is the God of the Gospel. Others do not even consider the problem of God: they seem strangers to all religious search, and they do not see any reason to be concerned about religion. Furthermore, atheism is often born, be it from an aroused protest against evil in the world, or from the fact that such an absolute character is wrongfully attributed to certain human ideals that they are taken for God. Modern civilization, itself, certainly not by its very essence, but because it finds itself too involved in earthly realities, can often render the approach to God more difficult.''[4] The Council mentions two other forms of atheism whose cause it analyzes at some length. I shall discuss them later.

It seems, then, that considered in its totality, the origin of atheism is not found in itself, but in the various causes which have just been mentioned. I shall keep in mind only the two most important, of which the others, moreover, are basically only complementary aspects: the progress of science and technology, on the one hand; the growth of culture, on the other. We discover the principal facts which have transformed and which cause the modern world to progress, and whose disadvantages and wrongdoings I am now going to raise.

Contemporary atheism is due, in the first place, to scientific and technical progress, not that atheism is a necessary product of technical civilization as such. In itself, technical civilization is neither favorable nor unfavorable to belief in God. It can, as we already know, bring much to religion, but it can, also, by its consequences, create a certain number of obstacles. Because of these consequences, Vatican II states: "the present progress of science and technology which, by virtue of their method, could not attain the depths of reality, can benefit a certain phenomenism and a certain agnosticism, while the methods of research proper to these disciplines are taken, wrongfully, as supreme guidelines for the search of all truth. It is, even, to be feared that man, relying too much on present discoveries, ends up by thinking he is self-sufficient, and that he no longer has to look for higher values.''[5]

In reality, modern science, with its discoveries and technical applications which have caused man today to be aware of his power of domination over the universe, risks causing him—and they have already done so—to bypass God, to eliminate Him on the intellectual level, as explanation of the world. It seems that, by seizing for himself little by little the secrets of creation, man will be able to succeed in explaining the universe scientifically, and, consequently, to remove from God's sovereign domain, at least such as He had conceived it, all that man formerly had not realized or was incapable of realizing. What is still impossible for him to explain or to do today will be possible for him tomorrow; thus, it is not impossible in itself. In these conditions, recourse to God becomes more and more useless and, thus, God, becoming without a reason for existence, science, in the future, will only deny Him more and more. This way of viewing things belongs to scientists. We shall see in another chapter that this is not the view of true intellectuals.

Pure science and technology are not prevented from being indissociable to each other, and the discoveries of even the most theoretical and abstract sciences are the source of the discoveries and realizations of technology. Now, technical progress, procuring each day more money, an easy life, comfort and all kinds of pleasure, has, without any doubt, made the world of today materialistic, and such a materialization leads sooner or later to denial of God. In fact, by letting oneself be captivated by this world made up of matter, by discovering and exalting its potentialities, by enjoying its riches, modern man, "filled with admiration before his very discoveries and his very own power," ends up bypassing and forgetting God. His great temptation, springing from the means of power he has created for himself, and which have given him an unlimited confidence in his potential, and in that of matter, is to be self-sufficient and not to have to depend on anyone. Modern man is really convinced that, by changing his conditions of existence, he will be able to substitute himself for God or Him for humanity which these same scientific and technical developments are in the process of uniting more and more.

Modern man is equally convinced that, in order to be completely himself, he must be man's highest value, and, in order to be genuine, humanism must be the negation of God: an atheistic humanism. Thus, we are approaching the second reason for contemporary atheism: the spread of culture insofar as it is the root of atheistic humanism.

We have heard the Council state that cultural progress in today's world has given rise to a new humanism. "Believers and unbelievers are generally in agreement on this point: everything on earth ought to be directed toward man as its center and its apex."[6] However, they differ on the idea of what man ought to become. Now a certain culture developed which favored a humanism that exalts man as an absolute norm: a humanism which worships man, and so negates God. Man no longer worships the elements, nor animals, nor things, not even God, only man. The passage from the Constitution, *Gaudium et Spes* quoted earlier speaks to the point: "Certain ones make such a case of man that faith in God is found debilitating; they are busier, it seems, affirming man than denying God."[7] Man is only man to the extent that God is denied. Such is existential humanism, as well as marxist humanism. The Council alludes to both in the same Consitution: "Often, when speaking of the first, modern atheism, also, presents a systematic form, an abstraction made from other causes, which pushes the desire of human autonomy to such a point that it places an obstacle to all dependence with regard to God. Those who profess this kind of atheism maintain that liberty consists in man being his own proper end, the sole lord and master of his own destiny. They pretend that this view of things is incompatible with the recognition of a Lord, beginning and end of all things, or, at least, that this view makes this affirmation totally superfluous."[8]

In this systematic form of contemporary atheism, the reader recognizes existentialist doctrine. In fact, existentialism, at least that which is not Christian, has a great influence on a number of contemporaries, and is openly atheistic. There is a Christian existentialism, stemming from St. Augustine, and, as far as France is concerned, coming down to the present, thanks to the efforts of Pascal, Blondel and Gabriel Marcel.

Indeed, according to this philosophy, there is nothing else for man than existing. Consequently, man has nothing else to do but construct his existence, using his liberty in order to realize this construction. "To do and by doing, to become, and to be only what he becomes," such is the motto of the non-Christian existentialist. For him, the acts of our liberty are absolute beginnings, and our existence depends only on our present decision. God and man cannot co-exist: one must deny the other. Even if God exists, that fact does not interest him. His presence or absence in the heights of heaven does not concern man. God does not have meaning for man's existence, or he would only be an obstacle to his liberty, and, thus, would only act in order to prevent him from constructing his existence, and, to bring harm to his dignity.

So, existentialist philosophy is given the primary task: to teach man to be truly a man, to exist in the true sense of the word. Man begins to exist, according to the meaning that existentialism gives to this word, only at the very moment when he becomes aware of his liberty and takes hold of realizing his own destiny.

This non-Christian existentialism is essentially atheistic. It denies God in the name of man's liberty and his dignity.

Alluding then to another kind of atheism, the Council says: "Among the forms of contemporary atheism one cannot pass over in silence that which awaits economic and social liberation. Religion, by its very nature, would be opposed to this liberation, to the degree that, arousing man's hope on the delusion of a future life, it would deter him from building an earthly city. That is the reason that, when believers of such a doctrine become masters of power, they attack religion with violence. In order to spread atheism, especially in what concerns the education of youth, they use all the pressure that public power has at command."[9]

In this last form of modern atheism, the reader recognizes the Marxist doctrine. The Marxists believe that we are moving toward a better world; they think that the interplay of natural and of social forces is operating for man's benefit; they are persuaded that "it belongs to History alone, that is, to human effort inserted into historical evolution, to succeed in procuring for men—through justice, liberty, solidarity— the deliverance that they are looking for." Indeed, it is a question of liberating man from economic and social captivity, and, at the same time, from his alienation and slavery to God by religion, because, for the Marxists, the religious need would only be the imaginary projection of social injustices and, because this attitude can only prevent man from working toward the construction of a better world here below.

One last reason for contemporary atheism, also emphasized by the Council, and, moreover, an outgrowth of the first two, is, and I quote the Constitution, *Gaudium et Spes*, "a critical reaction in face of religions, and especially in certain regions, in the face of the Christian religion. This is the reason that in this genesis of atheism, believers can have a considerable share, to the extent that, by neglecting the study of their faith, by false presentations of doctrine, and, also, by shortcomings in their religious, moral and social life, it can be said that they conceal rather than reveal the authentic face of God."[10] Actually, many Christians, let us acknowledge it, not only bad ones, but also those of mediocre faith, hope and charity, of a mediocre moral life, of a mediocre intellectual and religious background, alas, have contributed and still contribute greatly to presenting God, as they depict Him, as they speak of Him, and as they serve Him. This view of God is difficult to accept, and is really unacceptable for some men who cannot in justice conceive of God as a material and sensual reality, endowed with all the passions, all the reflexes, all the petty preoccupations and narrow limitations of a finite creature. These Christians make God a non-God, through abuse and anthropomorphism: they speak of Him as if He were a man. They give Him their own appearance and, making Him a being, subject to the same passions as they, but more powerful, they make Him take on all the evils and all the injustices that they encounter here below. To them is applied Voltaire's ironical remark: "God made man to His image and man has given it back to Him." There are others who, without reducing God to their stature, put Him in their service. They use Him for their profit, with a view to serving their own human interest, to make legitimate their most ambiguous enterprises, to legalize social inequalities, to justify injustices, in short, to perpetuate an established disorder from which they profit.

That "rather large" number of Christians in the genesis of atheism is the other side of the coin of progress accomplished in the realm of faith, a progress about which I spoke earlier, and which is realized thanks to the development of a critical spirit due to the social and cultural change in the world. However, this side of the coin—atheism born of progress—can be a help insofar as it instigates the Christians to a purification of their meaning of God, and to a betterment of their religious, moral and social life.

Dehumanization

The second series of dangers which the development in today's world of advances realized by sciences and technology brings about is that which I have stated under neologism and dehumanization.

It is not enough to better the conditions of material existence in order to change the human condition. Economic and technical improvements, if they are good in themselves and if they can, when put at man's service, make life more human, are also, capable, if they are used badly, of enslaving man and of harming him, of bringing injury to his dignity, liberty, and love, thus of making him less a man, in a word, of dehumanizing him. Even used in the best sense, they create more favorable conditions, but never do they resolve man's real problems. Also, as Vatican II notes,"The number is growing of those who, confronted by the present evolution of the world, pose the most fundamental questions, or they perceive them with a new astuteness. What is man? What is the meaning of suffering, evil, death, which continue in spite of so much progress? Of what use are victories paid for at such a high price? What can man bring to society? What can he expect from it? What will happen to him after this life?"[11] For that reason, if one must not condemn conquests of science and technology, more prodigious from month to month, and which stimulate and support the exaltation of our humanity, these conquests arouse great hopes, and, yet, at the same time, they give rise to great anxieties.

Anxiety, first of all, in the face of the formidable means of action which could be used for the destruction of all life on our planet, prompting the mania for domination of one single individual, or the desire for hegemony of one nation over others. In the preceding chapter, I remarked that the technical applications of science, while favoring the accumulation of scientific arms, serve paradoxically the cause of peace. Actually, in the face of the terrifying possibilities of retaliation, this accumulation of scientific arms, has had an unexpected result, the dissuasion of possible enemies having recourse to war. However, I added that, while pointing out this felicitous result of technical development, the Council has been convinced, but with a great deal of reservation. Rather than this process of dissuasion, it prefers the institution of a universal public authority, the cessation of the arms race, personal reform, the changing of mentalities, a change of heart: "Whatever may be this process of dissuasion," we read in the Constitution *Gaudium et Spes,* "one ought, nevertheless, to be convinced that the arms race, in which a rather good number of nations are involved, does not constitute a sure path toward the solid maintenance of peace, and that the so-called balance which results from it is neither a stable nor a true peace. Far from eliminating, thus, the causes of war, on the contrary, there is a risk of making them, little by little worse. While enormous amounts of money are spent in the preparation of ever newer arms, it becomes impossible to alleviate adequately so many present miseries in the world. Instead of really easing radically the conflicts among nations, the contagion spreads on the contrary, to other parts of the world. For this reason it is necessary to reiterate: the arms race is an extremely serious scourge of humanity, and injures the poor in an intolerable way. Indeed, it is to be feared that, if it persists, it will give birth one day to mortal disasters for which it is already preparing the means."[12]

Anxiety, also, exists, even in peace time, in the face of perils which menace the highest human values. Liberating certain men, technology, in fact, enslaves others. The exhausting work of the miners, the suffering of workers in metallurgic factories, the fatigue of women repeating the same gestures. Visiting an important automobile factory, Mr. X . . . having noticed that his guide, a foreman, was rather deaf, heard the latter reply: "We all become so at the end of a few years. It is the result of the dreadful and incessant noise." In another factory, also very modern, the same visitor watched the women controlling the rolling blocks. He wrote: "Their fingers manipulate the small steel balls with incomparable agility. Were they listening to the soft music in the background? I don't know, but their vague looks gave evidence of a wandering spirit, adrift, following some dream." Thus, subjected to soul-less mechanisms, millions of individuals risk being lessened not only in body but in spirit, of being dehumanized by the degradation of assembly-line work, and by this identification of man to a machine of which Virgil Gheorghiu, the well-known author of *Vingt-Cinquieme Heure*, has said: "When men will resemble machines to the point of identifying themselves with them, then, there will no longer be men on earth." Furthermore, technology does not exempt technologists nor beneficiaries from the inconveniences of their work. On the one hand, technological activity risks, if it is done in a feverish way, involving a plethora of biological and intellectual activities to the detriment of the highest activities of the spirit: contemplation, intuition, the gift of self. . . . "What do you think of my friend Mr. F . . . who on Christmas night, two years ago, was so absorbed in translating the plans of an American machinery which he wanted to construct in France that he forgot to come home; of Mr. V . . . a daring engineer, a progressive leader, who is undertaking some important experiments to the detriment of any detente, of all culture, of all family life, while his son is looking in the newspapers for answers to the initiation to life; of those two students at the Polytechnique one of whom spends his Sundays sleeping in the midst of a dismayed family, and the daughter of the other family confided to me sadly: 'I have never been able to talk to my father'?"[13]

On the other hand, objects produced by technology and which are good in themselves, can become noxious, be it because of an internal defect, such as the excessive power of an automobile which makes this latter more vulnerable to itself and to its user, be it by the perverse or excessive use that man makes of it, i.e. such as abusing movies, radio or television. Finally, technology runs the risk of making man lose the sense of his human condition, making him forget both the limits of science and those of human reason, as well as the essential problems of his personal destiny. It, thus, risks dehumanizing him still more.

Socialization, itself, the advantages of which, however, we have seen in the preceding chapter, advantages in what concerns the full development of the human person and the creation of truly personal relationships, not only does not always favor, as it should, this "personalization" of individuals, but even is not without danger to them.[14]

In fact, the development of social ties brings about an excessive amplification of the bureaucratic mechanism, a continually more minute multiplication of rules and regulations which govern human relationships in almost all areas of social life, and a continually greater use of techniques and methods: all things which risk transforming the individual into automatons. The result is a lessening of the scope of liberty, a narrowing of the sphere in which man can think for himself, act on his own initiative, exercise his responsibilities, judge independently of all exterior influences, expand his mental faculties by placing them in proper perspective, in a word, affirm and enrich his personality. The consequence is a grave risk of dehumanization.

This dehumanization is not without rapport with contemporary atheism. Quite the contrary. In fact, the negation of God leads to the suffocation of man. One cannot ignore God without impunity. God is the very source of personality. For man to exist, is to be only of and for God. His person is entirely relative to Him: it does not exist except by what it receives from Him, like a river which exists only because of the water it receives from its source. Man's relationship to God is, then, basic to his being, so that if he comes to disown it, he deprives himself of something essential; he mutilates a part of himself. In him, all the potencies of desire are disoriented; they go wild, for lack of being polarized towards God. Remaining made for God, whether he likes it or not, and his heart remaining restless until it rests in Him, but no longer being ordered to an infinite love, he acts in a frenzy before all that can satisfy him. Nothing satisfies him. He scarcely possesses the desired object when he is disgusted with it. He wants others. The more he obtains, the more dissatisfied he is. He is insatiable. The finite cannot satisfy his desire for the infinite. He is before a void. Not succeeding in filling it, he tries to divert his thoughts in order to forget his disappointments and his disgust. The unfulfillment of this desire for the infinite is the cause, in today's world, of many problems and many dehumanizing disorders, such as the use of drugs and stimulants under all forms.

In order to illustrate these assertions, I shall give as an example that of the nordic countries which I visited twice.

Useless to remark that what I am going to say about them applies equally, sad to say, to other countries. There, without bloodshed, all social and university problems, have been solved (a solution moreover never definitive for such problems cannot be solved once for all). There, life is easy, peaceful, apparently happy, but there exists an atheistic materialism, if not, in principle, at least, in fact. In order to create and to establish these marvelous conditions of existence, nothing has been forgotten except that "man does not live by bread alone, but also by every word that comes from the mouth of God." The result: they are dying of hunger; they drink; they have a good time; they divorce. Nothing is done about it. They are bored; they fall into anguish, despair, and end up insane or committing suicide. The number of mental institutions is very high. The number of neurotics is frightening, of suicides unbelievable. These countries are for me a proof not only of God's existence, but of the vital need that man has of Him.

These statements and this conclusion have been confirmed by the personal, spontaneous, sincere, and ever so moving testimony of a director with a world-wide reputation, and who, furthermore, is precisely nordic. I am referring to Ingmar Bergman.

In an interview on his film *Le Silence*, responding to the following question: "Why doesn't one ever see in your films contemporary Sweden, today's problems, the skyscrapers of Stockholm: doesn't society and the world in which you live interest you?" Ingmar Bergman responded: "Ah! Again a misunderstanding! It is difficult to explain. I myself feel that I am speaking of Sweden today in my films, that I am trying to respond to these problems and not to remain on the periphery. You see here in Sweden, we have everything, or rather, we live under the illusion that we have everything. However, in the midst of this full life, we have a great void, the lost illusion of God, call that whatever you want, it doesn't matter, a need for intellectual security which succeeds in compensating for all the inadequacies of material and social security. It is this void, and all that men invent in order to fill it, that I describe in my films, and I believe that it is a way of making films involved with contemporary problems and even with the one fundamental problem, that of giving spiritual or human meaning to a civilization of material happiness. In any case, it is my personal problem. Do not ask me to speak of anything else; I would not know how."[15]

From the hippie movement and the activities of May 1968, an analogous testimony is revealed.

This is the manner in which a hippie student explained the popularity of drugs: "When someone revels in the superfluous, this allows free time for reflection and for asking questions. For example, one looks for another reason for living than money or a washing machine. One no longer confuses comfort and happiness. One looks around finds nothing nor anyone to help him live: religion has become a ritual; politics is a game. . . . It is a total moral void. Our western civilization develops only the material level. It has lost its soul. We need true values and a great deal of spirituality. Our entire generation has become aware of this frightful void. . . . We were so steeped in materialism, so much a prey of gadgets and respectability that L.S.D. was, in the beginning, necessary to break with all that, and to rediscover love with a capital L, the universal love for all men."[16]

The day after the events of May, 1968, a student, Olivier Germain Thomas, explained them thus: "Our civilization is suffering from a terrible, perhaps deadly malady, which is called a spiritual void. . . . We have bread, a car, exterior liberty, but we are only molded into matter; the better part of ourselves is hungry. In my opinion, because of the collapse of essential, spiritual values (religion, art, love), the young went out on the streets. . . . They fought because of a lack in their soul. . . . Unconsciously, but profoundly and vigorously, the young of the entire world have arisen in order to safeguard their spirit. . . . Man's ascent ought to be a going beyond; he must be more than mechanical to live. To safeguard what, since the time of the caves, distinguishes us from an animal, we should, with the strength of passion, rediscover our soul. The real revolution will be a spiritual one."[17]

The atheism of the existentialists is just as dehumanizing as the scientific or practical atheism which I have just discussed. In order to be convinced of it, one needs only to glance at literature. Taken as a whole, it constitutes a shocking document on the condition of modern man in general. Daniel-Rops describes it thus: "Violence and the basest sexuality at the most elementary level of instincts. All human experience is reduced to these moments of disgust and of nausea, where everything and everyone seems pointless because everything is distorted and sullied. Definitely, what one ought to retain as the most impressive in this literature is the testimony that it gives of man's eluctable degradation, where he has betrayed the eternal part of himself. In all this literature, what moves one even to dizziness is a frightening lack, the feeling of a catastrophic oblivion: a presence is lacking which is Love. The general word which could be used for this venture, in a satanic sense, is comparable to Pascal's description of the despair of our condition as well as the meaning of this despair, itself: 'The misery of man without God.' "

Marxist atheism is, likewise, no less dehumanizing. In fact, Marxists have no respect for the human person. They have taken away this respect from humanity. For that reason, when they speak of Man with a capital M, they do not mean man in the singular, but, if I can so express, man in the plural, or Humanity. They have substituted for concrete man the idea of humanity. Marxism, then, is an idealism which has reduced the individual into a collectivity where persons cease to exist by and for themselves in order to lose themselves in this great whole called Humanity, which they have idolized. In the name of this idol which is only an idea, they force man to submit to everything. As has been said, for the Marxists "man is nothing more than carbon to be thrown into the locomotive of history." In fact, the Marxists believe, as I have recalled earlier, in a historic becoming, in humanity on the march towards its completion, and they hope to go beyond themselves in this collective conclusion. However, therein lies an enormous trickery, since, in order to build a future humanity, Marxism sacrifices individuals. Now, humanity, to repeat, is only an idea; it does not exist by and for itself, but by and for the individuals who compose and will compose it. The Council has recalled this fact several times in the Constitution *Gaudium et Spes:* "The social order and its development ought to work always for the good of people since the order of things ought to be subordinate to the order of persons and not the contrary."[18] Further: "Man, who, by his very nature, has absolute need of a social life, is and ought to be the principle, the subject and the end of all institutions."[19] A termination, on earth, of a future humanity, is, then, an illusion, since we are not members of a future humanity and when it will be, we will no longer exist. As has been said, so well: "There is no worse opium to give me than to soothe me with this kind of collective revival that I would experience in a future humanity of which I would not be a part." Actually, in this future humanity, I would no longer be conscious of myself since I would not be a member of it. Thus, there would not be for me a future humanity. What good would progress do me when I would not be able to benefit from it, when instead I would be sacrificed for it. They accuse Christianity of being the opium of the people because it soothes the pains of this life with the consolation of eternity. However, the true opium of the people, is it not rather Marxism which promises an earthly paradise which its followers will never know, which persuades thousands of men to accept a dreadful existence in order to work not for their happiness but for that of a future humanity?

This Marxist ideal does not lack a certain admirable grandeur and disinterestedness. God will take these qualities into account when admitting them to share His beatitude. Yet, it is no less fantastical, since does humanity have a future? Is it not mortal, just as the individuals that compose it? As has been said, "it does not have more promises of eternity than the individual. . . . There is not a collective immortality anymore than an individual one. It is just as useless to want to prolong the life of humanity as that of man. This great collective survival is only one long collective agony. Humanity is, thus, not worth more than the individual. Like the individual it is perishable. What must end one day can also end immediately. There will be nothing changed on the surface of the galaxies, whether humanity did or did not live for a long or short time, happily or unhappily. If there is no eternity, humanity will have been an incident in evolution."[20] Is it not to be against man to promise him a paradise that he will not know, which will happen perhaps and which, in any case, will disappear completely one day?

Thus, a world without God becomes little by little an inhuman world, and the world of that time will have shown in a new way that man, himself, cannot live, cannot become more of a man, without faith in God. We have seen the fatal consequences to which an atheistic and dehumanized world leads. To these consequences, it is necessary to add the instability of the home, the epidemic of divorce, so-called free love or other distortions, the profanation of conjugal love by egoistic hedonism, illicit practices shackling the generation, abortion, serious disorders introduced into the family today by economic, socio-psychological conditions, eroticism, the insatiable appetite for sexual excitement so peculiar to this time, the thirst for money which changes the economic life by exploitation and slavery, the desire for power and the domination of people. All these evils from which the modern world suffers, have, in fact, a religious root. Their manifestation is only the symptom of a more profound evil which is at the heart of man, the rejection of God.

Such are the main evils, dangers and ills that can involve and have already involved the very causes that have made today's world and that promote its advances toward progress. They are so serious that certain of our contemporaries would like to turn the clock back. The world will never go back, and our era will not deny its discoveries, in spite of the dangers that still menace it. "Who cares about foolish fears!" Louis de Broglie exclaimed not long ago, "We are launched on a great adventure and, like the snowball that rolls down the slope, it is not possible for us to stop it. We must run the risk since risk is the condition of all success."[21]

However, to run the risk imposes upon man some demands pointed out by the same outstanding French physicist: "The man of tomorrow should find in the development of his spiritual life and in the loftiness of his moral ideal, the wisdom not to abuse his increased forces." He was alluding to Bergson's celebrated and almost prophetic page where the illustrious philosopher already indicated in 1932, quite some time before his conversion to Catholicism, the only true direction to follow in order to resolve the impasse and to avoid the dangers of scientific progress. Here it is in its entirety: "Machines that operate on kerosene, coal, water power (Bergson did not know nuclear energy), and which convert into movement potential energies accumulated during millions of years, have come to give our organism an extension so vast and a power so formidable, so disproportionate by its dimension and its force, that surely nothing like that had been foreseen in the structural plan of our universe. Now in this body so fantastically enlarged, the soul remains what it was, too little now to fill it, too weak to direct it: from whence the void between it and this body; from whence the fearful social, political and international problems which are so many definitions of this void and which, in order to fill it, bring about today such disorganized and inefficacious efforts. . . ." Further on: "Let us add that the enlarged body awaits a spiritual supplement, and that the mechanical demands a mystical. The origins of the mechanical are perhaps more mystical than one would believe. It will not rediscover its true direction; it will only render services proportionate to its power unless humanity, that it has bent still more towards the earth, arrives, because of it, at the point of standing up and looking at the sky."

To look at the sky is to turn toward God. In fact, in Him alone, the modern world can hope for "the spiritual supplement" that it waits for. Because it lives no longer, or not sufficiently, of God, humanity is threatened by asphyxia and by death. Let it begin to live more of God: all will be saved. For that reason, the most urgent and most necessary task in today's world, without neglecting in any way, any of the economic, political and social reforms, is to help it find or refind the meaning of God; more precisely, the knowledge and love of the Father and of the Son, by the power of the Holy Spirit.

Footnotes

1. Const. *Gaudium et Spes,* no.1.
2. *Ibid.,* no. 4, par. 3-5.
3. *Ibid.,* no. 7, par. 3.
4. *Ibid.,* no. 19, par. 2.
5. *Ibid.,* no. 57, par. 5.
6. *Ibid.,*no. 12, par. 1.
7. *Ibid.,* no. 19, par. 2.
8. *Ibid.,* no. 20, par. 1.
9. *Ibid.,* no. 20, par. 2.
10. *Ibid.,* no. 19, par. 3.
11. *Ibid.,* no. 10, par. 1.
12. *Ibid.,* no. 81, par. 2 and 3.
13. Henri Rollet, "Le Divorce du progrés *et de la création."XIIIe, Semaine des intellectuels catholiques.*
14. *Gaudium et Spes,* no. 6, par.5; par. 2.
15. Express, March 5, 1964.
16. *Paris-Match,* Jan. 6, 1968.
17. *Le Figaro littéraire,* no. 1 161, 1968.
18. *Gaudium et Spes,* no. 26, par. 3.
19. *Ibid.,* no. 25, par. 1; cf. no. 26, par. 2; no. 29, par. 4.
20. Cf. L. Evely, Une religion pour notre temps, manuscript available through Dr. Ferriére, *"Les Rameaux" Ottignies, Belgium, 1966, pp. 121-126.*
21. *Louis de Broglie, Physique et Microphysique,* Albin Michel, Paris, 1947, p. 364.

Chapter 3

THE MODERN WORLD AND HUNGER FOR GOD

In the light of the Constitution *Gaudium et Spes* of Vatican II, as I have attempted to explain it in the preceding chapters, today's world has appeared to us, according to the terms of the conciliary text: "at the same time powerful and weak, capable of the best and of the worst." We have stated that "in front of it, a path is open to liberty or to slavery, to progress or to regression."[1]

Now, we have also stated that the causes of regression are found to be the very ones of progress. These causes are not harmful in themselves, since they are capable of producing good effects. They are linked to a fundamental cause which makes them beneficial as well as harmful. The evil is not in the development of science and of technology nor in the progress these have caused and continue to cause. The evil is "in man's heart," the Council affirms. It is also the conviction of Alfred Kastler, Nobel prize winner in physics. Questioned on the warlike applications of his discoveries, he answered: "The danger is not in the existence of arms. It is in the human heart." Another Nobel prize winner, Francois Mauriac, had already said: "Evil is in the world, and it is there because it is in man."[2] All these statements only corroborate Christ's: "It is within men's hearts that evil thoughts come; fornication, thefts, murders, adulteries, covetousness, wickednees, debauchery, envy, pride, foolishness. All these evils come from within and make man impure" (Mk 7:21).

This presence of evil in man's heart and in the world is the sad consequence of the sin of the first man, to which has been given the name original sin. "Established by God in a state of justice," we read in the conciliary Constitution *Gaudium et Spes,* "man, seduced by Evil at the beginning of history, abused his liberty, rising up against God, wishing to achieve his end outside of God . . . . What divine Revelation, thus, uncovers to us, our own experience confirms. If he looks into his heart, man finds, also, an inclination to evil, submerged within many evils which cannot come from his Creator who is good. Often refusing to recognize God as his source, man has, by that very fact, broken the order which directed him to his last end, and at the same time, he has broken all the harmony, be it in relation to himself, or in his relationship with other men and all creation."[3] Thus, "divided within himself, torn between good and evil, man, "by his pride and disordinate self-love,"[4] can cause to deviate from their true meaning, all values, and to change human activity, ordered for the service of God and man, into an instrument of sin."[5]

We have there, briefly formulated, the dogma of original sin,[6] that sin which is the cause of the existence of evil in and by man in the world. In order to save the world today and its values, it is, then, necessary to free men from this sin and from all slavery to which they have been subjected because of it. Now, Jesus Christ has already accomplished their liberation once for all by the power of His spirit, so that, in order to benefit from this liberation, all that is needed is for men today, as well as for men of all times, to give their allegiance to Christ the liberator.

This liberation will be discussed in the following chapters. We will see how, by permitting men to participate in God's very life, it can help avoid in today's world the harm and the dangers of progress realized in many areas by scientific development. This union in fact, can cause them to direct all these improvements for the service of humanity and for the glory of God, according to the admirable words of St. Paul who summarizes briefly the Creator's plan for creation: "All is yours but you are Christ's and Christ is God's" (Cor 1 3:22-23).

The Need for God

Before approaching the study of this liberation in itself, it is important to say why men today need to be liberated by Christ. We know that, like the men of yesterday and like men of all times, having been made for God, called freely to Him from the beginning, to be His children by sharing in His life of love, each one has sinned in the person of Adam (Cf. Rm 5:12). Indeed, out of pride, the first man refused the gift that God had given to him, as well as, to all men in his person. He fell and caused them to fall with him into the slavery of sin which deprived them of divine life and shut them off from God's love.

We know also that, immediately after this rejection, God, because He had not ceased loving His creature—because He is love, God cannot stop loving, because He would cease to be—promised, in mysterious terms a liberator which would come to deliver men from sin, and make them receptive again to His love. "And God said to the serpent: I shall place enmity between you and the *woman,* between your descendants and hers; she will crush your head, and you shall strike at her heel" (Gn 3:15). This prophetic announcement takes on its full meaning in the light of this statement of St. Paul: "When the fullness of time came, God sent His Son, born of a *woman . . .* in order to confer upon us filial adoption" (Gal 4:4-5). This statement means that, in spite of the original fall, God kept His plan to communicate to men His fatherly love, to make them His adopted children in His Son Jesus Christ. So, men remain called to be in the image and likeness of God, and destined to find their fulfillment and happiness only in a communion of love with Him.

Thus, because men today, like men of all times, remain

made for God, because they are hungry for God, in order to be able to satisfy this hunger, they need to benefit from the liberation accomplished by Christ.

However, according to a number of our contemporaries, God no longer interests men today. What interests them is the organization of the earth, the development of man, social questions, political action and sexual problems. They continue reiterating that God is dead. Indeed, if what is meant by that statement is that certain false aspects of God are truly dead or should be dead, I agree, and we ought to rejoice that they are dead, or that the anthromorphic God reduced to human dimensions is dead: the God who served and perhaps still serves to explain all that man cannot understand or master; the God of battles who orders us to kill for love of Him; the God who protects bank accounts, who legitimizes our egoism, laziness, pride, the will to rule and to dominate; the God who legalizes social inequalities, who justifies injustices and the most ambiguous enterprises, or, still more, God the policeman, and the God who is against man. We ought to be grateful to a certain atheism for having helped us to kill those gods.

However, that the God of Jesus Christ, the God who is the All-Other and the All-Love is dead, is what I question. In fact, I think there exists among men of our time an immense need for God. Concerning this need which our contemporaries resent, I shall begin by giving some proofs. Then I shall show that it is explained by another need which is characteristic of men not only today, but always: the need for love. Finally, we shall see that this need for love is precisely nothing else but a need for God.

Numerous indications reveal that the hunger for God has never been so alive as in today's world. Because of their great quantity, it would not be easy to record the films, television and radio programs, songs, novels, plays, newspaper articles, reviews, books of all kinds that directly or indirectly treat of subjects related to God. It is not unusual for this existence to be discussed in the most widely different types of work. Here are some examples collected by Jacques

Duquesne in his fascinating book on *Dieu pour l'Homme
d'Aujourd'hui:*

"Some priests fear that God is truly dead since 'His
existence is no longer discussed.' It is not so certain.

"A 21-year-old stenographer: 'No, I am not a Christian.
Of course, I went to catechism like everyone else. Then I left
it all, like everyone else. Actually not quite. That doesn't
prevent asking questions. I have a group of friends, boys and
girls. We go out together. You wouldn't believe it. We still
discuss God's existence when together. There's a boy in our
group, who believes in Him. As for me, I don't know. I
would really like to believe. I read a book called: *Dieu existe,
je l'ai rencontre'*.[7] The author explains that he was a
complete atheist: not baptized, no catechism, no communion, nothing. Then one day he went into a chapel by chance.
He saw an apparition, a great light. That man was lucky.
Why doesn't that happen to me? I would like to believe.
However, I'm not lucky. If there is a God, why does He show
Himself to some and not to others?'

"A 46-year-old business director: 'In my business circle,
our meetings are usually limited by precise objectives. We
scarcely have time to talk about anything more than our sales
or production problems. Yet, if you take a business trip with
someone for three or four days for example—then there is
time to know each other a bit better. It is not possible to
spend three or four days with someone without discussing,
in some way or another, basic questions. For instance, the
other week, I was in Finland, at the home of the director of a
factory, in the company of his young wife about whom I had
already been told: 'Before meeting her, become informed
about the latest record and the latest Parisian styles, that is
truly the only topic of conversation.' During the entire
evening, we spoke only about faith. The four or five men
who were there—engineers for the most part—truly
participated; you felt that it was a subject about which they
had reflected somewhat. When you have a profound
discussion with someone, it is difficult not to arrive, at some
time or another, at the ultimate preoccupation.' "

Andre Malraux:[8] "Modern civilization is in the process of attempting to drown the feeling of servitude — let it not drown at all, not even in alcohol — which is very much stronger than it, and thinking that it will last longer like that. Now I am persuaded that it cannot last. Either humanity will have found a new transcendence, that is, a new harmony between the feeling of servitude and, the cosmos, call it whatever we like, either that, or a new religion will be born, which comes back somewhat to the same thing. I believe that the state of the general thought of our civilization, in relation to the essential problems of the spiritual, is essentially a temporary one which succeeds only because science, which thought that it could become a total explanation of the world, has preserved a certain form of hope."

Marcel Maréchal, director of "The Theater of the VIII" in Lyons:[9] "I was raised in the Roman Catholic religion, and it has influenced me very much . . . . Even so, all that is far behind me, and, when I left that world almost fourteen years ago, it seemed to me very solid and very hierarchical. So I'm a little stunned, and, at the same time, amazed to see that, in such a short time, the flow of ideas has caused all that beautiful order to be called into question.

"What I ask is: why this questioning? If the reason is that the priests of the Catholic Church want to take a step further in the world so that the Catholic might become more 'Christian,' that is, closer to a true social action . . . if this broad movement is a progressive movement, if it is so that the Church might be more human, that does not seem important to me; that even seems deceptive to me. If, on the contrary, it is a widespread movement that causes the Church to want to rediscover her true mission, that is, to want to give priority again to people who see, to mystiques, that seems to be more interesting and more important. It is not by removing the cassock or by marrying that one will succeed in solving the problems of faith. If it is a leap forward, if the priest escapes from his duties in the Church clubs, of Catholic Action, etc. in order to say to himself: 'I am a man of God; I ought to give witness solely to my faith and to God,' then that interests me. In other words, if it is a mystical adventure, I find that exciting. If it is a social adventure in the style of the times, if the priests are suddenly touched by the socialist grace, that bores me; I find that it is a regression. . . . By his life, the religious ought to give witness to something else than his everyday life, than his political life. Let him give witness to the possibility of another dimension, of the divine life, if it exists."

"For my part, I shall remember for a long time that young girl who, right in the midst of a public debate on the conflict in the Church, stood up and shouted: 'All that does not interest me. Me, I'm an atheist. Why don't you talk to me about God?' The priests who organize conferences on social problems in their parishes, maintain that these discussions attract less than conferences on faith and on God."[10]

A study made among university students in the United States showed that eighty percent of them expressed the need for a religious faith.[11] Whereas, on April 8, 1966, the American weekly *Time* had asked the question: "Is God Dead?", three years later, on December 29, 1969, it asked the reverse; "Is God in the process of rising?", and it stated the signs of a religious renewal. In Germany, according to a survey taken at the end of 1967, eighty-six percent of the adults stated that they prayed. Max Horkheimer, the German philosopher with Marxist tendencies, who is acclaimed as the inspiration of the rebellious movement in the universities, declared, at the beginning of the 1970, in an interview in *Spiegel* it was necessary to turn to God and to theology in order to counterbalance the inhuman conditions of "the totally blueprinted society."

In the Scandinavian countries that I mentioned in the preceding chapter, there has been, for about thirty years, a great spiritual, actually Christian, reawakening, especially among the intellectuals who already hope for the foundation, or rather the restoration, in their country of the contemplative and monastic life. In Sweden, several religious houses have already been established; they have abolished a law that forbade such foundations. There is a sign that proves the depth of yearning for the spiritual life in these countries because, provided that it is lived seriously, the monastic life is one of the most authentic witnesses that can be given to God's transcendence.

A similar spiritual awakening is, likewise, in the process of occurring in Russia: "After almost 45 years of a regime exclusively and violently anti-religious, the communist leaders, themselves, are being forced to submit to facts and figures; there exists in Russia a "religious phenomenon" not only in a survival but, also in a revival state. The following are the most important events establishing this fact: In August, 1957, there was a large secret meeting in Moscow, bringing together 350 theorists and activists, specialists of atheism, from the fifteen republics of the Soviet Union. . . . On the podium were all the great stars of atheism. . . . The president, Mr. Mitine, began by declaring forthrightly that, such a conference was necessary because the situation was serious. 'The influence of religion,' he said, 'continues to make itself felt today . . . among many of the Russian people. In many places, an increase in the number of believers is noted; . . . certain young girls and boys are being influenced by religion; a good number of Komsomols (members of the Communist Youth Party) not only call themselves believers, but have the audacity and the arrogance to flaunt their religious behavior; certain local committees are giving evidence of a culpable tolerance toward certain *Komsomsltzi-Bogomoltzi* (that is, 'Communist Youth praying to God'. . .); they do not denounce such 'turncoats'. . .; they allow their members not only to marry in the Church, but, even, to attend and to participate in all religious rites.' The delegates admitted these crushing facts. Certain ones (such as Ramme and Priadko) declared the damage irreparable. They were denounced publicly for their 'fatalistic pessimism.' " Faith in the God of Jesus Christ has, then, remained alive among the Russian people. The most dramatic example is that of Alexander Solzhenitsyn who gives witness, in the most direct way, of his Christianity, especially in the last chapters of his *Gulag Archipelago.*

As for those who call themselves atheists, many are only with regard to the God whose death is proclaimed and who, in fact, does not exist. I have already spoken about this God, or rather, about these false concepts of God at the beginning of this chapter. Besides, the God in whom they do not believe, or in whom they no longer believe, is not God such as He truly is and Whom they fail to recognize where He is through lack of power, will, or for various reasons. It is the God such as they imagine Him, the results of caricatures that have been made of Him, or the false notion of Him that has been unfortunately given to them. I have already mentioned certain Christians, poorly informed about their religion through their own fault, or the fault of those who should have instructed them. "They represent God to themselves," says the Council when speaking of these atheists, "in such a light that by rejecting Him reject a God Who is in no way that of the Gospel."[12]

Basically, the religious need is the most essential need of humanity, and a need that is entrenched in the innermost depths of every man and that one can overlook only if one denies it purely and simply; it exists in those very ones who call themselves atheists. It is, likewise, not surprising to read this remark of Roger Martin du Gard: "The human conscience is religious in its essence. It must be admitted as a fact . . . . The need to believe in something . . . that need is in us just as the need to breathe."[13]

Now, atheists must, indeed, place this need on whatever object. Not believing in the God of the Christians, they look for this object elsewhere than in the Christian religion, and they make an actual God of it. However, to this unknown God whom they search for and discover gropingly, to use St. Paul's word, to this God "that their conscience reveals obscurely as the ineffable source of all truth and beauty, of all justice and goodness," they give one of the following names: conscience, justice, duty, honor, truth, science, beauty, art, life, work, philanthropy, altruism, party, country, race, society, or humanity. In fact, they attribute "wrongly to these human ideals," as Vatican II says, "such an absolute character that they come to accept them as God."[14] Likewise, to them these ideals seem to merit the consecration of their life and, even, if such be the case, sacrificing it for them. At the same time they affirm the Sovereign Good, and it can be said that, without knowing it, they believe in God; they become part of a group of the godless. After all, the name God is only a name, like all names, it is conventional. Add to that the fact that the word God has, in French, no descriptive meaning and says nothing of the reality that it signifies. If these atheists, then, give another name to their absolute, if they do not wish to recognize in it our God, the reason is that the word God has been dishonored and does not correspond, or no longer corresponds, in their mind, except to the false ideas that they have made for themselves or that were given to them about Him.

These false notions of God are the reason, in good part, that so many men search outside of the Christian religion for the satisfaction of their religious aspirations, for a purer, more reasonable, and more spiritual religion. For many atheists, atheism indicates the reaction against men's abuses of the idea of God. For all of them "atheism is, then, much less the pure and simple negation of a transcendent reality for man of an Infinite, of an Absolute, than the rejection of a certain representation of God which seems to them incompatible with man's dignity, but so much the more with what God ought to be." As one of them has expressed it so eloquently: "God is God for only him who surmounts the temptation of degrading him by using Him in his service (Leon Brunschvig)." "It's not God whom I hate," said another, "it's the use that the faithful make of Him." Thus, for that reason a non-Christian philosopher was able to write: "There aren't any atheists; there are only men who refuse to recognize in the deformed image of him that is presented to them, the God, the concept of whom they carry in the depth of their being."

However, it will probably be said that the ideal of many is only commonplace. Impossible to discover in them the least need for the absolute. That is not completely true. There is, in every man, a secret urgency which results in his being dissatisfied with anything that he attains or possesses, and everything, some day, deceives or bores him. Needing something to fulfill his desire, and lacking knowledge of God, man, consciously or not, hopes to be satisfied making his God whatever he wants. His idol can be an idea, a passion, a fad; it can be money, power, a creature of flesh and blood; it can be only the pleasure of a meal, as seen in those people of whom St. Paul spoke that "their God is their belly" (Ph 3:19). All these idols which are an insult to the true God, basically give homage to Him, and prove that there is in every man, no matter how materialistic he seems, a desire to project beyond what is real, even when he is mistaken by the object. However altered and deviated it might be because of the first fall, this desire is no less a sign of the presence in every man of a religious yearning.

The religious need is then a universal fact. Everything indicates that the recognition of a certain superior reality, of a certain absolute, responding to this most essential need of humanity, is as old as humanity itself. Attempts have been made to prove the contrary. However, neither ethnology nor prehistory can furnish precise facts to support the thesis according to which there would have been, from the very beginning of human history, a period when any kind of religion would have been missing. Likewise, religion would have been born one day by man's exploitation, at the same time as it, thanks to progress. "Nothing more inaccurate," writes Teilhard de Chardin, "than to look at religion as a primitive and transitory stage which humanity goes through during its infancy. The more man is man, the more necessary it will be to know how and to be able to worship . . . . The religious phenomenon is an irreversible cosmic grandeur" (*Comment je crois*, p. 31). Elsewhere: "Arrived at a higher level of self-mastery, the Spirit of the earth discovers a more and more vital need for worship: from the universal Evolution, God emerges greater and more necessary than ever" *(Sauvons l'humanite')*.

Men of our day are not on the verge of giving up God. What is happening is, even the contrary. "Perhaps," writes Jacques Duquesne, "we are at the dawn of a new age of humanity in which God will be necessary."[15]

It is not until the hippie phenomenon, the phenomena of drugs, violence, eroticism that there is a deep indication of the need of the absolute which dwells in every man and which is nothing else but the need for God. The remarks of authorities in all these matters clarify some perspectives that, indeed, must be called metaphysical and religious. Actually, whether they wish it or not, men are made, for the infinite, for the absolute who is God, and their heart remains restless, says St. Augustine, as long as they do not rest in Him. The young, as well as adults, cannot escape this truth. In order to proclaim, I suppose, their independence and their personality by anticonformity, the boys let their hair grow, and the girls shorten their skirts, to no avail. They are no less created to the image and likeness of God; they, too, remain made for the absolute which is God. However, for a variety of reasons, not succeeding in becoming conscious of this need, or in identifying it and directing it toward God, since it was repeated so often that God was dead, today's youth succeeded in repressing it. Thus, this need for the absolute having been repelled but not gratified, the young—and the not so young—attempt to satisfy it by the awkwardly expressed rejection of the society of abundance and of consumption, by all kinds of stimulations, by revolt and violence, by depraved and perverted practices of sexuality which is eroticism. As proof of this affirmation, I need only to recall, with regard to the first three phenomena, the witnesses quoted earlier,[16] and to quote, with regard to the fourth, the remark of a sociologist, Roger Bastide: "when the gods cease to speak, the libido speaks."

This same repression of the need for the absolute explains, also, the development of sects, the success of astrologers, clairvoyants, spirits and other kinds of mediums. The famous American astrologer, Zaltan Mason states: "For the past five years, the average age of my clients has fallen from 45 to 25." He adds: "These are men who search for God, and lament the present chaos in the world."[17]

Such then, is the feeling of emptiness and anguish of man become materialistic by the advances of technology, when he should have received happiness from them. The surge toward the Far-Eastern religions, the thronging to sects of all sorts as a substitute-religion, the animosity of Marxism against all religion, the resistance that the latter encounters in all countries, the revivification of faith that is produced, and the religious character which cloaks Marxism itself, the deviating phenomena of the modern world, all these facts prove to us that man is an essentially religious being. They allow us, then, to affirm once more that in those very ones who, for various reasons, call themselves atheists, there exists the religious need.

The Thirst for Love

How to explain this need, this hunger for God? By the thirst for happiness which is a thirst for love.

It is a commonplace that we are creatures avid for happiness, as well as, that for us there is only one problem in the world: happiness. With regard to this problem, all others are subordinate or derivative.

No matter what demand, no matter which occupation, no matter what part of the world, no matter what moment of life and of the day, there is no one who is not inspired by the conscious or unconscious desire to be happy.

Is it not this thirst for happiness that is described in the famous expression which has always fascinated man: to live life? If there are several ways to understand the meaning and to feel the richness of this life, all of them include the desire to be happy. To be happy, according to Pascal, "is the incentive of all man's actions, even those who are going to be hanged."[18] For his part, Claudel wrote: "For a rather long time, along all the paths of the Universe, you have exercised this ability of attention and intelligence at the service of this deep craving for happiness which the most austere philosophers recognize as the basis of human nature."[19]

The thirst for happiness is, then, a universal fact, although life proves powerless to satisfy it, and, if all men are agreed in demanding for themselves and for others, laughter and song, even in the depth of misery, the reason is that they are profoundly convinced that joy exists and that man is made for happiness.

However, in reality, what is happiness? What must be understood by this magical word that, from the beginning of time, has fascinated humanity?

Happiness is a certain state of contentment resulting from the rather complete, and more or less perfect satisfaction, from many and varied desires which exist in each human being, a satisfaction obtained, thanks to the possession of goods which are the objects of these desires. The big problem is to discern which of these desires, the realization of which, by the possession of its object, will make us the most completely and the most perfectly happy.

First, I shall state that human aspirations are diverse and contradictory, not only by—another well-known thought of Pascal: "All men search for happiness without exception. They use different means, but they all tend toward this end. What causes some to go to war and others not, is the same desire which is in both, (as well as in each individual), accompanied by different viewpoints."[20] Sometimes these diverse and contradictory aspirations are simultaneous; sometimes even, certain tendencies are deviated; certain pleasures accompany some apparent and relative good— such as the fact of hanging oneself—which, in reality, are found to be absolute wrongs. In fact, because man is a sinner he is mistaken in his objective, and he attaches himself to caricatures of his good and of his happiness.

This remark having been made, let us return to the question: what is, of all the desires that human beings share, that one whose satisfaction obtained by the corresponding good, can procure true happiness for us? We will not ask the philosophers for the answer to this question because we find it somehow, close at hand, in our personal experience and in others. There is no need in fact, of a long study of self and of others to affirm that the need to which we aspire and whose possession ought to make us happy, is love.

Effectively, human experience allows us to declare that all of man's aspirations lead definitely to that of loving, and to be loved, and that the solution to the problem of happiness — and thus of existence — is found in love.

Have we not said, actually, that, when our heart is satisfied, we are completely happy, while on the contrary, when our heart hungers, all of earth's advantages are of little value? Is he who only knows the most opulent life incapable of giving happiness? Is he happy, he who has not known or heard about these people surrounded by every advantage that the world can give and who, however, lead a disturbed and sad life, made up of constant changes which seem to them like so many checkers? Inform yourself, and you will have no difficulty discovering that their heart is empty. So, a life without love is no life.

On the contrary, for hearts filled with love there is no miserable life which does not seem to them rich and beautiful. "It is truly beautiful," writes a young woman whose home is very unpretentious, "it's truly beautiful — the simple life where one is loved deeply . . . . Looking at us from the outside, they think us deprived of everything, while we have so much."

Such a general statement ought to find its explanation in the very nature of the human person; in fact, we do find it there. If we look for what is in our soul, the good that surpasses all other, we observe what it is that satisfies the heart. That is not surprising: created to the image of God Who is love, man has been molded with love. Not that this good is the only one that attracts us! How to deny that sensible satisfactions do not unloosen in us violent and sometimes dominating appetites! However, man — and there is his nobility — could not find in his senses the ultimate end of his desires. Sensible pleasures shake him completely; yet they contain a triple deficiency: they pass quickly, they excite the appetite more than satisfy it, and their excess even engenders disgust.

On a higher level, we find the satisfactions of the spirit: the force of science, the joy of discovery, the delights of beauty. Certainly, those are objects most worthy of the human intelligence, whose possession gives to man his proper position on the scale of human beings. However, it is apparent that, of themselves, they do not give happiness. We know very well that the most studious mind and the most artistic spirit find taste in work, beauty in art, only because of the fervor that they have in their heart. If the latter lacks love, the spirit is confused; if it is overwhelmed, science, genius and art are only surplus goods whose esteem derives, above all, from the brilliance that they add to love. "Glory always causes pleasure. People have talked about my modesty. In his subconscious each man is ambitious. I am happy to be a Nobel Prize Winner." After having shared these confidences with a journalist come to interview him, Alfred Kastler replied to the same interviewer who asked: "Since receiving your prize, what question has given you the most pleasure?" The answer: "That of a Spanish journalist. He asked me what was the greatest event of my life." Mr. Kstler continued smiling: "He waited for me to say: the Nobel prize. Certainly, it is an immense personal satisfaction. However, I believe that it is a rare satisfaction. There is something more beautiful than ambition and work . . . it is love. The most beautiful day of my life was that of my engagement."

In brief, the consideration of human nature leads us to the conclusion that, for every man, the supreme good is that of the heart: it alone is above all other goods—nothing replaces it. Experience is there to tell us that, in the midst of their research and anxieties, their crimes and their virtues, their laughter and tears, men are occupied with loving. To love well or badly, sublimely or basely, the instinct of loving is the constitutive part of their nature.[21]

Thus, the desire for happiness, the desire that seemed to

us universal and constant, implicit under every aspiration, common to all men in spite of the divergence of their views, is the desire to love and to be loved. That is the reason why St. Augustine summarized all the aspirations of his being, of every being, precisely in these words: *"Amare et amari*: to love and to be loved."[22]

The thirst for happiness which is a universal fact is, then, a thirst for love. Towards what object does this love, which drives every human being, lead our heart? We can respond immediately: to the search for reciprocal love, capable of responding to his own. Until he has found it, man searches. Like the Spouse of the Canticle of Canticles, he goes through the City, that is, this world, and asks all passers by — creatures around him — the same anguishing question: "Have you seen the one whom my heart loves?"

Would the object of his love be perceptible goods which obtain what one is accustomed to call advantages and the pleasures of life: health, beauty, fortune, luxury, comfort, rank, glory, honor, power? Would love be in the possession of this vast and marvelous world which is offered to him?

When questioned, these creatures answer: *"Quare super nos*: search above us." In fact, man notices very quickly that, even when he might have all the comforts, money, honors, and sensible joys that he could desire, he would lack the perfect exercise of his own human faculties: intelligence and will.

Actually, it is in this exercise that is found man's end which serves for nothing else, and which leaves nothing to be desired because it involves all other ends. These are only the means which lead to it, or elements which constitute it. To find his complete contentment in an inferior end is exceptional, indeed. It is contrary to nature: the person is, in this case, unnatural, monstrous, at least, completely atrophied.

Is man then going to find in the object of his intelligence and of his will, the very object of his love? It seems so. What the intelligence searches for is the knowledge of the Beautiful and of the True; what the will desires is Goodness.

However, Beauty, Truth and Goodness, when viewed closely, are only three aspects of the same reality, of the unique reality which, according as it addresses itself to the intelligence or to the will, is expressed by Beauty, Truth and Goodness. That is the reason why these three terms are attributable to each other, and that it can be said: Beauty is true and good; Truth is beautiful and good; Goodnesss is beautiful and true. Now this unique reality which irradiates, thus, in Beauty, Truth and Goodness, which is subject to them, is a reality at the basis of love, an amiable and, in a certain way, a loving reality.

Indeed, through the intermediary of the senses, the spirit, put in contact with Beauty, gives it its consent, at the same time as Beauty is given to it; placed before Truth, it gives it its consent, at the same time as Truth is given to it. The will placed before Goodness, gives it its approval, at the same time as Goodness is communicated to it. In these three cases, there is a gift — it is said that one is "smitten," "delighted" — there is even a reciprocal exchange, a union and possession. Now love is the same thing. The three exclamations that escape from us in these three instances: it is beautiful! it is true! it is good! are prolonged in this same cry: I love! One could add: "and I am loved" — in a certain way, obviously — because Beauty, Truth and Goodness, if they kindle our desire, they themselves do not feel any desire for us, any conscious and free love: they give themselves without knowing it, but to the extent that they give themselves, it can be said, in a certain way, that they love. Thus, this remark of the poet:

But there is nature who invites you, and who loves you.

Can Beauty, Art, Harmony, Truth, Science, Goodness, Virtue, Justice, and Duty, satisfy my thirst for Love?

The same answer is given to us: *Quaere super nos*: search above us.

Search above us. Not that we do not have anything to give you, but we are incapable of satisfying you completely and forever.

In reality, without being like those who regard creation as bad and dangerous, and who separate themselves from it with fear, who consider all earthly foods as poison, and who reject them with an absurd disdain or a morbid fear, one must admit that beauty, even if it is never clouded by a shadow, is always fleeting; that truth, even if it is never sullied by error is, however, incomplete; that goodness, even if it is not impossible, is often difficult to follow.

How short-lived is the beauty of creatures! the poet says:

> The fascination of eyes is too quickly taken from them.
> With today's charm, tomorrow comes to distract you,[23]

A beautiful landscape delights us, but time is pressing, and we must leave it, or day ends and all returns to shadow.

One hardly begins to enjoy the music of a beautiful concert when the instruments are silent! We are scarcely under the spell of a powerful choir of warm and melodious voices when they stop: it is already finished!

> Do not love anything for its song: songs have only one hour![24]

Time passes, and the face of the world passes with it: "Where are the snows of yesterday?" Where is:

> The rose which this morning had unfolded
> Its crimson robe to the sun?

Human faces, and human beauties pass with the face of this world. "All flesh is like the grass," the prophet Isaiah used to say, "and all its grace, like the flowers of the field: the grass dries up and the flower wilts" (Is 40:6-7).

Beauty fades even when man's hand tries to hold on to it by painting it on a canvas, on stone, or on paper so that at least sometimes, alas, its passing might be delayed! . . .

Our thirst for beauty remaining unsatisfied, our heart searches elsewhere for fulfillment.

Might this fulfillment be truth?

All the Athenians of the first century A.D., reports St.

Luke, and the foreigners settled in the city, spent their time talking about, or listening to the latest news (Ac 17:21). This situation, need it be said, is not peculiar to the Athenians alone. When we reflect on the use of our time, we admit without difficulty the considerable importance that men attach to the new which comes to them constantly. The reason is that man is a very curious and restless being. "This restless monster, man," Peguy used to say. He wants to know without restriction, what was, what is and what will be. He needs truth in order to resolve the problem of his life, the human problem.

Philosophers have attempted to solve this problem.

Certain ones among them, in the last century, believed that the solution would be given by science. "To organize humanity scientifically, such is the last word of modern science, such is its audacious but legitimate claim." It was, at least, Renan's thought. Indeed, before long "the failure of science" was announced (Brunetiere). The growing disorder and the great anguish of contemporary society are the cruelly ironic response to Renan and the scientists. Science itself, in the twentieth century, far from succeeding in explaining everything, causes scientific spirits — true ones — today, more than ever, to have the limits of their knowledge tapped, even because of its progress and technical applications. A growing number of intellectuals state openly that what they know is little when compared to what they do not know. "Without doubt," writes Oppenheimer, "the notion of universal knowledge has always been an illusion, but it was favored by the monistic conception of the world where some great central truths determine others in all their amazing and astonishing proliferation. We are no longer tempted today by the keys of the totality of learning and man's experience. We know that we are ignorant."[25] For his part, Alfred Kastler, confided: "Without a doubt, I am like everyone else: I ask myself questions about the origins of the world. Yet, since I do not know how to answer them, I prefer to remain silent."[26] Not only modern intellectuals recognize the limits of their knowledge, but they deny formally the absolute character that science wants to attribute to scientific certitude. Science gives only probabilities, and its dogmas are affected by a certain relativism. At the world congress of the Philosophy of Sciences, held in Zurich in September, 1954, Ferdinand Gonseth, the famous Swiss mathematician, declared that "principles are no longer fixed at the point of departure, but only temporarily defined, according to the science of the moment. From whence it follows that science reveals only the relative and the probable." Leprince-Ringuet, in his book, *Des atomes et des hommes*, shows that scientific certitude, "appearing at the start from a convergence of somewhat fragile indices"—which is equally true of very complex disciplines such as biology, as well as, geology, paleontology and physics—can be held in check because of, and by, other discoveries. He recalls that Maxwell's famous theory which includes in the same synthesis light and electro-magnetic phenomena, considered formerly as sacrosanct, no longer, holds the same value today as formerly after Max Planck; in any case, the atom escapes him completely. "However," he says, "whoever would not have considered, around 1900, the Maxwellian theory as a certitude would have been accused of stupidity by all intellectuals!" Analogous statements are to be found of Louis de Broglie, as well as of the Italian intellectual Francesco Severi. "Classical science," says the latter, "used to speak of evidence and of necessity; today it speaks of probability."[27]

Thus, by the very admission of the intellectuals, the most developed science is incapable of giving any absolute certitude; it cannot explain everything. Furthermore, scientific progress and technical realizations, themselves, pose problems that science as such, is still more incapable of resolving. If, in fact, placed in its domain of matter, science reveals itself incapable of attaining real truth, how could it pretend to solve problems which arise in other areas? How would it be able to answer man's fundamental questions about the meaning of the world and its proper destiny? "The development of the physics of particules," says again

Leprince-Ringuet, "leaves certain problems intact. It gives no new element in response to the question of knowing what we have come to do on earth. Even should we go with our anguish to the moon, this anguish would remain the same."[28] For his part, Jean Guitton writes: "Let us suppose that we know perfectly the how of all changes, what would this accomplished science allow us to answer to the question *why* and even the question *what*? What is the cause of matter, of life, of human existence; what is the basic reason for all that? Let us suppose a fatal science explaining and even causing one to know the concept of an egg . . . As for me, I won't be satisfied in the least. There would still remain for me to understand what is, essentially, the cause of life, and evolution; why are there laws and not chaos; why did the thought arise; why does all that exist rather than nothing; why am I; for what am I destined, and what is the meaning of this universe, and what is death for a thinking being? Secretly these are the questions that every man asks. Certainly science never answers them."[29] Besides, that is not its object nor its end, and true intellectuals refuse to philosophize about such. Recognizing its limits, science does not prevent its devotees from turning to other areas: that of philosophy and of faith. Indeed, there are many true intellectuals whom physics leads, as one of them said "to the burning shores of metaphysics." Likewise, numerous intellectuals, after having wandered on the paths of doubt, have ended, like Charles Nicolle, by turning towards God. "Since reason," he wrote to his friend Leon Daudet, "is incapable of explaining biological facts which have led to the genesis of the living, useless to look for other explanations than the traditional. After all, I do like you, I hug the shore."[30] Thus, it remains true that, left to itself, science, which has made a great deal of progress in the knowledge of inanimate matter, leaves us in serious ignorance about ourselves, as Dr. Alexis Carrel notes in *L'Homme, cet inconnu!* The enigma becomes more serious to the degree that science progresses; the mystery becomes deeper instead of disappearing.

The positivists, together with Auguste Comte, believed in solving the problem by suppressing it, practically, in order to give the illusion that it was resolved. However, there are problems that cannot be suppressed.

The idealist themselves have concurred with Kant about the incapacity of our intelligence to resolve the problem in question.

There remain the existentialists and the Marxists.

What answer does existentialism bring us, that is atheistic existentialism? As response to all problems that existence poses, we receive regularly the fatidic: it is absurd. "Existence is without reason, without cause and without necessity," writes Sartre in *l'Etre et le Né*ant. In *La Nausée*: "Everything existing is born without reason, is prolonged by weakness and dies by coincidence." Life is "a lost under-taking from beginning to end," "something completely indifferent, insipid, and tasteless, which when one takes stock, upsets your heart and makes you nauseous." Love, reduced to egoism, attempts to make itself "a fascinating object" with regard to another in order to make itself loved by him, all the while desiring that this other makes itself an object, also, so that it be loved in its turn; love "seems nothing more than a series of indefinitely deceptive attempts which leave the individual a stranger to all the joys of the communion of souls in a true love." So, to our need for happiness, joy, life and love, one responds with a doctrine of nothingness, nausea, absurdity, egoism, anguish, despair, suicide and death. The Christian is well aware of these conditions of the soul. Every Christian, above all, the saints, the Christian par excellence, knows more or less these circumstances. However, with him, they emerge into those states which are called Christian confidence, love hope, joy, the Christian way of life—or of death, not through distaste for life, but because of love of life. These states allow him to overcome by going beyond the conditions of the soul where existentialism fails.

The marxists are happily more optimistic. They have a faith in man, and a faith in the future of humanity. The first is translated by the will to liberate man from economic and material servitude; the second consists in this idea that there is a progress that is irrevocably realized by History, that is, by men's effort inserted into historical development. Crises and revolutions can happen: they are part of this development which will extend over an incalculable number of years, and, at the heart of which, progress is accomplished. The important thing is to have confidence in History, to believe in this progress, but the essential thing is that it is being accomplished. Unfortunately, we know that there is a captivity worse than the economic: it is the spiritual captivity that is man's slavery to the powers of evil which he carries within himself and to those outside, and which St. Paul calls "the princes, the powers, the dominations of this world of darkness (Ep 6:12). Now we do not see that Marxism has liberated its followers from that captivity. We know what anguish and what despair exist under the so-called economic liberation which is settled definitively by the alienation of the human person to collectivity, by the subjection of man body and soul, "to the socialized and rationalized production of material goods without any other perspective than to consume the part that an equally socialized division will give to him."31

Scientism, positivism, idealism, existentialism, Marxism are, besides Christianity, the principal inclinations of modern minds; they are positions which cannot satisfy our spirit athirst for truth, nor satisfy, consequently, our heart thirsting for love.

Can the Good that our will desires satisfy the need of this heart?

It seems that there would be no doubt about it, Goodness being essentially kind, and more so than Beauty and Truth. It must be remembered that the goodness in question here is moral goodness. Indeed, "goodness," writes Father Garrigou-Lagrange, "is not only what is desirable, what is capable of attracting our desire, and of making us happy; it is also what ought to be desired, what has a right to be loved, what demands love imperiously and establishes duty."32

First of all, let us state that, if the fact of sin is perhaps the most evident of all facts, the tendency to good is no less essential and universal.

Now this inclination toward good, while one obeys it with complete fidelity, gives to life a great nobility, and gives interiorly profound satisfactions. Experience tells us so.

However, in addition to the fact that good is not always easy to discern, neither is it always easy to follow.

Basically, wanting the good, man, as St. Paul says, tends toward evil, in spite of himself, dominated as he is by another law that he feels within himself, and which fights against the law of his reason. "Exhausted and fatigued by the useless search for the true good" (Pascal), his heart remains restless.

Furthermore, as long as it remains in the sphere of simple, human morality, the tendency toward good leaves us to face ourselves, or the implacable commandment of duty. Now that state cannot satisfy us, for goodness represents an ideal too cold for our heart, as long as it does not show itself to us under the form of a person who would give to the moral law a more kindly aspect. Besides, beauty, not more than goodness, would be without a shadow and eternal. Beauty and the whole truth, could not satisfy our heart as long as they remain abstractions.

In fact, love cannot be content with the intellectual representation of its object. The human heart wants beauty, truth and goodness, but under the form of a living person, capable of knowledge and love, having a heart of flesh similar to his, conscious of the gift that the receives and capable of giving him a conscious response because as we have seen love requires and always must demand a reciprocity.

Would the human person then be the object of my love? "It seems obvious," says Bossuet, "that man's pleasure is man."

The fullness of human love seems, actually, to bring us the answer. What is more satisfying to a heart than the love of a father, mother, husband, wife, brother, sister, friend?

However, this is rare and it passes quickly.

This love is rare. What does the human heart really encounter most often, if not egoism, isolation, misunderstanding, indifference, miseries, injustices, hatred, jealousy, deceptions, separation, doubt, infidelity, lies? All are things that cause him to suffer and which drain him indefinitely.

Even with persons, the most favored in every respect, love lacks a fullness because it is fleeting, and because our heart needs a love that is stable, definite, eternal, in a word, absolute.

"Let them be sweet," affirms Chateaubriand melancholically, "but let them quick, the moments that brothers and sisters pass together during their childhood, united under the protection of their parents! Man's family lasts only one day; God's breath disperses it like smoke." Children scarcely know their parents, parents their children!

What about final separations that we hear about here on earth. Don't they occur rather often prematurely? Moreover, at whatever date they take place, they are always premature, aren't they? . . . How many couples, for example, have been suddenly separated by death before being able to enjoy their incipient love? How many eyes "blue or black all loved, all beautiful," to use the poet's words, were scarcely filled with light and life when already "they were filled with shadow?"[33]

While they last, how many painful tests these affections have experienced! However, at least, during the short length of time that he lives with his love, doesn't our heart enjoy it as much as it wishes, and does his joy, still only ephemeral, leave anything to be desired for the moment? Experience answers no. Actually, what a true and great love asks for is total union, the perfect compenetration of souls. Now, without talking about complete solitude which, sad to say, disturbs so many hearts, it can be said that absolute intimacy does not exist, even between two beings who are one. The reason is that the human heart is incapable of expressing itself, even to itself, incapable, then, of communicating itself entirely, incapable, also, of penetrating the depth of another heart, even if the latter strains to surrender itself. "The heart of all men is impenetrable; who can fathom it?"(Jr 17:9). Thus, there does not exist a living person who is not more or less alone. "The solitude of lovers and of friends. The mother's solitude embracing her son with a ferocious clasp, and of the father seeing himself in the eyes of his daughter. The solitude of the priest cloistered in his black cassock and of the Don Juan caressing a beautiful body . . . . We go from the cradle where we were alone, to the coffin where we will be stretched out alone."[34]

Thus, then, his search ended, man makes the same declaration as the Spouse of the Canticle:

> I have searched for him whom my heart loves
> And I have not found him.

When asked, all creatures, from whatever level of Creation, have been invited to look elsewhere, to look higher: *Quare super nos*, look above us!

This statement impresses us with its double meaning; first by its gravity and universality, even really, by the fatality of the remark. Because the thought expressed contradicts absolutely our most profound aspirations, to such a degree, what amazes us most is not, perhaps so much the superhuman character of our aspirations as the reality and the awareness of our failure: proof that the failure is not essential to our nature, but rather that "the creature does not measure up to the standard of our heart"[35] and that man was made only for the infinite. The writer Aragon who certainly would never be accused of mysticism says of one of his heroines that she "wanted to find ultimately and at any cost the incarnation of her dreams . . . . The infinite in the finite." In order to attempt to explain this wish, he adds: "There is a passion so consuming that it cannot be described. It eats whomever contemplates it. All those who are captivated by it are caught. One cannot test it and recover. One shivers just talking about it; it is the taste of the absolute. It can be said that it is a rare passion, and frenzied amateurs of human grandeur will even add: unfortunately. It is necessary to undeceive oneself. This passion is more widespread than the flu. There is no microscope to examine its microbe; we do not know how to isolate the virus, which, for lack of a better word, we call the taste of the absolute.''

That fact does not prevent this novelist from seeing in this taste of the absolute only an accidental malady of the soul, whose symptom is ''a total incapacity for the subject to be happy,'' even though he says that it is more prevalent than flu. It would have seemed more just, if he had recognized, with Paschal, that this hunger for the absolute is a constitutive element of human nature, an innate aspiration of the human heart. ''What then,'' says the author of the *Pensees*, ''do this avidity and incapability shout out to us, if not that, formerly, there was in man a true happiness whose mark and completely empty trace, alone, now remain for him. He tries in vain to fill it with all that surrounds him, looking for, in absent things, the help that he does not receive from present ones, but which are all incapable of help because the infinite chasm cannot be filled except by an infinite and unchangeable object.''

Thus, for us Christians, the taste for the absolute — this passion which dwells even in hearts where no sounds reveal it, but where it is no less protected than a fire under the ashes — is a hunger for God, a hunger which gnaws at every man, which is, as has been said so forcefully, ''the very definition of man.'' Everything in us calls for the absolute, for an absolute of love, for an absolute love. It is this call that is the most essential and the most noble aspiration of our nature; it is this need of an infinite love, which gives us our highest value, and causes us to perform our greatest activity. It is not then something artificial or illusory; it is really in us, even though it is not of us.

However, it will be said, are you really sure that someone ought to respond to this call: that to our infinite need for love ought to correspond an objective reality? Wouldn't this be only a projection into the reality of a being that we would dream up, an ideal creation of our spirit in order to respond to this call, in order to satisfy this need, this desire of our nature?

No, it would be very strange, indeed, that a dream which encompasses in it the most fundamental aspirations of all mankind is only a dream. A need of nature, a natural desire cannot be fruitless and without an end, because it would have no reason for existence, and something without a reason for being is a contradiction. Could one pretend that the need, for example, to drink or to eat can be without a purpose? It could be frustrated, but it could not be fruitless. Thirst supposes drink; hunger supposes nourishment. Likewise, "the eye implies the existence of light; the lung, the existence of a respirable atmosphere."[36] Andre Gide is right in saying:

> I know that I have not a desire
> That has not already its readied response. . . .[37]

Likewise, our need for an absolute love, also, implies the existence of a being capable of gratifying it. This need is not, then, the cause, but the effect of the reality toward which it tends. It is not our need of this being that makes it exist; it is this existing being that places this need in us.

So, the depth and universality of this need, alone, are a proof that to this need ought to correspond an objective reality, an absolute being, an infinite love.

Besides, the powerlessness of Creation to satisfy this need is another proof of it. Like Claudel's character, Creation says to us: "I am the promise which cannot be possessed, and my grace consists in that very thing,"[38] That is, creatures cannot give this absolute being, this infinite love; they promise and do not give: it is a grace that they give us forcing us to turn toward someone higher.

"Having scarcely surpassed them," says, once again, the Spouse of the Canticle, "I found the one that my heart loves" (Sg 3:4).

This absolute being, transcendent and, at the same time, immanent, that is, present in our most innermost being, who alone can give the truly satisfying response to our desire to love and to be loved. Reason, moreover, proves to us that this infinite love that our heart calls intensely and of which it has such a great need, exists, and faith, furthermore, gives us the certitude of its existence. It is faith that has put this call and this need in us. It is none else than He whom we call God, and whom Christianity, with the Apostle St. John, calls precisely: Love. "It is necessary to love," writes Pascal, "a being who is in us and who is not ourselves. This need is true of each and every man. Now, only the universal Being is such. The kingdom of God is in us: the universal good is in us; it is ourselves, and it is not we."[39] Elsewhere:"The God of Abraham, the God of Isaac, the God of Jacob, the God of Christians, is a God of love and of consolation. He is a God who fills the soul and the heart of those whom He possesses; He is a God who unites Himself in the depth of their soul, who renders them incapable of another end than Himself."[40] We will see in the following chapter, to what degree it is true that God merits this name of Love, and that, like St. Angela de Foligno, "there is nothing in Him that is not love."

Footnotes

1. *Gaudium et Spes*, no. 9, par. 4.
2. "Bloc-note," *Le Figaro*, April 1-7, 1965.
3. *Gaudium et Spes*, no.13, par. 1
4. *Ibid.*, no. 37, par. 4.
5. *Ibid.*, no. 37, par. 3.
6. Cf. my work: *Le peche Originel, Peut-on y croire encore?*
7. Andre Frossard, *Dieu existe, je l'ai rencontré*, Fayard.
8. In an interview retransmitted by the O.R.T.F. national French radio and television, cf. *Le Monde*, Oct. 27, 1967.
9. Excerpt of an interview published in *Lumiere et Vie*, monthly journal, no. 93.
10. Jacques Duquesne, *Dieu pour l'homme d'aujourd'hui*, Grasset, Paris, 1970, pp. 88-92.
11. Rose Golden, *What College Students Think*, Nostrand, Princeton, N.J.
12. *Gaudium et Spes*, no. 19, par. 2.
13. Jean Barois, *L'Age critique*, La Pléiade Edition, p. 502.
14. *Gaudium et Spes*, no. 19, par. 2.
15. Jacques Duquesne, *Dieu pour l'homme d'aujourd'hui*, p. 93.
16. Cf. above, p. 39.
17. Quoted by Jacques Duquesne, *Dieu pour l'homme d'aujourd'hui*, pp. 52-53.
18. *Pensées*, Brunschvicg edition, no. 425.
19. Paul Claudel, *Seigneur, apprenez-nous a prier*, Gallimard, Paris, 1942, p. 53.
20. Pascal, *Pensées*, ed. Brunschvicg, no. 425.

21. Cf. Snason, *Marie-Madeleleine*, Albin Michel, p. 23.
22. St. Augustine, *Confessions*, Book II, Ch. II.
23. Marie Noel, *Les Chansons et les Heures*, Stock, Paris, p. 150.
24. *Ibid.*, p. 150.
25. Quoted by Jean de Fabregues in *La France Catholique*, Jan. 16, 1959.
26. In *Nouvelles et Images du monde*.
27. Cf. *Documentation catholique*, 1952, p. 678.
28. Quoted by Luc Baresta in *La France Catholique*, Nov. 20, 1964.
29. In *Arts*.
30. Charles Clerc, *Charles Nicolle, prix Nobel de médecine*, p. 12.
31. Riquet, *Conférences de Notre Dame*, Lent, 1947, 5th conference, p. 23.
32. Garrigou-Lagrange, Dieu, *son existence et sa nature*, 2 vols., 11th edition, Beauchesne, Paris, 1950, Vol.1, p. 308.
33. Sully Prud'homme, A. Lemerre.
34. Edouard Estaunié, *Solitudes*, Perrin, Paris, 1930, p. 238.
35. Mauriac.
36. Francois de Curel, *La Nouvelle, Idole*, Albin Michel, Paris, 1931, p. 66.
37. A. Gide, *Les Nourritures terrestres*, Gallimard, Paris, 1942, p. 40.
38. Paul Claudel, *La Ville*, in *Théatre de Paul Claudel*, Gallimard, Paris, 1947, Vol. 1, Act. III.
39. *Pensées*, no. 485.
40. *Ibid.*, no. 556.

Chapter 4

GOD IS LOVE

In spite of what appearances might lead one to believe, men of today are hungry for God because, like men of all times, they are hungry for love, for an absolute love, and God alone is capable of satisfying completely this hunger. Now, if God can thus satisfy men's hunger for love, the reason is that He, Himself, is this love. St. John defined Him thus: "God is love." In order to understand this definition well, we must examine carefully the mystery of God's intimate life, in other words, the mystery of the Blessed Trinity, as Jesus Christ has revealed it to us.

Introduction to the Study of the Trinitarian Mystery

There is value in recalling beforehand what we can know about God with the help of Christian revelation. Men can look for and discern God in the light only of reason or of science or of conscience, thus, without the help, I do not say, of his grace, but of the revelation made by Jesus Christ. Vatican I states that it is something completely possible, basing this affirmation on St. Paul's letter to the Romans. Speaking of the pagans, the Apostle says: "What can be known about God is visible to them, God having manifested it to them. In fact, since the creation of the world, His invisible perfections, above all, his eternal power and divinity, let themselves be understood and contemplated in creatures. Pagans are, thus, inexcusable since, having known God, they have not glorified Him as such, and have not rendered glory to Him" (Rm 1:19).

This, then, is what we can know about God with natural knowledge, that is, without help of the divine word publicly revealed. God is the only being in whom essence and existence are identical, that is, He does not receive His existence from another but He possesses it without a beginning of any kind, neither temporal nor logical; the only being who exists of Himself, who has no cause, who has no source, who has always been, who will always be. He is the only eternal being, infinite in time as well as in eternity, a being, independent, absolute, transcendent, the unique one, the most high, inaccessible in Himself. When speaking of God, a Moslem mystic expressed this transcendence thus: "He could not have anything *above* hanging over him, nor anything *below* which lessens Him, nor a *limit* confronting Him, nor *alongside* disturbing Him nor *behind* censuring Him, nor *ahead* limiting Him, nor *before* causing Him to appear, nor *after* Him causing Him to disappear, nor an *all* repressing Him, nor a *he is* making Him found, nor a *he is not* depriving Him. There is no *attribute* to describe Him. His act has no cause; His being has no limit. He remains removed from the stages of creation. His acts do not admit of improvement; he turns aside from them in His transcendence, just as they turn aside from Him in their contingency."[1] God is still the one who gives movement without being moved Himself; the one in whom there is no change, no perfecting, because a movement and a development would suppose that He has not always been perfect. He is the one who cannot be and not be, that is, the necessary being. He is the one who is for all beings the source of being, of goodness and of all other perfection. He is the one who orders all things, that is, the ordering Intelligence. He has the fullness of life, of truth, of goodness and of beauty. He is the all-powerful, the just, the holy and merciful being. He possesses all perfections in their perfection; He is Perfection; He is the Perfect One.

However, this natural knowledge of God is incapable of telling us all about God because it cannot enlighten us concerning that part of divine truth which we cannot know unless God is disposed to reveal it to us. It is impossible to penetrate the mystery of God's intimate life. God alone can allow us to penetrate it; He alone can lift the veil that conceals it from our eyes; in a word, He must reveal it to us. Now, God was pleased to reveal Himself. It is knowledge by means of faith. Thus, we are going to examine as much as possible, this mystery of God's inner life, the mystery of the Blessed Trinity. We have been created to know and to contemplate this mystery here below and in eternity. Moreover, how can we announce Jesus Christ and the God of Jesus Christ if we are incapable of responding to someone who asks us the reason for our faith in this mystery, for example, one of our Moslem brothers, or Jews, or unbelievers for whom this mystery is a stumbling block? Witness this man who, having asked one of his fellow office workers — a Christian — if he believed in the Blessed Trinity, and having received an affirmative response, said to him: "What is this monster with three heads?" The other man was speechless.

For that matter, the Christian mysteries are truths that we ought to believe, even though we cannot understand them, and they will not be revealed to us until eternity. These are truths that we cannot understand perfectly, and that we could not know if God had not revealed them to us. By saying that we cannot understand them perfectly, one infers that the Christian mysteries do not escape completely our understanding. A mystery is a truth that was hidden, but which has been revealed. This fact stems from several passages of St. Paul. Now God has revealed to us the mystery of His intimate life by His Son Jesus Christ. St. John, after having affirmed: "No one has ever seen God," adds immediately: "His only Son who is in the bosom of the Father, He it is who has revealed Him" (Jn 1:18). He alone could do it because He alone knows Him. "No one," he says, "knows the Father except the Son and He to whom the Son is willing to reveal Him" (Mt 11:27; cf. Jn 6:46). If He knows Him, the reason is "that He belongs to Him" (Jn 7:29).

This revelation has not been made only for intellectuals and theologians. Knowledge of the Trinity is accessible to the most humble, to the "little ones" of whom Christ speaks: "I bless you, Lord of heaven and of earth, for having hidden it from the wise and clever, and revealed it to the very little" (Mt 11:25).

It is no less true that knowledge of the mystery of the Blessed Trinity, like that of other mysteries, moreover, will always be imperfect. We cannot understand perfectly the Christian mysteries which surpass all created intelligence. No one will be surprised not to be able to fathom the depth of the interior mystery, even in heaven, for we will never finish penetrating God's infinity.

This rational study, even though imperfect, is, however, of great help to human reason; it allows it not only to explain fully the mystery, but to furnish motives for admitting it, reasons for believing it. Besides, the contemplation of the trinitarian mystery is very enriching for our spiritual life. As Vatican Council I states, "While reason, enlightened by faith, seeks carefully piety and moderation, it acquires, with God's help, a certain very profitable intelligence of the mysteries, as much by analogy to things that it knows naturally, as by the liaison of the mysteries among themselves and with man's ultimate end."[2] Strongly supported by the authority of this Council, I shall, then, try to penetrate into the mystery of God's intimate life with my reason enlightened by the gifts of faith, and, for a precise starting point, an analogy drawn from Sacred Scripture, itself; the analogy of the human soul.

Before developing this analogy that will allow us to understand a bit better what God's intimate life is, I believe it useful, as well as necessary, to write briefly about life in general.

Taken in its universal sense, life designates four things,

namely, the very principle of life, the special state created by this principle, the peculiar activity caused by this state, and, finally the faculties demanded by the exercise of this activity.

Life denotes, in the first place, the immanent principle which distinguishes the living from the dead, the internal cause which animates the living being, builds it and produces the phenomena accomplished in it. In this sense, we say that the soul is the life of the body, and grace is the life of the soul.

Secondly, life designates the effect produced in the living being by the mysterious principle of which I have just spoken. Furthermore, the latter has as function to make itself master of the elements which enter into the composition of this being, to form this being into a determined type and according to a master plan, to give it form, to animate it, and to establish it in a special state proper to a living being.

In the third place, life designates the totality of acts proper to this state, the special activity of the living. In reality, everything living produces actions conformable to the life that animates it. It passes constantly from potency to act. It changes unceasingly, if not always place, at least, according to existence. In brief, it is in perpetual motion because to move itself means precisely not only to change one's place, but, also, oneself, to change on the level of being. For that reason, philosophers say that life is in movement: *vita in motu.* Furthermore, they say it is an immanent movement, that is, one that comes from the interior of the living being: *motus ab intrinseco.* This statement means that the living being contains in himself the principle of his movements and of his changes. In other words, the cause of the actions which are proper to the living being, which express and reveal his life, which enable its recognition and the evaluation of its force, is interior to the living being. It is this immanence, this interiority of the principle animating the living, which distinguishes it from the non-living.

Finally, life, in general, denotes the appropriate structure of the living, that allows him to accomplish the actions of which I have spoken. Actually, in order to produce these actions, the living being is gifted with various faculties: he will have eyes, ears, arms, a jaw, legs, etc. in a word, an organic apparatus adapted to his environment and to his own nature.

Such are the various meanings of the word "life." It can be stated that these meanings are coordinated among themselves: the principle that animates the living, forms him into a state that is proper to him, and which determines in him a special activity which appropriate faculties allow him to exercise. However, let us emphasize that what characterizes the living is the immanence of the activity, and that the essential element of life to which all is directed, in a word, is action. This latter expresses and interprets life; it is the sign of life, and, at the same time, the ultimate product. It is the sign, since it is the action that manifests life; it is the ultimate product, since even the repose of the blessed in heaven consists of an action, of the most immanent action, that of the intelligence and will, which unites us to God by knowledge and by love.

This highlight of somewhat abstract philosophical ideas is going to enable us to study our subject more clearly and more in depth.

Let us proceed now to the analogy of the human soul.

When creating man, God said that He made him "in His image and likeness" (Gn 1:26). It is a question of using the light that shines from this biblical verse like a projector, so to speak, on this vast screen called the human soul and, thus, to look for and to rediscover the traces of God, of the One God in three persons. Indeed, it is impossible that some traits similar to His are not to be found there, because of the fact that it (the soul) has been created in His image, and it received this original imprint, rudimentary as it might be, but sufficiently indicated to justify the expression of Sacred Scripture.[3]

First, let us state what we understand by soul. This term ordinarily means three things: *anima, spiritus, mens*. Here it is not a question of that aspect of our being, which we share with animals, of the *anima*, that is, of the life by which we are joined to a body and which animates this body. Neither is it a question of the highest part of our being, of the *mens,* that is, of our soul in relation to God, as living for God. It is a question of the soul as spirit, *spiritus,* that is, the soul as living in and for itself, made of these two wonderful things: intelligence and will.

The soul, thus defined, I shall state first what it *is:* it is one and spiritual. It already has those characteristics in common with God who is, who is one, and who is a spiritual being.

Then I shall note that this spirit that is my soul thinks; by thinking, it conceives thought. Thinking about something other than itself, it conceives a thought similar to this thing. Thinking about itself, it conceives a thought similar to itself, for the thought is made similar to the object thought. My spirit perceives the thought that it has of itself, then, as identical to it since it is an expression of what it is. At the same time, although the thought remains in it, and, even when he expresses it outside of himself, he perceives it as distinct of himself, since in the spirit that thinks there is something more than in the spirit that does not think. So, there are two: the spirit that conceives, the father of the thought, and the thought, daughter of the spirit that is called, also, its word, its remark, its interior speech. The human spirit corresponds, then, to God the Father, the thought to God the Son.

If the spirit thinks all by itself, its thought, embracing it completely, will be, although born of it, equal to it, and it is his very self that he will recognize in it. Here is a comparison. If, instead of looking at myself in a small mirror where I shall see only a part of myself, I look at myself in a full-length mirror, the image that the latter will reflect of me will be, since it is sprung from me, as tall as I am.

I suppose that this spirit, recognizing itself, thus, completely in its thought, is replete with perfect qualities, and without any pride, it admires itself in this thought: it admires itself in the thought since the latter expresses its perfections and it is pleased. This complacency is love. Since it is the thing itself that the spirit conceives, it is also this object thus conceived that it loves: its love embraces its entire thought.

If this thought, instead of being, as in us, an inconsistent modality of the spirit, could lift itself to being, as in God, a living person, then someone conscious of himself and capable of knowing and of loving, it could return toward the spirit that engendered it, and recognizing itself in it (the spirit) as the source, the principle of this perfection that it expresses, it would love this father with this same love that the father loves it. Since this thought embraces the entire spirit, it is the entire spirit that it would love.

This love of the spirit for its thought and of the thought for the spirit, embracing the entire thought and the entire spirit, would be as great as this spirit and this thought, and each being distinct from each other, it would remain in one another since this latter would be one in the other.

This love which would proceed from each one, which would join them to each other, without being lost in each other, would correspond to God the Holy Spirit, and would achieve this replica of the human trinity.

To sum up, such is one of the rational explanations that human intelligence can give to the mystery of the Blessed Trinity, using as supporting evidence the well-known verse of Genesis: God said: "Let us make man to our image, according to our likeness," and admitting, of course, what it already knows by revelation of God's secret. As Bossuet says, "without this revelation, who would dare cast his eyes upon this wondrous secret of God? However, with faith, we dare not only to contemplate it, but moreover, to see in us an image of it."[4]

The Mystery of the Blessed Trinity

Let us now try to obtain the knowledge of this wondrous secret of God, which Jesus Christ revealed to us.

The study of this mystery, we are going to attempt, will

necessarily be abstract; it will, even, seem to some like a game of wits. A game of wits? Not at all. What we are going to say on this subject has a basis in reality, such as we know it by means of Revelation. An abstract study? Certainly. Indeed, it is not an experimental knowledge of God that I intend to offer the reader. That knowledge is the fruit, not of philosophical speculation, but of the exercise of theological virtues, and of the gifts of the Holy Spirit. On the other hand, being pure spirit, God could not be perceived by the senses nor understood by the imagination. God a pure spirit, can only be known by a spiritual faculty: the intelligence. Knowledge of God in His trinitarian life, the point in question here, is, then, an intellectual and speculative knowledge. Such knowledge could only be abstract because it is the fruit of a reflective work of the intelligence which, in order to do it, utilizes pure ideas whose verbal expression will, inevitably, be abstract. However, this knowledge does not clarify less, for that reason, the mind which is used to acquire it, especially if the intellectual consideration of the mystery results in the experience of God. Give some courses to the young on love, marriage, the psychology of man and of woman, on sexuality, whatever. Of all these topics, they will have some knowledge — perhaps profound, very interesting — but this knowledge will be theoretical. It will lack something essential: experience. Indeed, in order to have a more complete knowledge of these questions, they will need to experience love; they must marry, and live their love. Then, they will have an experimental knowledge of conjugal love, which will perfect their intellectual knowledge. However, this latter will not remain less desirable, even necessary and indispensable for the success of their marriage.

Thus, the Bible compares knowledge of God and the relationships between God and man with a human marriage and conjugal love. Intellectual knowledge is very desirable, if not necessary, but it is absolutely insufficient. Experimental knowledge is necessary: God must be experienced; one must live the trinitarian life. Therein, lies another question.

This experience is a personal affair; it is the appropriate work proper of all Christians, accomplished under the guidance of the Holy Spirit operating in them by His gifts, as I have just said.

Like all life, that of God is, at first, a state.

The God of whom Jesus Christ speaks as being the Father, is a God who "has life in Himself" (Jn 5:26), who possesses this life in its absolute plenitude. Now the plenitude of life is not conceived without thought or love. These two vital operations belong, then, to God the Father by virtue of His nature. This work of thought and of love is so extraordinary and so great in Him that, by the fact of thinking and of loving, there are two divine persons who spring from His inner being, and who spring from it without leaving it, just as human thought springs from man's spirit without leaving it, even when he verbalizes it; just as human love springs from his heart but remains in him, even when he expresses it exteriorly. In God, there is, then, other than the Father, two persons who are the very expression and the perfection of His internal vitality: they are the fruit of the turning in of God the Father on Himself in order to think Himself and to love His thought and to be loved in it. These Persons are uniquely spiritual spirits. Thus, their acts are uniquely spiritual. They know and they love; they only do that: know themselves and love each other.

Actually, having, in an absolute manner, the plenitude of life and, thus, of being — because the Living One par excellence, is Being "the Being who is" — the Father knows Himself and thinks about Himself, of necessity. Otherwise, He would not really *be*. Yet, knowing Himself, He knows Himself as He is; the thought that He has of Himself is in conformity with Himself. He is the thought; the latter is He, without confusion or inadequacy. In fact, the thought that the Father has of Himself, explains the Father completely without, however, confusing itself with Him; no more than man, when he conceives himself, what he conceives and he who says "I" does not confuse himself completely with the one who is conceived and with the one who is designated by "I."

So, like us, and infinitely better than we, the Father is aware of who He is. He represents Himself to Himself, and in this representation, perfect as all that is in Him is perfect, He produces and conceives another. This exact thought that the Father has of Himself, He pronounces it actually, although silently, within his own interior.[5] It is pronounced, as are pronounced in us, in a certain way, thoughts of which we have a very clear awareness. It is pronounced in a word; it is a word, the word by which the Father, Himself, speaks to Himself completely.[6] It is His Word. This Word constitutes a reality as perfect and as conscious as the Father, a Person like Him: His Son to whom He communicates His nature and all His perfections, except that of being Father.

By thinking about Himself and by contemplating His infinite perfections, the Father thus engenders His Son, and it is this Son that He contemplates definitively since this Son is His exact image, "the splendor of His glory, the imprint of His substance" (Heb 1:3), and in him, He finds Himself completely. Seeing Himself, thus, in His Son, as in a perfect mirror, in another self possessing all that He possesses, He delights in him; He cannot help delighting in him; he cannot help loving him.

Indeed, the Son, being the expression of the Father, personifies Beauty, Truth and Goodness, in a word, the Sovereign Good that is the Father. Now, by his very nature, all good, of necessity, arouses in those who know him a love of desire, because He can gratify a need in them, and this love is perfect in a love of complacency in the good possessed. The Father, then, loves His Son of necessity with a love of desire because He finds in him His good, that is, the possibility of being what He is, that is, Father, of being in other words, as far as principle (that is, source, origin), the Sovereign Good that the Son is, in so far as he is begotten. He desires His Son because He needs him in order to be a Father. Let us note, immediately, this need does not constitute an imperfection in the Father; it does not indicate a lack in Him, but expresses simply an exigency, itself, of His Person without which He would not be Father.

In this Son loved thus, the Father's love rests, and takes pleasure no less of necessity. At Jesus' baptism and the day of his transfiguration, the Father will declare: "This is my beloved Son in whom I am well pleased" (Mt 3:17; 17:5).

However, this love of desire and the love of complacency, flow from another love, the love which is the gift of self.

On the one hand, if the Father needs His Son in order to be the Father, He has given him first of all — of course, it is a question of a logical precedence—Sonship; He engendered him; He gave him life: such is to love with a love of a gift.

On the other hand, if the Father is pleased with His Son, the reason is that He sees in him His very essence. Now the Father's essence which the Son possesses has been given to him from all eternity by the Father Who gives it to him perpetually, since He always was and always will be the Father. In other words, always and forever, He has a Son since He cannot be a Father if He does not have a Son: you might as well say that He possesses His being only by communicating it to His son, that He is the Father only by giving Himself to His Son: It is again a love of gift. The Father, then, loves this Son whom He needs and in whom He is well-pleased, of necessity, with a love diffusive of self, eternal and without limits.

For his part, the Son, because he is someone capable of knowledge and of love, contemplates within the bosom of the divinity the infinite perfections of His Father of which he is the perfect expression. He finds in Him the source and the principle of this infinite Beauty, Truth and Goodness which He is and which He personifies. This knowledge that he has of the Father draws him toward the Father in a reflected outburst of love, the love of desire and of complacency, but also the love of gratitude for the gift of the Father, a love that prompts him to make to Him in return the gift of himself.

So, the Father loves the Son, and the Son loves the Father. Now their mutual love — which is also unique since it is in the same love by which the Father gives Himself to the Son and by which the Son gives himself to the Father (just as with the same glance that I look at my image in a mirror, my image looks at me—constitutes a third Person who is the Holy Spirit. Revelation shows us effectively that the Holy Spirit acts like a person, that is, like someone who performs actions that stem from a person. Consequently, the Holy Spirit is love in person. Indeed, the activity of love is so intense in God that it results in a new person. In other words, the love produced co-jointly by the Father and the Son is so powerful and so complete, that it is separated from them, in some way, in order to form a distinct person who exists only as love. He is formed by what the Father and the Son possess as the dearest and the most appealing: their personal love. It is the personal and living expression of the love which is God. We shall try to penetrate a little better into this mystery of the personification of this love.

All true love involves a desire for ecstasy, in the etymological sense of the word, which means going out of self. It forces those who love to go out of themselves. "Love," writes an anonymous author, "fces the lover outside of himself, and places him in the beloved in such a way that the soul is more present in the one loved than in the one loving."[7] So, those who love each other, want to go out of themselves in order to pass from one to the other. This desire drives them farther than themselves. With the "I" and the "You," it causes them to form, beyond themselves, a "we" which is made of their very own love.

Divine love, too, carries within itself this desire, and it alone can realize it in all truth and perfection. By loving each other, the Father and the Son go out of themselves, so to speak, and form, beyond their persons, a reality which is born of their love, a reality which, in order to be perfect, as all that is in God is perfect, constitutes a person like them. It is the person of the Holy Spirit. The Holy Spirit draws, from the common origin that he has from the Father and the Son, the perfection of personal existence. He is the personified ecstasy of the Father and of the Son. Far from being an abstract person without magnificence, he appears to us as being the personification itself, of exaltation and of dazzlement, of intoxication and of wonder, which is a proof to lovers of the love that dwells within them. Consequently, he is the song of the Father and of the Son, their common jubilation and their common joy, sprung from their happiness of giving themselves to each other, of possessing each other: their joy of loving and of being loved.

This third Person of Blessed Trinity is called the Spirit not only and, first of all, because he is immaterial, free from all matter, a pure spirit; thus understood, this name would not be his own name for, in this sense, the Father, also, is a spirit, as is the Son. If he is called Spirit it is according to the etymological meaning of this word, breath. He is so-called because he is love incarnate, love at its culminating point, and because love, at his extreme degree, no longer speaks or sings: it is silent, or rather, it exhales like a sigh, like an inflamed breath (*spiritus*) where the soul fades completely. In an active way Christ, Himself, has applied to the Holy Spirit this symbol of breath by breathing on His apostles in order to communicate the spirit to them (Cf. Jn 20:22).

The Holy Spirit is, then, at the same time the breath of love exhaled by the Father and the Son, and the fruit of their love, union and sanction. He is in a word, the kiss, simultaneously common and unique — like the mutual and unique kiss which a child and his image, reflected in a mirror, give to each other — the kiss which seals, in the indivisible unity of the divine nature, the trinity of the Person in the eternal ecstasy of infinite joy.

Now what constitutes the divine Persons, as such, are the relationships which exist among them, and which distinguish them, each one from the other two.

First of all, the divine Persons are formed by their relationships. Indeed, the Father is only a father because He has a Son. He exists only relatively to His Son, to whom He gives all that He is, except His paternity, that is, the fact of being a father; the Son is equal to the Father, but he is not the father. The filial relationship of paternity constitutes the Father's personality alone.

For his part, the Son is a son only because he has a Father.

He exists only relatively to his Father, to whom he gives all that he is, except his sonship, that is, the fact of being a son; the Father is completely equal to the Son, but is not the son. The filial relationship alone, constitutes the Son's personality.

The Holy Spirit, also, is constituted by relationship, by relationship to the unique origin, to the unique principle: Father-Son. He is but the infinite breath of love which proceeds from one and from the other, and in which he communicates to them—to the Son by the Father, and to the Father by the Son—all that he is, except his procession, that is, the fact of proceeding from one and the other by the exhalation of love: the Father and the Son are all that the Holy Spirit is, but neither the one nor the other is the Holy Spirit. The proceeding from love constitutes the Holy Spirit's personality alone.

However, in spite of the real distinction that exists among these Persons, there is among them a no less real union which is more than a union: a unity.

Indeed, given that there is only one God, this oneness of the divine Being unites the Persons of the Blessed Trinity in the most complete unity.

Actually, although they are distinct from each other, the relationships which exist among the divine Persons, and which constitute them as such, do not distinguish them from the divine Being: they are identical to Him. It is not the same with human persons. Relationships which are established among created beings are pure accidents. They exist, indeed, in a subject, but they distinguish themselves from it. The paternal relationship, for example, is not essential to Peter. It is accidental that he can have it; for that reason it will be distinct from him. In God, on the contrary, where nothing is accidental, where everything that exists is his Being and belongs to His essence, relationships are not accidental; they do not exist in a subject; they exist only in the divine Being, in the divine essence, and become one only with it. Consequently, the divine Persons who are formed by these relationships are, themselves, identified, also, with the divine Being, with the divine nature. Each one of them possesses all this nature; it is, even, all this nature: the Father is God; the Son is God; the Holy Spirit is God. Now, the divine nature, with which the Persons identify themselves, is one. It is one not only specifically, but also numerically, that is, the divine Persons, the three of them, possess only one and the same nature, a nature not only similar, just as human nature exists among human beings, but, also, unique. "It is he the Holy Spirit who will glorify me because he will take what is mine and will announce it to you. All that the Father has is mine. For that reason, I said that he will take what is mine and will announce it to you" (Jn 16:14-15; cf. 17:10). That is the reason that, while each is truly God, the divine Persons are, however, only one God.

From this oneness of the divine nature results the unity of the Persons of the Blessed Trinity. Being, indeed, identical in the same and unique nature, the divine Persons are united to each other by the relationship of this nature, at the same time, distinguishing themselves, from each other, by the conformity of their relationships.[8]

Now, and this is the point that I wanted to make, this unity of the divine Persons, which flows from this identity with their common nature, is expressed especially in the fact that these three Persons are present and live each one in the other two, by the resemblance of the human spirit, by the thought that this spirit conceives, and by the love that he has for it: spirit, thought, love which, they, too, being completely distinct among themselves, remain each one in the other two. Each of the divine Persons, in reality, finding himself complete in his nature, finds himself, by that very fact, in the other two, since these Persons, the three of them, have only one and the same nature. That was the reason that Christ could say to Philip: "Don't you believe that I am in the Father and that the Father is in Me?" (Jn 14:10; cf. 10:22-29; 14:21). They penetrate each other really and totally; they are blended without being confused, each one in the other two. Here is the manner in which St. Augustine formulated this mutual presence when speaking of the divine Persons:

"Each is in each one, and all are in each one, and each one is in all, and all are in all, and all constitute only one." He adds: "May he who sees that, even imperfectly, even through a mirror, and, like an enigma, rejoice in knowing God, honor him as God, and render him thanks. Let him who does not see, try religiously to see and not to remain blind."

The trinitarian life consists, then, in the presence of the divine Persons, each one in the other two, in their mutual dwelling (from the Latin *in habitare:* to dwell in) or immanence (from the Latin *in manere:* to remain in); a presence that makes God's life, a state, a state of intimacy, the most profound intimacy established by the most perfect knowledge and by the equally most perfect love.

God-Trinity is Love

However, the trinitarian life is not only a state, something static. An intense circulation of love animates this dwelling where the divine Persons reside; it is this dwelling, itself. Indeed, like all life, God's life comprises an activity, a movement. "Life is in the movement." Yet in God, life is, according to Cardinal Bérulle's forceful expression, "a movement without movement." Otherwise, God would be imperfect because it would be necessary to distinguish in Him, as in us, the aptitude to act and action, which would be an imperfection. This distinction does not exist in God. God's act is permanent, without loss, respite, fatigue. "God acts unceasingly," affirms Christ. He is the pure act. However, "if, on the human level," as Cardinal Danielou said, "movement is the expression of a lack—and, thus, unworthy of God,—this represents only a deficiency of it. However, in God, movement exists in its eminent value, as pure act, intensity of life, immanent operation." A spiritual master of our time, the Cistercian, Dom Augustine Guillerand explains what meaning must be given this word in this manner. In speaking of God, he writes, "His movement is not our movement. I am in a new world where nothing begins nor continues nor ends." Again: "Our rectilinear spirits are, at first, disturbed by it. We think that to advance is to go from one point to another, and that is true when the initial point is nothingness or indigence. When it is Being, itself, development cannot be done except in Him, in communication . . . with His Being."[9] He, also, says: "This movement is not a certain form of life such as I know it: it is not the movement of a being; it is the movement of Being, itself, and it is the reason that it is Life, itself."[10] A comparison will allow me to illustrate this truth: it is quite ordinary, God forgive me! If I make a wheel, of a bicycle for example, turn not too quickly, I can see the movement of rotation. However, if I make it turn as fast as possible, it will be impossible for me to know if it turns or not, because the movement will be so rapid. My comparison is very poor, but it makes us grasp a little what is the intensity of life in God.

The reciprocal presence of the divine Persons supposes, then, a true dynamism and not only a simple sojourn and a rest. It is, in the trinitarian life, what constitutes movement, and the very fact that it is presence, because whoever says presence, says relation, and whoever says relation, says movement, specifying that, as I remarked in the beginning, to move oneself is not only to change places, but also to change on the level of being. I will explain.

Presence is not defined essentially by space, by the fact of "finding oneself in a stipulated place," still less, when it is a question of persons who are outside of space. Presence is defined by the relationship, by the connection which exists between two or more persons: for example, the relation of friendship and the relation of love. It will be so much more intimate as the relationship becomes closer. The localization interferes only to the extent that it creates, supports or draws relationships closer.

Now, what establishes a relation between two people is the change that whatever cause produces, either in the one or in the other, or in both. This cause can be, for example, the knowledge that one has of the other, or that they have of each other, or the love that one has for the other or that they have for each other. The relation established by this change is, then, presence. Now the change which creates a relation in a being consists in the passage of this being, from this aptitude to act, to action. This passage, from potency to act, as the philosophers say, is the very definition of movement. Thus, then, movement is at the root of the relationship which constitutes presence.

Such is the presence by which the divine Persons are present one in the other two. It results from the relations which exist among them: paternal, filial, paternal-filial. These relations, too, are due to a change but without change, to a movement but of a special nature: it is "the movement without movement" about which Bérulle used to speak, and that we have tried to define earlier. These relationships are established by knowledge and by love. In fact, the paternal relationship is due to the engendering, always as action, of the Son by the Father, operated by the knowledge and the love of the Son by the Father. In other words, it is due to the gift, without intermission as well as unreservedly, that the Father makes to his Son of His being and of all His perfections. The filial relationship is due to the always present fact that the Son welcomes the Father's gift and returns it to Him always and completely in a burst of grateful love. The relation of procession or paternal-filial is due, likewise, to the constantly present fact that the Holy Spirit is exhaled conjointly by the Father and the Son, in other words, he is their mutual gift, their love personified, in which they recognize each other in knowing him, like parents who, by looking at their child—the personification of their love—recognize themselves in him.

Now these relations, by distinguishing completely the divine Persons from each other, involve them, move them each toward the other two, in a movement of a love so intense that it gives them, the one to the other two, and unites them, thus, in the most complete unity.

Actually, the relationship which, by definition, as I have already said, establishes a rapport between two things, could not act except if these two things are opposed (I do not say contrary) that is, placed one facing the other, not mingled, thus distinct. Yet, at the same time, because it joins them one to the other, because it puts them in relationship one with the other, it links them; it unites them, of necessity, with each other because the relative, the thing referred, united, "related" cannot exist nor be conceived, at least as such, without the thing to which it is referred or related. If there is no son, he could not have a father. For that reason, in God the paternal relationship, by completely distinguishing the Father from the Son, unites Him to the Son since it makes Him Father of this Son. The filial relationship, by distinguishing completely the Son from the Father, unites him to the Father, since it makes him Son of this Father. Finally the relationship of procession, by completely distinguishing the Holy Spirit from the Father and from the Son, unites him to them since it makes him the love of the one for the other. Thus then, what distinguishes the divine Persons — that is, their reciprocal relationships — is, at the same time, what unites them. In other words, nothing distinguishes the divine Persons if not the reciprocal relations which make them different among themselves, and which, at the same time, unite them to each other.

I have already, also, said that the relationships which unite the Persons of the Blessed Trinity are the relationships of knowledge and of love. They are born of the knowledge, by the Father, of His son who is His "image," and of the knowledge, by the Son, of the infinite perfections of his Father; and this mutual knowledge is fulfilled in the mutual love of the Father and of the Son consummated in the ineffable embrace of the Holy Spirit.

So then knowledge and love are definitively the movement which leads the divine Persons one toward the others. In the words of Dom Guillerand, "It is the very movement of their being. This movement is infinite, as is their being; it is their very being, but their being which moves in order to give itself . . .; both are only love and gift of self. They give infinitely to each other this being which is only movement and love . . . ." Eternally, the Father, the Son and the Spirit "contemplate this gift of self, and they delight in giving themselves, in their being one in the other, one by the other, one for the other. No measure, no restriction in this gift of self"[11] and, of course, no egoism.

No egoism, is there, neither in the Father, nor in the Son, nor in the Holy Spirit. Effectively, the Father does not love Himself, neither does the Son. As St. Bonaventure writes, "the love which is the Holy Spirit does not proceed from the Father, as the Father loving Himself, nor from the Son as the Son loving Himself; it proceeds from the one loving the other. It is a knot; it is the love by which the lover tends toward the other." No egoism is there between the two either, since the mutual love of the Father and of the Son does not stop with them; it does not close them in on themselves like a closed society; it leaps, on the contrary to the breaking forth of a third person to whom the two communicate all their being.

Neither is there egoism in the Holy Spirit. Far from being complacent in itself, his Person is the complacency of the Father in the Son and of the Son in the Father. It is true that he does nothing of himself, not being himself the origin. However, he is no less directed toward the unique origin Father-Son from whom he proceeds, no less generous in his love than the Father and the Son. The Holy Spirit is the love which is completely given to the Father and to the Son, to the Son by the Father and to the Father by the Son. Because the Holy Spirit is the total gift of the Father to the Son, and of the Son to the Father, the Trinity completes itself with the third Person.

O Trinity! O Unity! O Love! Where to find the least egoism—there where the person is only pure relationship and living, perpetual communication. Rather, how to conceive of a gift, of a more complete, more disinterested, more generous love than this existing love, than this continual divine impoverishment, than this permanent, divine poverty?

So, it can be affirmed that not only the third, but the three Persons in God are love. Yes, truly "there is nothing in Him that is not love." Love is "the essence of His essence," His unique and very same nature, possessed entirely and indivisibly, but differently, by each of the Persons. Each of them is identified by this substantial love. He distinguishes Himself from the others only by possessing, in His own way, this unique and very same Love. The first is Love possessed by the Father as Principle and Source, and given by Him: it is paternal Love. The second is the Love possessed by the Son as begotten of the Father, and given back by him; it is filial love. The third is the Love possessed by the Holy Spirit as proceeding from the Father and the Son, Love thus given and given back: it is personal Love, the paternal-filial Love.

The trinitarian life, life such as it is lived in and by the Blessed Trinity, is, then, essentially a movement of love. It consists in that the three Persons are pure relations each to the other two, completely ordered, completely given each to the two others, in the mutual possession of a knowledge and of a love, that are infinite.

Footnotes

1. Quotation of Al-Hallaj. Cf. Massignon, *Al-Hallaj, Martyr mystique de l'Islam,* Paul Geuthner, Paris, 1922, p. 368.
2. Const. *De Fide catholica,* ch. IV, Denz, 1796.
3. Cf. Landrieux, *Le Divin Méconnu,* Beauchesne, Paris, 1921, pp. 3-12.
4. *Elévations sur les Mysteres,* second week, 4th elevation.
5. "The Father spoke only one word and it is His Son. He spoke it always and in an eternal silence. It is in silence that the soul understands." (St. John of the Cross).
6. In God, the word is not distinguished from the thought any more than the thought is distinguished from the divine being.
7. *De adhaerendo Deo,* ch. 12.
8. This unity is symbolized by the three-branched candle which certain Eastern churches use in their divine liturgy. These three branches actually form only one because they have one single base.
9. André Rouvier, *Dom Guillerand, un maitre spirituel de notre temps,* Desclée de Brouwer, Paris, 1965, p. 123.
10. *Ibid.,* p. 128.
11. *Op. cit.,* p.126.

Chapter 5

LIBERATION FROM SPIRITUAL DEATH

Men have been invited, and continue to be invited, to participate and to communicate in this life of love of the divine Persons. Now, we know that in the person of Adam by disobeying God, they fell into the slavery of sin which has deprived them of this communion. This privation consisted in a two-fold death: death to divine life, or spiritual death, and death to physical life, or corporal death. We, likewise, know that, by His sacrifice, by His death and resurrection, Jesus Christ liberated them from this sin and, thus, from this two-fold death. "When you were the slaves of sin," writes St. Paul in his letter to the Christians of Rome, "you were free with regard to justice (in the sense of a virtuous life). What fruits did you produce then? Fruits which embarrass you today because the result of all that is death. Yet, now, liberated from sin and become God slaves, you have sanctity for your fruit, and the result is eternal life. The reward of sin is death, while God's gratuitous gift is eternal life in Jesus Christ Our Lord" (Rm 6:20-23).

Thus, it is by receiving, through faith in Jesus Christ, the gift God made gratuitously to them of eternal life in His Son, that men today, as men of all times, can be freed from the slavery of sin and from all other slaveries to which sin has subjected them. To them, also, as to all of the Jews who believed in Him, Jesus said: "If you live in my word, you will truly be my disciples; you will know truth and the truth will make you free men. . . . Indeed, I tell you truly, whoever commits sin is the slave of sin. The slave does not remain forever in the home; the Son remains there always. If then the Son frees you, you will truly be free. . ." (Jn 8:31-36).

By infusing into men eternal life, Christ frees them from spiritual and corporal death. In this chapter and in the following, I shall discuss only the liberation of the first of these two deaths. The liberation of the second will be discussed later.

If, as has just been seen, man's liberation from spiritual death is brought about by the infusion of eternal life into his soul, we must know in what this life consists, this life that is called both Christian and spiritual.

In order to give this life a clear and concrete definition, I believe it necessary to state beforehand what it is not. I shall do so in this chapter by showing, on the one hand, that the spiritual life, properly so-called, is not reduced to what is called "the religious life," nor to what is called "the interior life"; on the other hand, neither is it reduced to any kind of "spiritual life."

At first sight, even though these three expressions: "spiritual life," "religious life,"[1] and "interior life" overlap, more or less, they do not coincide exactly.

"Spiritual life" Is Not Identical To "religious life"

Actually, as has been observed, "we ought to affirm that there has existed, that there still truly exists, forms of 'religious life' which imply no 'spiritual life,' nor any 'interior life' properly so-called." Without speaking, for example, of the old Latin religion, that of the pagan peasants of Latium, which only consisted of the correct fulfillment of certain rites and the exact pronunciation of certain formulas, we find with the Christians, be they

Catholics, orthodox or Protestants, persons whose religion, indeed, consists, above all, if not exclusively, in "exterior practices" or in "good works." Is not Mass on Sunday, fish on fast days, candles, kissing statues and icons, the veneration of statues, the rosary, Easter Communion, social conformity, affective fidelity, if not the whole at least, the main point of the religion of a good number of Catholics, to speak only of them? They can be very sincere, and even pious in their own way, but one can recognize in their religious life only an embryo of the spiritual life.

For others, whose number grows from day to day, religion consists, above all in a charitable activism where they spare no effort in all kinds of social action. It is reduced to love of neighbor; it is to be found more and more among Christians.

Certainly, love of neighbor is an essential element of Christianity. Did not Christ declare that it is the distinctive sign of the Christian: "By the love that you have for each other, will all recognize you as my disciples" (Jn 13:35). Furthermore, this love which was already the object of a commandment of the Old Law: "You will love your neighbor as yourself," must be practised according to the new dimension Christ gave it: "I give you a new commandment: to love each other, yes, to love each other as I have loved you" (Jn 13:34). However, even thus understood and practised, the love of others cannot be the whole of Christianity.

In fact, before the commandment of love of neighbor, Christ recalled one He said was the first and the greatest: "You shall love God with all your heart, with all your soul, with all your strength.' " If He loved His own to the end, even to giving His life for them, it was, first of all, out of love for His Father. It is so true that authentic love of neighbor cannot be conceived without love of God who is the source of it, according to this statement of St. John: "Beloved, let us love one another since love comes from God" (1 Jn 4:7).

Thus, to reduce Christianity to charitable relations with the neighbor, to what is called today the horizontal dimension, is to mutilate what constitutes its first and fundamental dimension which is its vertical one: the relation to God. It is to make it, paradoxically, as all the believers of the "death of God" want, an atheistic Christianism, which implies obviously the negation, if not in theory, at least in practice, of Christ's divinity.

Without going that far in actual fact, many Christians, today, have put so much emphasis on the horizontal dimension of their Christianity to the detriment of the vertical, that they have ended up by relegating God to a second plane. This lack of interest for the appropriately religious dimension of the Christian religion is manifested in the loss of the meaning of adoration, contemplation, thanksgiving, praise, prayer in general, as well as, in a great indifference to the sacraments. Likewise, an increasing number no longer goes to Mass on Sundays and holydays, or to confession. Those who do go to confession, almost always, acknowledge failures in charity, but rarely think about confessing not having prayed or assisted at Mass. These seem much less important to them than to sin against the love of neighbor. Loving one's neighbor is good; it is even very good; it is indispensable. However, it cannot dispense with the love of God, nor, consequently, with faith in Him, with hope in His grace and in the life to come.

Furthermore, this love of neighbor, in order to be authentic, ought to be modeled on Christ's love: "Love one another as I have loved you." Now why did Christ love, and love, even to giving His life? Not directly to better our living conditions, nor to suppress suffering and temporal death, but to save us, that is, to deliver us from evil, to free us from sin and from eternal death, and to make us His brothers and, thus, children of His Father, loved by Him as He loves the Father and with the same love. Is that not the eternal plan of God's love, such as St. Paul revealed it (Ep 1:3-6) and that Christ came to accomplish? True love of neighbor, the Christian love, in other words, authentic charity, does not consist essentially in devoting oneself to others. It is not necessary to be a Christian for that. Do we not find tremendous self-sacrifices among non-Christians? Christian love of neighbor includes something more essential, namely, to want for others this reason why Christ loved them to the point of giving His life: to want them to become sons and daughters of His Father, and, thus, to establish among themselves and Him the relationship which constitutes precisely the vertical dimension. For that, one must want, first of all, for oneself this relationship with God. For that reason, the Christian religion, lived in practice without this dimension cannot constitute a true spiritual life. The latter, in fact, consists in the exercise of the theological virtues of faith, hope and charity, which have, precisely, God as object.

Finally, for other Christians, religion is reduced, above all, if not solely, to a more or less sustained effort to acquire a certain manner of life in conformity with, a more or less, exalted ideal of perfection. It is only ethics. It is not always their fault. Instead of talking to them about God, about the God of Jesus Christ, of teaching them to live exactly the theological virtues of faith, hope and charity, in a word, to live with and for God, parents and educators have spoken to them only of duty and of the moral virtues. They have preached to them only obedience, sincerity, effort, purity—all things which are certainly good, but which are not the Christian "spiritual life," and which do not distinguish essentially the latter from any non-Christian, even pagan, religion, which preaches a, now and then, very exalted morality. How right Cardinal Daniélou was to reiterate in every way possible: "A Christianity which would reduce itself to a human morality would lose the essential of its interest. We do not need one more professor of morality. We have had them since the beginning of the world, and they have never saved anyone. St. Paul says, even in the Epistle to the Romans, that professors of morality only serve to make us sin more by teaching us what is virtue. What we need is a Savior. Christ alone, because He is the Son of God, saves us. If Christianity is only ethics, I have no conclusive reason for not preferring Marxist morality."[2]

So then, the reaction of this young student is understood.

Sent into a university environment with not many Catholics, he wrote not long ago to a priest: "How amazed I am to discover, among my colleagues and my professors, all atheists, this awareness, this dignity of life that my parents taught me, and that I believed to be especially the distinctive sign of a Catholic. Those that I see here are much better than many Catholics whom I know. Likewise, I no longer understand very well the justification for the sacraments and for religious exercise." This young student did not comprehend that, what distinguishes a Catholic from an upright man, is not the, more or less, perfect practice of moral virtues but the living faith in God Who is love, and Who loved men to the point of giving to them His Son to make them divine, by making them participants in His divine nature, according to St. Peter, and making them live by His own life. It is one thing to know ourselves loved by God, like sons, like His very own Son, and with the same love, called to enter, from this life into His intimacy, by knowing Him as He knows Himself and by loving Him as He loves Himself; it is another thing to reduce the Christian religion to the practice of moral virtues alone. For many Christians, Christianity is transformed into moralism, and the consequence is so many failures and defections. Indeed, we encounter many men and women, baptized or unbaptized, with a naturally religious spirit, thirsty for the absolute, who look for intimacy with God, but who, confronted by the morality of too many Catholics, as well as, by their formalism, conformity and activism, turn from the Christian religion to Far Eastern religions, or toward cults of all kinds which are proliferating everywhere, and where they hope to find what will satisfy their legitimate aspirations. What a shame and what a mistake!

What a shame! By becoming involved in these different directions, one cannot help taking the wrong path. If the Hindu religion, to speak only of it, implies a spiritual and interior life of some value, it cannot satisfy completely the human heart. In fact, the human heart which looks for a religious life, which looks for God, needs to encounter a personal being who is not only superior to creation and to himself, but also absolutely distinct from it and from him. If love wishes the perfect fusion of creatures who love each other, it, nevertheless, rejects a confusion, an identification which, by abolishing all distinction of persons, ends up by destroying love itself. Now, in the Hindu religion, as, moreover, in many other Far-Eastern spiritualities which are, more or less related, such as Chinese Taoism, the spiritual man leans toward an absorption of his own personality into an impersonal deity. Actually, the God of India, is so immanent and so present to the world that, he penetrates all, that he is all. He is, likewise, in man so that he becomes man, and man becomes he.

In order to be able to relate to God and to be united to Him, the Hindus, having no other means to achieve it — not believing, like the Christians, in the mystery of the Incarnation, in the mystery of God's Son made man — are led to identify God with the universe, and to identify themselves with one another. The result, then, is an annihilating pantheism: the absorption of God in the world — and then this God is no longer a God — or the absorption of the world and of myself in God — and then, of what use is this God to me if I no longer exist?

Certain ones among them, it is true, recognize not only God's unicity and immanence, but, also, His transcendence. They have, rightfully, concluded that divine reality surpasses infinitely all others. Spiritual reality is apart from the world, apart from all that exists, so above all that experience can attain, all concepts, and all names in use to designate the things of the world, even the concept of being, nothing of all that can be applied to God. Unfortunately, preoccupied as they are with stripping the Divine Being of every name and of every conceivable attribute, by reason, and with purifying Him of all imperfection, they are led to relegate God to the depth of the unrecognizable, of making Him an unconscious or, at least, an impersonal entity, an unconsciousness and impersonality that bring Him close to nothingness. Yet, an impersonal God, a God incapable of knowing and of loving us cannot satisfy completely the demands of the human heart, of this "heart which is restless unless it rests in God," as St. Augustine said so eloquently.

I have just alluded to God's personal character. God is a person; there are, even, in Him several persons — three, to be exact. It seems to me absolutely necessary to dispel any misunderstanding on this subject. Catholic theology is entirely in agreement with those Hindus whom I just mentioned, and with all those who, like them, affirm that none of the concepts used in contemporary speech can be applied to God. Every time we affirm something about God, it asks us to deny it at once. It is so, and it is not so. This is called "negative" or "apophantic" theology. For example, if I say that God is Love, I must state immediately that God is not love, because God does not love in the sense that man loves. His love resembles human love, but it is, at the same time, completely different from it. Otherwise, I would assimilate God to an object of my experience, and then God would, no longer, be the true God. However, Catholic theology does not allow the usage of concepts, rendered in current speech, to speak of God. It only uses them, such as they are, analogically, which means: when Christians, in order to express all that relates to their knowledge of God, use terms designating concepts elaborated by human reason from natural experience — they might be the most refined concepts of the most abstract metaphysics — they must take care that these terms are not understood in their colloquial sense, and that the concepts which they express are appropriate to the divine being only by analogy or by "means of eminence." In other words, the concepts expressed in these terms, are only analogous to the concepts that they ordinarily designate, that is, they are lifted to the divine plane, and, consequently, they do not mean exactly the same thing as the latter, but something which resembles it, while surpassing it. That does not mean that they do not have a positive context, and teach about God only in the manner of images or of pure allegories. It does mean that it is necessary, first of all, to eliminate from their context all that is finite, limited, relative, proper to the created being, and contradictory to the creating, absolute, unlimited, infinite Being. That means, then, it is necessary to regard this context as expanded to the infinite into a perspective whose limit is not discerned.

Thus, when we say God is a person, or that there are persons in God, we depart from the principle that any perfection in the creature must be found in the Creator, and we affirm that the person ought to find itself there surely, being the highest form of being we know. We transpose into God a notion drawn from our experience of the human personality. Yet we deny, in this notion that we apply to God, all that is negative and limited, in order to keep what is positive and capable of infinite dimensions. To say that God is a person is not to represent Him in the manner of a human person, like an individual made of flesh and juxtaposed with others, having qualities that others do not possess, and not having the qualities of others; it is not seeing the Good Lord with a white beard, seated on the clouds, the God of a certain popular imagery, or the dignified pastor of a famous film, with a tall hat and frock-coat. It is to say that He possesses, to a supreme degree, (to a degree of which we cannot have a clear idea) the values of the human person: a free subject (and supremely free without any of the limitations of human liberty); a subject of relationship with other persons, like us (without these relationships putting him in a state of dependence, as in our case), etc. It is saying that He possesses eminently *the* personality, since He is the source of it. It is, also, saying something very positive about Him, which is meaningful to us, although we catch only a glimpse of its direction. It is, in every instance, affirming a practical consequence of the greatest importance: we ought to act with regard to God, like persons with regard to a Person, more of a person than they themselves and source of their personality, not like towards a great *All* or a first *Axiom* or an indifferent, blind, unrecognizable *Absolute*. Speaking thus, we do not want only to say that we ought to act *as if* that were, but *because that is,* in an eminent manner surpassing all our conceptions.

It is for failing to criticize the anthropomorphism of the notion of person, as I have just done, that a number of people, I think, deny the personal character to God, and refuse, consequently, to believe in the God of Jesus Christ in order to acknowledge only the God of philosophers and intellectuals: the Supreme Being, or the great Architect of the Universe.

What a pity! But, also, what a mistake! Far from this religion being deformed — formalist or moralist — from which so many persons are turned away, the Christian religion is precisely, as we shall see in greater detail in another chapter, the "form of 'spiritual life' where our most personal and most interiorized relationship with God, Himself, the most personal in His transcendent reality, is fully recognized and formally cultivated . . . . The Christian tends to a complete blossoming of a life fully human and, at the same time, completely personal, in the discovery of a God who is not only also, a person to him, but the personal Being par excellence."[3] Likewise, these souls would not be directed towards less pure sources, if they had known that the Christian religion could, and even must, blossom into a spiritual life, under pain of remaining radically incomplete, and the true spiritual life is not reduced to a "moral life," not even to a "charitable life," still less to a "ritualistic" or "formalist" life.

"Spiritual Life" Is Not Identical To "Interior Life"

The truly spiritual life is not reduced, any longer, to any kind of "interior life." Indeed, if there exists forms of "religious life" which do not imply either an authentic "spiritual life" or an authentic "interior life," there exists, also, forms of an "interior life" without a truly religious life, which is to say, without God, because there cannot be religion without some kind of God who would be its object, even if, like the Romans of the decadence, the real existence of this object can be doubted, or that this object is badly known or poorly loved among certain Christians.

The "interior life" could only be a, more or less rich, psychological current, a more or less profound psychic life. It can be found among unbelievers, even among notable materialists. Poets, artists, musicians, writers-novelists, dramatists or philosophers — can experiment and communicate a richness of imagination, of sentiments, of thought, which is, indeed, their sometimes exceptional, even amazing wealth. We are forced to recognize that they have an "interior life," although it is, from time to time, strange, even monstrous. Yet, this life, in any case, is not a "religious life" nor a "spiritual life," if one understands by that expression, at least, "the approach to a reality other than that of the sensible world, and which surpasses the individual."[4]

Let us observe that not only poets, artists and writers succeed in possessing an interior life which is neither religious nor spiritual. Many men, in fact, if not all, especially in their infancy or their adolescence, live an "interior life," that is, a dream world, very much their own, that they fill with people and things consonant with their most intimate desires, but that the real world does not realize. This life is surely not religious in its essence, and cannot be called a "spiritual life." Certainly, it has an excellent value, that of meditation and retreat. However, the danger is to reduce meditation to the single occupation of self, to an indefinite introspection, to an exclusive cult of our egotistical way of seeing and of feeling. If we remain thus enclosed, all alone with ourselves, what sterility, and how far we are from the authentic spiritual life!

It is necessary to say as much for this other form of life that can be qualified as interior, insofar as it is opposed to this exterior activity which makes lives superficial. Yet it cannot be one in reality, if it is content to develop in the abstract in the pursuit of an intellectualized ideal and without reference to the real life, if it locks up relationships with God within the interior of self. Indeed, in order to be an authentically Christian spiritual life, the interior life ought to try to be concrete by the practice of virtues; it ought, above all, to tend toward establishing and developing relationships with the neighbor; in other words, it ought to express itself effectively — except for a psychological incapability — in love of others. In fact, it would be abnormal that, living by the love of the Father and of the Son, one would not be drawn irresistibly by this love to love those whom they love.

The Christian spiritual life is not identical to just any spiritual life

Thus, then, true spiritual life is not the same as just any religious or interior life. It must be added that all spiritual life is not necessarily a spiritual life, appropriately Christian.

First of all for a Christian, the spiritual life is not to be understood like a philosopher for whom it consists in the normal exercise of the highest human faculties and in the activity of this spiritual substance which is the human soul. Understood in this sense, the spiritual life has nothing specifically Christian, although certain Christians are tempted to let themselves be seduced by the nuances of this meaning. The spiritual life of the follower of Christ is not reduced to mere acts, even supernatural acts of his intelligence and of his will. It would exclude from its influence body and matter, for, according to this notion, what is of the soul is spiritual, and thus opposed to the body; what is of the spirit is spiritual and thus opposed to matter. Now we shall see that it is not like that, at all, for the authentically Christian spiritual life. Consequently, contrary to what certain ones think, especially those who want to reduce Christianity only to its horizontal dimension, far from diverting temporal action, values and earthly tasks, from the construction of a more human and more fraternal world, the truly spiritual life contributes and ought to contribute to forming men more completely because they are more fully Christian, more fully sons of God, thus more at the service of their brothers. It gives them a more urgent obligation to fulfill their temporal tasks, all the more urgent that, as has been already said, the improvement of conditions of existence can create more favorable situations in this life itself.

Then, all spiritual life is not necessarily a life implying a "religious life," because forms of "the spiritual life" without religion and, thus, without God have been found and are to be found more and more frequently.

Such seems to be that particularly pure and primitive form of Buddhism that is called *Hinayana* (that is, "the little vehicle"). It is a spiritual life without any religious foundation. The Buddhist does not deny the gods: he is simply not interested, just as he is uninterested in all distinct existence. The "spiritual life" that he preaches consists precisely, at least in principle, in this absolute dis-interestedness and in this complete detachment with regard to all cosmic, human or divine existence. Such a form of "spiritual life" is certainly paradoxical. Yet, it exists, and it is necessary to recognize what it has been and what it still is, at least, for a certain number of people: an experience whose psychological reality, or a certain grandeur, cannot be denied, even though one must deplore and contest the final inanity, and, in any case, all so-called religious character, and thus, refuse it the so-called name of "spiritual life."

Such is, likewise, the case of those unbelievers and atheists, growing in number, who, being mistaken about His true nature, separate God from their spiritual life. This form of spirituality could be called a spiritual life, implying a religious life but without God, as this idea will appear in what follows. To tell the truth, this name is poorly chosen. It has no meaning since, as I have already said, there cannot be any religion without a rapport with some superior, transcendental reality. Also, we will see that, finally, it is the same with atheists, even though they distinguish religion and belief in God.

In a conference with the significant title, "The Religion

of the Unbelievers," a non-Christian writer, author of *Années obscures de Jésus*, says "that at the root of, or at the heart of all, even atheistic, thoughts, is found a doubt or religious emotion." He adds: "If it were not so, we would not have to talk today about the religion of the unbelievers, but, at the very most, this would be a truism of their religion." Further on: "It seems, indeed, that what characterizes the religious anguish of our times, what renders possible at the same time, among certain ones, the sclerosis of the religious spirit, and let us hope, its eventual renaissance, is no longer the distinction between faith and reason, but rather the distinction between the religious spirit and belief in God. The chief fact of our time, it seems, is that the religious spirit and belief are no longer closely linked, as they were in the ages of faith, or of equilibrium in the faith, but that one can be a believer without having a religious spirit, and inversely, what is even more significant, that one can have the religious spirit without, for that matter, being a believer." After having spoken of believers, or so-called believers deprived of a religious spirit, such as Voltaire and Julien Benda, he approaches the study of unbelievers, of "those spirits". . . who, in the divorce that occurred between religious spirit and belief, have taken the side opposed to that of Voltaire or of Benda. They retain the religious spirit, even if they no longer believe in God." Aron, then, gives "some examples of these spiritual, and actually religious, dramas which touch the most profound and the most serious of our epoch," quoting some texts of these unbelievers, texts which "constitute without paradox one of the most amazing religious anthologies: the religious anthology of unbelief!" The unbelievers whom he quotes are Proudhon, then some, free-masons, next Nietzche, and, finally, Hitler. Here is the first of these two texts that Aron chose "in order to allow us," as he says, "to measure the gravity and intensity of the religious sentiment of Proudhon, blasphemer and atheist." It is taken from *La Justice*, and relates the last moments of Proudhon's father.

Proudhan wrote: "At sixty, my father, exhausted from

work, in which, as is said, the blade had worn out its scabbard, felt that his end had come. I must say that I had never noticed in him a word or a gesture that smacked of impiety, any more than devotion. He neither prayed nor blasphemed, being completely involved in his business, expecting nothing except from his work, and importuning with solicitation neither heaven nor men. Sometimes, on great feasts, I saw him go to Mass like everyone else; he was bored there, understanding nothing, as much a stranger to everything as a deaf mute. If the priest mounted the pulpit, he could stand it no longer, and without laughing or giving it a thought, left quickly. Certainly, the weight of his devotions was light. The day of his death, he had a presentment of his end; a thing which is not unusual. So, he wanted to prepare himself for the big trip, and he, himself, gave the instructions. Relatives and friends were invited; a modest dinner was served, enlivened by gentle conversation. At dessert, he began his farewell; he spoke regretfully of one son who had died ten years earlier, much before his time. I was away on family business. His youngest son, not understanding very well the reason for his emotion, said to him:

'Come on, Dad, forget those sad thoughts. Why are you sad? Aren't you alive? Your time hasn't come.'

'You're wrong,' replied the old man, 'if you think that I'm afraid of death. Listen; it's all over. I feel it, and I want to die among you. So, let someone bring in the coffee.' He tasted a few spoonfuls. 'I've done a good deal wrong in my life,' he said. 'I have not succeeded in my undertakings. I have loved all of you. I die without reproach.' A not too devout relative of the family thought he ought to comfort him by quoting from the cathechism that all does not end with death, and that it is, then, one must realize that God's mercy is great. 'Cousin Gaspard,' replied my father, 'I don't know what it's all about; I don't think about it at all; I feel neither fear nor desire. I die surrounded by those whom I love. I have paradise in my heart.' About ten o'clock, he fell asleep, murmuring my name for the last time. Friendship, a good conscience, hope for a better future for those whom he left behind, all gathered to bring a perfect calm to his last moments."

After what I just said, it seems that interior and spiritual lives can be conceived with a religious life, but they would be Godless. We will see that, in fact, it is not like that, and it is truly necessary because, once again, so that one can speak of a religious life, it is necessary that the latter admit of a relationship, whatever it is, if not with the God of Revelation, at least with a superior, transcendent, real or supposed being.

Likewise, "what is striking . . . when one studies the whole of human history," writes Father Bouyer, "or when one fathoms the psychology of any individual, is the interior life, itself, that tends to develop into a spiritual life," that is, into a relationship with a spiritual reality which overflows the individual's conscience, even if this reality is not recognized as divine, even if this character is expressly refused to him. In its turn, the spiritual life is oriented no less spontaneously, towards some form of "religious life," where this spiritual reality is recognized not as "something" but as someone."[5]

Thus, these artists, poets, writers, that I have mentioned, can be militant materialists. Yet their sole passion for "doing" an artistic, poetic, literary, scientific or philsophical work expresses the need inherent in all intense, interior life of surpassing the limits of the individual, to become communication and communion. Nothing is more striking in the interior dream of so many men than their passionate tendency toward a world whose reality surpasses, subsists, and exists independently of them.

On the other hand, the primitive form of Buddhism, to which I alluded and which is "like the most amazing effort that humanity has ever made in order to provide a spiritual life without God," reveals, surprisingly, to what extent an endeavor of this type is contrary to nature. Conceived very precisely in order to satisfy the need in man for a spiritual life outside of all religion, it has been incapable of holding to its initial atheism. From the primitive *Hinayana*, deliberately a-religious, Buddhism evolved toward *Mahanyana* (or "the big vehicle"), that is, towards a new form of popular religion, capable, moreover, of the highest subtleties in the amidism, for example. Buddha becomes a god, the god-savior par excellence, in place of all the gods that he had caused to disappear from the preoccupations of his followers.

As for unbelievers, and atheists to whom I have alluded, what they discard, basically, from their spiritual life, emptied of God, is not God as He really is, the God Whom Jesus Christ revealed and Whom they do not know or know poorly; they make, for themselves false images or false ideas that have been given to them about Him. Basically, the religious need exists in them, only they assign it, as an aim, one of the ideals which ordinarily attract a human being, and to which they attribute such a certain, absolute character that they come to accept them for God, as, for example, love of neighbor, conscience, duty, justice, science, Humanity, etc. Witness the Proudhon family, father and son. The incident quoted earlier about the son at his father's death, reveals indeed an implicit aspiration towards God the remunerator, in whom, says the Epistle to the Hebrews, it suffices to believe in order to please him and to be saved (Cf. Heb 11:6). This aspiration is contained in the obedience to the moral conscience, which is a participation in God's will, insofar as it rules human actions in conformity to this wisdom. This witness manifests, moreover, a genuine love of neighbor, which love can be in certain instances, a love of God of which one is unaware.

The "spiritual life" of unbelievers of which I have just spoken is not deprived of all religious life. As we were able to affirm, it implies, no matter what the appearances lead one to believe, a relationship with God — a relation that I have said is necessary in order to be able to talk about a religious life — although this God, under the circumstances, is only an impersonal reality, an idea, an ideal, that one affects, to such a degree, of the absolute coefficient that one ends up by confusing it with God.

Yet this God whom I will call the God of conscience or of natural mystics, or even of unbelieving mystics, this God for whom it occurs, however, that one sacrifices his very life, is not quite the God that our heart searches for, the true God. He stands in need of being, if not transcendent, at least, personal, that is "Someone," a living being who is not only distinct from the created, and infinitely superior to him, but also intelligent and free, conscious of himself, in a word, a person. Now we have seen, in a preceding chapter, that our aspirations needed to concentrate on a person, more exactly on a personal being par excellence.

So, although one cannot deny to the atheists' form of "spiritual life" a very properly religious character, one, cannot, however, give it the name of "spiritual life" properly so-called, because, in order to be authentic, all religious life ought to be joined to a personal life with God: it ought to be, as Francois Mauriac has said, "a story between someone and Someone."[6] That is not the case. The same Mauriac was correct in writing: "There exists a supreme truth to be revealed to men today, who have admitted, once and for all, that they are atheists. It is: they are only atheists with regard to the God of the philosophers and of intellectuals, of the God whose death Nietzche proclaimed, and who, indeed, does not exist. However, the Father Whose Son revealed to us that He exists by this one invocation: 'Our Father Who art in heaven . . .' this God to Whom Claudel used to say: 'There, you are suddenly Someone!' "[7] this God, I will add, Who is not only Father, but also Son and Holy Spirit, this living God Whose life is an exchange of love among these three Persons and Who wants, as we will see by what amazing way, us to participate in it.

Footnotes

1. As will be seen later, this expression does not designate here a state of life based on the three vows of chastity, poverty and obedience, but the life of prayer whatever its form; in other words, it designates the expression of man's relationships with God.
2. Cardinal Daniélou, *l'Avenir de la Religion*, Fayard, Paris, 1968, p. 22.
3. Bouyer, *Introduction a la vie spirituelle*, Desclée de Brouwer, Paris, 1960. I was inspired by this work in the drawing up of certain passages of this chapter.
4. *Ibid.*
5. Cf. Bouyer, *op. cit.*
6. Francois Mauriac, "Bloc-Notes," *Le Figaro*, Oct. 13,1966.
7. Francois Mauriac, *La Pierre d'achoppement*, Rocher, Monaco, 1951, pp. 120-121.

Chapter 6

LIBERATION FROM SPIRITUAL DEATH (CONTINUATION)

After having made the distinctions which allowed us to say what the spiritual life is not; it is a little less difficult for me to talk now about this life with more precision, attempting to say what it is, at least, by outlining the essential elements which constitute it.

I will gladly define the spiritual life — which is, also, called "life in the Spirit," or "life according to the Spirit" — as a participation or a communion in the life of the Blessed Trinity through a participation or a communion in Christ's filial life, both realized by the Holy Spirit, who, by making us beloved sons of the Father in His Son Jesus Christ, transforms us — in our entire person and in our relation to the world — to the image of this same Son.

Communion in the Trinitarian Life

The Lord's magnificent proclamation is known: "I have come so that they may have life," He said, speaking of all men, "and that they may have it abundantly" (Jn 10:10). Another: "God so loved the world that He gave it His only

Son so that every man who believes in Him may not perish, but may have eternal life'' (Jn 3:16).

Evidently, the life in question here is not natural life, but supernatural life, the life of grace, in other words, eternal life. Indeed, St. Paul affirms that ''the grace of God is life eternal in Jesus Christ Our Lord'' (Rm 6:23). Also, the eternal life referred to so often in the New Testament does not mean the future life in heaven so much as future, ''the life of the world to come''; it designates the life that will not end, but which has already begun, and of which the life in heaven will only be a total unfolding. It is from and in this world that men can possess eternal life, according to those words of Christ: ''Truly, truly, I say to you, he who believes in the Son has eternal life'' (Jn 6:47; 3:36). ''My sheep hear my voice; I know them and they follow me. I give them eternal life'' (Jn 10:27-28). St. John echoes the Master when he says: ''God has given us eternal life and this life in His Son. He who has the Son possesses life; he who has not the Son of God, does not possess life. I have written it to you in order for you to know that you possess eternal life, you who place your faith in the name of the Son of God'' (1 Jn 5:11-13).

What is this eternal life that is also called Christian life, and spiritual life? Our Lord Himself defined it: ''Eternal life,'' He said, addressing His Father, ''is that they know You, Yourself, the only true God, and the One Whom You have sent, Jesus Christ'' (Jn 17:3).

Eternal life consists, then, in knowing God and His Son Christ. Yet, it is necessary to define what this term ''to know'' means in biblical language. Actually, here, knowledge has the usual meaning: information of the mind by means of abstractions. However, it must not be forgotten that the language of the sacred writers is, above all, existential, and their vocabulary is concrete. Also, knowledge flows over into abstract knowing: it expresses an experimental knowledge. To know someone is to enter into personal relations with him, relations which can take many forms and be more or less intimate. So, knowledge can imply love, the possession, through love, of the known object. That is the meaning of the verb "to know" in St. John's statement which I have just quoted. The knowledge, in question here, is experimental; it is a communion of love. To know and to love God and Jesus Christ, such is, therefore, eternal life.

Of course, it is not a question of a knowledge through human reason left to its own natural resource, nor of a love stemming from a heart left to its own sensual forces. Christ wishes more and better for us. He wants us to know God as God knows Himself, and for us to love Him as He loves Himself. Then, the eternal life that Christ possesses in its fullness, and that He came to give us, is the life of God. St. John who had come the closest to the Word in Whom is life — *In ipso vita erat* — says expressly: "Life manifests itself; we have seen it; we give witness to it, and we announce to you this eternal life which is with the Father and Who has become visible to us" (Jn 1:2). St. John adds, showing indeed, that, if the life which is in the Father, manifests itself to us, and that, if the Apostles announced it to the world, it is so that we may participate in that very life: "what you have seen and heard, we announce it to you, so that you, also, may be in communion with us. As for our communion, it is with the Father and with His Son Jesus Christ" (Jn 1:3).

Thus, then, the eternal life that Christ came to communicate to us in abundance, is communion and participation in God's own life. Also, it is from the very beginning a state like this latter.

Indeed, as is known, it is baptism that caused us to be born to eternal life. Let us recall the Lord's words to Nicodemus: "No one can enter the Kingdom of God" — according to St. John, that means: no one can have eternal life — "unless born of water and of the Spirit." Now, baptism communicates to the baptized a grace called sanctifying, or habitual or divinizing grace. Indeed, it is a principle of being and of life which establishes the baptized in a state of grace, which is nothing less than a communion, a participation in the divine nature, according to St. Peter's expression, in a word, a divinization.

This is the way in which this divinization is realized, and

what is its nature.

Let us note, first of all, that the doctrine of divinization is the keystone of Christianity. This truth is forgotten very often. There is a great tendency, in fact, to reduce salvation to the mystery of the Redemption. It is affirmed that Christ came to redeem us and to expiate our sins. However, what is omitted is that He came, also, and, above all, in the end to make us children of God, thus divinized beings. Redemption is one thing; divinization is another. The one could have existed without the other. If men had not sinned, they would have been called to participate in the divine nature without its having been necessary to heal them of evils which they had inflicted upon themselves. Their divinization would have been realized in Christ even so, as we will see, but Christ would not have needed to be crucified, and to redeem them. However, in reality men did sin. They needed to be purified of their fault and delivered from its consequences. That is the work of redemption. The latter is now necessary so that divinization may operate and be accomplished in the redemptive act, itself, that is, in Christ's death and resurrection.

By taking an infinitely pure body in Mary's infinitely pure womb, the Word of God united all of humanity to Himself, according to the thought familiar to the Eastern Fathers, and he deified, divinized it. These Fathers found the heart of their doctrine in Christ's words: "The Kingdom of heaven is like leaven which a woman took and mixed into three measures of meal until all of it rose" (Mt 13:33). By uniting Himself to a single human nature, the Word inserted Himself in all of humanity: He deposited there a divine leaven which would cause the dough to rise, which already, by right or by power, extends His good deeds to all of humanity. St. Athanasius writes: "Just as the Word, having taken a body, became man, so we men, taken by the flesh of the Word, are divinized by Him." St. Gregory of Nyssa: "God united Himself to our nature so that, thanks to its union with the divine, our nature is divinized."

Yet, in fact, it is baptism that divinizes us. It is not

enough that the leaven has been placed in the human dough; it still needs to extend its action to each element of the dough. It is not enough that the Word assumed human flesh and thus He became part of all humanity, in general, so that all flesh be "His flesh," divinized: each body must be taken by the body of the Word; the divine life which assumed Christ's human nature, and through it, human nature, as a whole, in its entirety, must be extended to every single being; each human being, in particular, by personal effort must unite himself effectively to the Word Incarnate. If, in fact, every man has been truly divinized, thanks to the union of the Divine Word with all humanity by the intermediary of Christ's particular human nature, he has been as man, being a part of human nature in general, and not so much as a single man. Insofar as man, he has only been divinized virtually; divinization ought to attract each man individually, as the leaven causes each element of the dough to rise, as the sap takes each branch at its birth. Now, it can only be done, thanks to the redemptive Passion which breaks through the obstacle of sin preventing the penetration of the leaven or of the sap, that is, of divine life. Each human being, in particular, receives the influx of this life only by faith and the sacraments, especially baptism. By this sacrament, we are in some way, as St. Paul says, grafted on Christ, joined to Him, fused with Him; we truly receive the Incarnate Word; "we become participants with Him" (Heb 3:14). Thus, we are deified, divinized, thanks to our union with Christ.

Of course, divinization, according to Christianity, differs essentially from what it is in a pantheistic system.

According to pantheism, the world is ontologically consubstantial to God, and souls are parts or modalities of the divine substance: they are divine by nature, originally. "From the One, from the Absolute, proceeds eternally and necessarily modes and beings who are consubstantial to Him. Wisdom consists in recognizing the substantial identity between the individual and the absolute, Self, between the individual spirit and universal Spirit, between atman and Brahman. Salvation consists in causing the multiple to return, the latter being apparent to the One from whom it proceeds and from which it fell, to blend itself into the unique divine substance, by losing its individualism which is the sign of a fall."[1]

According to Christianity, man is called to participate through grace, in the life of God. He is invited to become "a participant in the divine nature," according to St. Peter's expression. St. Paul expresses it well, that at the end "God will be in each and in all." Yet, on the one hand, one must, indeed, guard oneself from confusing with pantheism what could be called pauline pantheism, which in order to affirm God's immanence in all, does not affirm less His transcendence. According to Christianity, divinization is accomplished without confusion of natures or of persons. The personal distinction remains, which makes love possible. On the other hand, the Apostle does not say that, from the beginning, man came from the substance of God, that he is ontologically consubstantial to God. Only the Word, the Word Incarnate Jesus Christ, is God by nature, and possesses originally the same and unique divine substance. To Him alone, the Father communicates His nature which becomes, without division or partition, without diminution or multiplication, Christ's own substance, and who causes Christ to be consubstantial and equal to the Father. Our participation in the divine nature, which makes of us divinized and deified beings, is not the consubstantiality of our soul with God, the ideal of all pantheism and of false mysticism, but only a certain likeness which makes us, not God's equals, but deified beings, or like God; it is not an emanation nor a flowing into us of the divine essence, or of the same reality which would exist in God, and which would pass from God into us, but it is the communication to our soul of an image of God comparable to the communication of the imprint of a stamp on wax.

However, if we remain creatures, if we do not become "God," by blending ourselves with Him in the unity of being and of person, we are truly divinized by an essential transformation which, without causing us to lose our own "subsistence," unites us to God in a substantial union, not in the sense of a confusion of substances, but of a union "of substance to substance." The Father divinizes our soul by making it like His through spiritual contact brought about by His Spirit, from the substance of His Son who is His very substance — since the three divine Persons have only one and the same substance — with the substance of our soul, as the wax is rendered similar to the imprint of the stamp by contact with it.

This comparison of the stamp or of the seal, completed by that of the image, and used like it by St. Paul, meant a great deal, also, to the Eastern Fathers. It helps very much to understand the intimacy of our union with the divine nature, or, in other words, of the presence in us of the Blessed Trinity. The stamp is the Holy Spirit, as the Fathers of the Church tell us, by relying on St. Paul. The imprint is that of the Son, but it is also the Father's, since the Son is the Father's image. The Holy Spirit is, then, like the stamp which bears the image of the Father and of the Son, and which imprints it on us. How does He imprint it? By His presence, because He is the image of the Son, as the Son is the image of the Father: "The pure image of the Father," writes St. Cyril of Alexandria, "is the Son; the natural likeness of the Son is His Spirit. That is the reason that, remodeling human souls as on Himself, He strikes on them the divine form, and imprints on them the seal and the substance that is above all substance."[2] Furthermore, he states precisely: "The Holy Spirit engraves on us the image of the divine substance, but He does not do it like a painter; he does not paint on us the divine resemblance, as if it were a stranger to him. No, that is not the way that He leads us to this resemblance; being God and proceeding from God, He imprints Himself invisibly on the heart of those who receive Him, like a stamp that is imprinted on wax. By, thus, communicating Himself, to human nature and by giving it His resemblance, He refreshes the beauty of the model in this nature, and restores to man the image of God."[3] It remains but to state precisely that the divine substance whose image the Holy Spirit imprints on us is this substance possessed as much by the Son, as by Christ. "The Holy Spirit," writes St. Athanasius, "carries the name of the stamp. It is He, indeed, because He expresses the Son's image in such a way, that he who is, thus, stamped carries in him Christ's form."[4] This precise detail has its importance. I shall return to it later. The definitive formula of the comparison of the stamp is, then, this one: the Holy Spirit is like the stamp which carries the imprint of the Son, which is the image of the Father, and which imprints on our soul, as on a soft wax, by imprinting Himself, being Himself the Son's image.

However, the image on the stamp is one thing; the image imprinted on the wax is another. The Fathers of the Church, also, distinguish the divine substance whose imprint is stamped on the soul, and the imprint thus produced, which transforms, in reality, the substance of the soul, and is called habitual, sanctifying, or even created grace. Yet, they affirm that this stamp is imprinted and maintained in the soul by the intimate presence in it of God Himself, a presence called uncreated grace. The soul is like a transparent paper which reproduces an object by transparency, but which does not reproduce it, and keeps the image only as long as the object is present to it with an intimate and permanent presence. Here is another comparison. The sun's image which is reflected in a mirror, and transforms, in a certain way, this latter, represents created grace, that is, the divine imprint which is produced in the soul and which transforms and divinizes it. The presence of the sun in the mirror, which makes possible and maintains the transformation of the mirror, thanks to the image which is reflected in it, represents uncreated grace, that is, the intimate presence of the Holy Spirit Himself.

By imprinting on our soul the image of the divinity, the Holy Spirit makes us like God, and, in and by that very fact, the Father and the Son come to dwell in us in the unity of this same Spirit, in a strict and permanent way, without any intermediary other than their imprint: "If anyone loves me," says the Lord, "he will keep my word and my Father will love him, and we will come to him and establish our dwelling in him" (Jn 14:23).

Thanks to baptism, a change is, then, effected in our nature. Now this change establishes new relationships between God and us; it puts us into new relationships with the Persons of the Blessed Trinity. These relationships result from a new knowledge and a new love which this sacrament communicates to us. Knowledge which permits us to know God and creatures as God knows Himself and them: I have called it the virtue of faith. Love which allows us to love God and creatures as God loves Himself and loves them: I have called it the virtue of charity. To these two virtues is attached a third: hope which is only the desire of faith to always know God more perfectly, and the desire of charity to unite itself to Him always in a more intimate union. These virtues constitute for the Christian life the active appearance that we have recognized all our life; they form for this life what are, for every living being, faculties with which he is endowed by virtue of the actions that he must perform.

So, faith and charity transform interiorly our intelligence and our heart, making us capable of thinking and loving like God. One single difference exists, which is merely a difference of degree not of nature: Of degree, for, as St. Paul says, "Today we see in a mirror, in a confused manner, but then it will be face to face. Today, I know in an imperfect manner, but, then, I shall know as I am known" (1Cor 13:12). Not of nature, because faith and charity are not only an objective communion with God's thought and love, but still and above all, as we will see, an interior communion and a real participation with this thought and love

Eternal life implies, then, an abode, a real sojourn, a substantial dwelling of the Blessed Trinity in us. Such is the element which makes of it a state, the special state created in us by baptism: the state of grace, a state of intimacy with the Father, Son and Holy Spirit, established through knowledge and love. "That day, Jesus declares to His Apostles, "you will know that I am in my Father, and you in me and I in you" (Jn 14:20). To His Father He says: "As you, Father, are in me and I in you, that they, also may be one in us . . . . I have given them the glory that you have given me, so that they might be one as we are one: I in them and you in me" (Jn 17:21-23).

Yet this presence in us of the three divine Persons is not only something static. Like the presence of each one of these Persons in the other two, it is, also, dynamic because it causes us to participate in the impulse of love which draws these Persons each towards the other two.

Indeed, in our soul, thus inhabited by the God-Trinity, is continued the eternal begetting of the Son by means of the Father and the eternal spiration, that is, exhalation, of the Spirit of love by the Father and the Son.

Better still, God's presence in us makes us capable of participation in activity proper to the divine Persons: we find ourselves associated wondrously with this begetting and with this exhalation, and introduced in that way, into the current of the trinitarian life. Not only does the Father beget continually His Son in us, and the Father and the Son exhale unceasingly upon us their common Spirit and love, but, also, assimilated to the Son and the Holy Spirit, we are, by means of participation, without a doubt, continually but actually engendered by means of the Father as sons, and exhaled by the Father and the Son, as a term of love, at the same time that, as we shall see, we exhale unceasingly with the Son, conjointly with the Father, their common Spirit of love. To repeat: the life of the divine Persons being to know and to love each other, we, too, are put into a state of knowing and of loving them, not only as they know and love each other, but by truly participating in the very knowledge and very love that God has of Himself. The Father and the Son not only know us with the very knowledge by which they know each other in the Holy Spirit, but, also, we ourselves know the Father and the Son with the same mutual knowledge by means of this same Spirit: "I am the good Shepherd," Christ says, "I know my flock, and my flock knows me, as the Father knows me and I know the Father" (Jn 10:14). The Father and the Son not only love us with the same love with which they love each other in the Holy Spirit, but we, also, love the Father and the Son with the same love with which they love us by means of this same Spirit: "You have loved them as you have loved me," says Jesus to His Father when speaking of His disciples. Again: "I have made your name known to them, so that the love with which you have loved me before the creation of the world might be in them" (Jn 17:23-24).

Thus, then, we are divinized, not by a vague participation in the divine nature, but by a relationship with the Persons of the Blessed Trinity, by means of a real union with them through knowledge and love, be they actual or habitual. This is a response to the objection made about baptized infants, about the just who sleep or who are distracted, as well as about individuals who are, consequently, actually incapable of supernatural actions. Indeed, it suffices that the just soul be directed, at least, habitually to the knowledge and love of God so that it realizes God's presence in it by means of grace. St. Thomas writes: "God is said to dwell spiritually, like in an intimate dwelling, in the saints whose soul is *capable* of uniting itself to God through knowledge and love, even if they do not know Him, and do not actually love Him" — as is the case of baptized infants, the sleepers and the distracted — ; "it suffices that they have, by means of grace, the character of faith and charity."[5] God's presence in us by means of grace is, then, a new and special relationship which establishes us in an intimate union with Him, a relationship which results from the gift that He gave us of Himself in and by grace which transforms us, and divinizes us, making us capable of knowing and loving Him as He knows and loves Himself by means of an actual participation in His knowledge and love.

Such is the eternal life which baptism has us live. It can be defined as the movement, the impulse kindled in the innermost part of our being by the three divine Persons present within us; a movement which, by making us participate in their relationships of knowledge and love, draws us toward the Father, in the Son, through the Spirit. It consists of communion with God by knowing Him and being known by Him with the very knowledge by which He knows Himself in the mystery of His being one and trinitarian, and by loving Him and being loved by Him with the very love with which He loves Himself.

It is that divine life in us that St. Elizabeth of the Trinity, a Carmelite who died in the odor of sanctity, said: "This is what makes my life an anticipated heaven: 'To believe that a Being who is called Love, dwells in us at every instant of the day and night, and that He asks us to live in union with Him.'"[6] How many persons, disturbed by solitude, would find peace, if they really took to heart this overwhelming truth of the presence in them of the three divine Persons by means of grace! What exclamation of surprise and wonder would they utter the day that they would discover all these riches that they carry within them, and which they have been unaware of for so long, or in which they did not dare believe! It is there that the secret of joy, of true, unending joy, is to be found.

This presence, it is true, is not clearly perceived at once. The difficulty, for those who, having caught a glimpse of this doctrine, want to live it and live it to the full, is not in the obscurities of the mystery, but, rather in what this mystery presents of incredible wonder. Furthermore, it is all in the realm of the invisible. As Father Plus has remarked: "it is necessary to ponder it twice, even several times, in order to say to yourself: 'I am not dreaming. It is true. It is like that.' Only, little by little, by dint of returning to it, do the splendors become clear." "Oh, would that I could say to all souls," writes again Sister Elizabeth of the Trinity, "what sources of strength, peace and, also, happiness they would find, if they consented to live in this intimacy. Only, they do not know how to wait. If God does not give Himself in a sensible way, they leave His holy Presence; when He comes to them, laden with all His gifts, He finds no one; the soul is out involved in exterior things. It does not dwell within its very depths." Actually, at first, God does not seem to us far away and abstract. Then, He is in us, so to speak, in a latent and hidden state, in the manner of a picture on undeveloped film that must be "revealed," and which is only revealed under certain conditions. God, too, needs to be revealed, and He only allows this revelation progressively, and, likewise, under certain conditions, thanks, above all, to the constant and always more perfect exercise of the theological virtues of faith, hope and charity.

Thus, it is that, little by little, I will be able to feel not only with a sensible sensation — one might even be able at times to test such sensations — but with an interior religious sentiment, kindled and supported by faith. I will be able to feel "someone who is in me more myself than I am," because, then, there is less and less I who will live, it is the God-Trinity who will live more and more in me, and will bring me to further union in their own life, in the encounter of the love of the Father and of the Son in their mutual Spirit.

Communion in Christ's Filial Life

Now, this union is realized, thanks to the communion of love which the Holy Spirit establishes betwen the Word of God and us. Indeed, St. John has told us that our communion is not only with the Father, but also with His Son Jesus Christ. St. Paul, for his own part, writes to the Christians of Corinth: "Faithful is God Who has called us to communion with His Son Jesus Christ our Lord" (1 Cor 1:9). Thus, it is our participation in the Son of God that makes us participate in His divine nature and divine life. "If the Word became flesh," writes St. Ireneaus, "If the eternal living Son of God became the Son of man, it is so that man might enter into communion with the Word, and, receiving adoption, become a son of God."[7]

In what does our communion with Jesus Christ consist?

Our communion in the trinitarian life is due, as we have just seen, to our deification, in other words, to the participation that the divine Persons give us in their nature by means of the stamp that the Holy Spirit imprints on our soul. Although I have already mentioned it, it is appropriate to emphasize once more: the divine nature whose image is, thus, stamped on us — this unique nature which belongs completely and indivisibly but diversely to the Father, to the Son and to the Holy Spirit — is this nature as possessed by the Son incarnate in Jesus Christ. The Fathers of the Church, especially of the Eastern Church, insist a great deal on this idea that God's image, according to which God made man in the beginning and which he restored to him when "the plentitude of time" came, is the Son's image. (St. Ireneaus goes, even so far, as, to say that the corporal nature, itself, has been created in the image of the Son made man, and present as such, in God's mind when He created the first man). For example, here is what St. Athanasius says on the subject: "It was not necessary that he who had once been a participant in the likeness of God perish. What had to be done for what God had made? What had to be done was to renew what was imprinted of God's image on man made according to His image, so that men could again know God by means of it. Yet, how could that be done, if not by the coming of the very image of God, our Savior Jesus Christ. In fact, it could not be done by men since they are not images but in the image of God, not by angels because, even they, are not images of God. For that reason the Word of God came by means of Himself, so that He, the Father's image, could restore man made to His image . . . . Thus, no other could perform this task except the Father's Image . . . . The very holy Son of the Father, image of the Father, came into our dwelling in order to renew man who had been made in His image."[8] So, the Fathers repeat that, what the just grasp at first in Him, is the imprint of the Word, the Father's image, and by it only, the Father's image. It is in the Son's image which he carries in him, that the just recognize the Father. To quote once again St. Athanasius, "When the soul discards all the blemishes of sin which cover it, and keeps only what is pure and in conformity to the image; when the image shines, it sees there, rightfully, as in a mirror, the Word, the image of the Father; and in Him is represented the Father whose image the Savior is."[9] The Lord had said: "He who sees me, sees the Father."

Again: "No one knows the Father except the Son, and he whom the Son is willing to reveal Him."

Having, thus, become participants in the divine nature, as belonging to the Son, we, too, become sons; we are made "sons in the Son," according to the strong expression used by Father Mersch. The sacred writers speak often of our divine sonship through our union with the only Son. St. Paul writes to the Galatians: "You are all sons of God by faith in Christ Jesus. All of you, indeed, who have been baptized in Christ, have put on Christ" (Gal 3:26-27). St. John's statement, speaking of the Son of God made man, is known: "To those who have received Him, He has given power of becoming sons of God." The Fathers of the Church wrote prolifically on this subject. It is impossible to choose, since the texts are numerous and inspiring. Their teaching is summarized in this pithy sentence: The Son of God became man so that man might become son of God. However, I shall quote a passage of St. Cyril of Alexandria commenting on St. John's text which I have just mentioned: "By the fact that they have received the Son through faith, men receive the power to be counted among the sons of God. Because the Son wishing to signify His love for men . . . gives them the power that belongs to Him alone and is proper to his nature; they are lifted to His level. Otherwise, we would not have been able to avoid corruption, we who carried the earthly image, (that is, of Adam corrupted by original sin), if we had not been imprinted with the beauty of the heavenly image (Christ) by means of the call to sonship. Having become participants with Him through the Spirit, we are struck in His likeness . . . . Thus, we are elevated to the supernatural dignity by Christ, but it is not exactly like Him that we will, also, be sons of God, but in His likeness through grace."

In order to try to make this mysterious reality understood, St. Paul speaks about filial adoption: "When the fullness of time came," he writes to the Galatians, "God sent His Son, born of a woman . . . in order to confer on us filial adoption" (Gal 4:4-5). Ephesians: "Blessed be God, the Father of our Lord Jesus Christ, who has blessed us with all kinds of spiritual benedictions . . . determining in advance that we would be for Him adopted sons through Jesus Christ'' (Ep 1:1-5).

As Abbot L. Lochet writes: "it suffices to have penetrated into a family where an adoption has been realized, in order to grasp all the beauty of this new situation in God's family. The little adopted one truly belongs to the family; he is treated exactly like the others. He receives the same care, affection, and, later, the same inheritance. Whatever his origin, differences of wealth or even race, he is treated by his parents as their own child, by the children as one of them, by everyone, as part of the family."[10] Thus, according to St. Paul, since we have received this grace of baptism, "we are no longer strangers, nor guests, we belong to God's family" (Ep 2:19).

By making our divine sonship and the intimate bond which unites us somewhat better understood, thanks to it, and to our Father in heaven, this idea of adoption has, furthermore, the advantage of defining well the difference that exists between Christ's sonship and ours. Our sonship is one only of grace, as adoptive sonship. Indeed, only Christ is son by nature, by a natural sonship. To Him alone, the Father communicates in its fullness the divine nature which becomes the nature proper to the Son. "By our origin and according to our nature," writes St. Athanasius, "we are creatures. Later, we are taken for sons, and, then, our Creator becomes, also, our Father. Thus, it is apparent that it is not we who are sons by nature, but rather the Son Who is in us, and that, as for God, He is not our Father by nature, but Father of the Word Who is in us, in Whom and because of Whom we cry: 'Abba, Father.' "[11] This is the reason that St. Cyril of Alexandria says: "all sonship comes by means of the Son because he is, by sovereignty, the one true Son."[12] In him dwells the fullness of the divinity, in such a way, that he is consubstantial, equal and coeternal with the Father, thus, begotten and not created. Although we are sons, we are and we remain creatures; for that reason, our sonship is only adoptive.

Besides, this idea of adoption is far from taking into account completely the reality of our sonship, any more than defining fully our filial relationship to the Father. Divine adoption is much more perfect than human, legal adoption. It must even be said that it belongs to another category. A person adopts a child who, a stranger at adoption, becomes his child. He receives his name, is surrounded by affection, and can become his heir. Yet, all that is only a juridicial convention, pure fiction. Legal adoption does not change the nature of the adopted one. It does not infuse the blood of the adopted father; it does not make him a new being. The adopted one remains what he was before the adoption, in spite of all the love with which he can be surrounded.

Filial adoption which makes us God's children is not a figure of speech, a lovely metaphor, a purely exterior name. By divine adoption, the Father makes us participate in the natural sonship of His only Son. Indeed, because the divine substance with which the Holy Spirit imprints on us His likeness, is I repeat, this substance possessed by the Son become man, Jesus Christ. Between Him and us a union is established, the very closest that can be conceived, second to the personal union of the Son with the human nature assumed in the womb of the Virgin Mary; a more than moral union (like that which consists in the conformity of our thought and of our will with God's thought and will); a more natural union (like that of our soul and body): it is a "physical" union, in the Greek sense of the word, that is, essential, ontological. It is a union by means of identification with His being and life. Between Him and the Christian, there is a community of being. According to the formula, dear to St. Paul, the Christian is "in Christ," he exists in Him; he becomes "one same being with him" (Rm 6:5). Christ and the Christian form one single and the same Christ, but in two persons. Although it does not eliminate the personal distinction, identification with Christ is then very real since it is a community of being. It is, consequently, a living community. Because he is in Christ, the Christian lives Christ's life. Every Christian can say with St. Paul, if not to the same degree, "It is no longer I that lives, it is Christ who lives in me. Although there are two living beings, namely, Christ and the Christian, there is only one sole life which is Christ's own life. Through faith and baptism, Christ enters into the Christian to become the soul of his soul, the life of his life.

Identity of being, identity of life, as amazing as this doctrine seems, and now so easily reconcilable with the rigorous other-ness of Christ and of the Christian, it is, however, undeniable that St. Paul teaches it. Furthermore, his teaching is coupled with that of Christ: "He who eats my flesh and drinks my blood, dwells in me and I in Him. Just as my Father Who sent me is living, and that I live by the Father, the same way he, too, who eats me will live by me" (Jn 6:56-57). On the eve of His death, He said to His disciples: "I will not leave you orphans; I will come back to you. Still a little while and the world will no longer see me, but you, you will see me because I live and so you will live. On that day, you will know that I am in my Father and you in me, and I in you" (Jn 14:18-20).

From then on, all the reality of divine adoption is understood. It is not, like juridical adoption, pure fiction, which causes the adopted one to be considered as if he were the child of the adopter. It is an effective reality; it brings about a transformation of our being; it communicates to us a new life, thanks to a regeneration, "a birth of water and of the spirit" which is a "birth from on high," a "birth of God." As St. John says, "Christ has given the power of becoming sons of God to those who believe in His name, who are born not of blood, nor of the will of the flesh, nor of the will of man but of God." It is, consequently, a much more convincing proof of God's love and, at the same time, the effect of this love: "See what great love for us the Father has shown," says St. John, "that we are not only called children of God but we are His children" (1 Jn 3:2). Not only have we been adopted, but beautifully and well engendered. The Father begets us by giving us a share in the nature of His Son.

Thus, our divine filiation is so real that it can be

considered as being a positive participation in the eternal begetting of the Son in the Father's bosom. Not only does the Father engender always His Son, in us, but he also begets us forever as sons in this Son, as by a prolongation of His own generation, according to our union with Him. Origen writes: "Consider the Lord; the Father has not begotten Him once so that He ceases to be begotten, but begets Him continually; He is the same, of course. The Savior is "the effulgence of the Father's glory," and the effulgence does not cease being engendered . . . . If, then, the Savior is perpetually engendered by the Father, so you, if you have the spirit of adoption (filial). God begets you continually in Him in each work, in each thought, and he who is, thus, begotten is perpetually begotten as the son of God in Jesus Christ."

To this engendering is linked exhaling, the Spirit's breathing upon us through the Father and the Son, in which breathing we are also exhaled, breathed upon this same Spirit by the Father and the Son as expressions of love: thanks to this begetting and exhalation, we enter into participation in the trinitarian life, source and model of all spiritual life. By and in the Son we enter into the life of the three divine Persons: "As the Son is in the middle between the Father and the Holy Spirit," writes Bérulle, "he has wanted to be in the middle between God and men. We must, then, cling to Him, as we cling to the Father; we must emanate from Him, as we emanate from the Father; we must receive His Spirit, as being the one who produces it with His Father." I have already spoken of this miracle, but I must add here that theologians are not afraid to say that our divine sonship in Christ, that is, our being begotten as sons in the Son, is such that we are associated in the act by which the Son, in the depth of the trinitarian life, exhales the Holy Spirit conjointly with His Father. St. John of the Cross writes: "The Holy Spirit renders the soul capable of producing in God the same breath of love that the Father produces with the Son, and the Son with the Father, and which is none other than the Holy Spirit Himself. . . .So that He might bring us to this depth of glory, God has created us in His image and likeness". . . namely that, in the Holy Trinity where Christ introduced us, we accomplish, through participation, the same work He accomplishes by nature, that is, that we breathe, that we exhale the Holy Spirit. Christ had said: "He who believes in me, from his heart, as Scripture says, will flow rivers of living water." He said that, explains St. John who recalled this statement, of the Spirit, whom those who believe in Him ought to receive (Jn 7:37-39). He had already declared to the Samaritan woman: "He who will drink of the water that I will give him, will never be thirsty; the water that I will give him will become in him the source of water springing forth into eternal life" (Jn 4:14).

Now one understands a little better at what point we are, according to St. John, children of God. How right Péguy was in having the Father say, when speaking of men:

And all these sinners and all these saints
  together march behind my son
And behind the joined hands of my son.
And they have their hands joined as if they
  were my son.
At last, my sons. At last, each one a son
  like my Son!

How right, also, was Claudel in writing: "You have a Father in heaven Who no longer knows how to distinguish you from His Son!"

Likewise, one understands a little better to what extent and with what consequence, Christ Who is the "only Son," "the only begotten" (Jn 1:18), is, at the same time, the "first born Son. . .of a number of brothers" (Rm 8:29). St. Cyril of Alexandria writes: "Christ is at the same time 'only Son' and 'first-born Son': he is the only Son as far as God; he is the first-born Son by means of the salutary union that he placed between us and him by becoming man; so that we, in and by him, were made sons of God, both by nature and by grace, by nature, in him and in him alone; by participation and by grace, because of him, in the Spirit. Just as the quality of "only Son" became appropriate to humanity in Christ because it is united to the Word according to the economy of salvation, so it became appropriate to the Word to be "firstborn" and to be so among many brothers because he united himself to the flesh."[13]

Such is the expression of divine filiation that procures for us the communication that made us from God's nature in His Son Jesus Christ: This sonship is a true participation in Christ's sonship: it brings us to a communion in Christ's personal relations with His Father in the Spirit; it causes us to live a filial life in Him; better still, it causes us to actually participate in His very own filial life, and by it, in the trinitarian life. We enter into the movement of love which draws the Father toward the Son, and the Son toward the Father under the impetus of their common Spirit.

In fact, "if, on the one hand," as St. Gregory of Nyssa notes, "the Father loves the Son, and, if, on the other hand, we who, by faith, form Christ's Body and we are all in the Son, it follows that He who loves the Son, loves, also, the Son's Body as His very Son." For his own part, St. Augustine writes: "The Father loves us in His Son . . . , for He who loves His only Son, loves, also, the members of His Son whom He has adopted in and by him . . . He loves the Son insofar as He is God because he has begotten him equal to Himself; He also loves him accordingly because he is man, for he is always his only Son, the Word become flesh. . . .He loves us because we are members of the One whom He loves." St. Paul had already said that the Father made us agreeable to His eyes in His well-beloved Son.

Our Lord insists on this love of complacency of the Father for those whom He made sons in His Son by concluding with the similitude between this love and the love which His Father loves Him: "You have loved them," He says to His Father, "as you have loved me." By inferring even their identity: "I have made known your name of Father to them, so that the love with which you have loved me before the creation of the world might be in them." One can go further in the conclusion and say that the Father has loved us with this love, likewise, from all eternity. St. Paul says:

"God has chosen us in Christ since before the creation of the world, having, in His love, predestined us to be His adopted sons in Jesus Christ."

However, the Son is, likewise, all love for His Father. He loves the Father with that eternal and limitless love with which He, Himself, is loved by the Father, and which is their common Spirit. "My Father loves me, and I love my Father:" Christ can make this statement from the first instant of His conception. Thus, it must be concluded that united to Christ in baptism, we are, from that instant, drawn by, with, and in Him towards the Father. From henceforth, we can love the Father as He does, with a tender and filial love, with this same love which proceeds from Him, and which is, consequently, called the Spirit of the Son, as well as, the Spirit of the Father. "The proof that we are sons," writes St. Paul to the Galatians, "is that God has sent into your hearts the Spirit of His Son, who cries out: 'Abba,' that is, Father!" (Gal 4:6). To the Romans: "You have received a spirit of adopted sons, which causes you to cry out: 'Abba, Father!' The Spirit in person is joined to our spirit in order to testify that we are God's children" (Rm 8:15-16).

So, by entering, through baptism, into union with Christ, we share in His filial relationship, thanks to which the Holy Spirit proceeds from the Father through the Son, by means of love. These direct and personal relationships, by means of knowledge and love, with the Persons of the Blessed Trinity, make us, thus, participate in their very life, since they make us capable of knowing God and His creatures as He knows Himself and them, and with the same knowledge with which He knows Himself; capable, likewise, of loving God and His creatures as He loves Himself and loves them, and with the same love with which He loves Himself.

The spiritual life will consist, if not in becoming conscious of and experiencing, in any case, of living by this begetting in us of the Son, in which we ourselves are begotten as sons in Him, and of this spiration or exhalation in us of the Spirit, in which we are, also, exhaled in this same

Spirit as expressions of love, and we, too, exhale Him.

We are now at the source of prayer. Indeed it is a classic expression to call prayer a "breathing of the soul." St. Francis de Sales, forexample, writes about prayer: "By it we aspire to Him—God—and we breathe in Him and mutually He inhales in us, and upon us."[14]

Prayer is for the spiritual life of the Christian what breathing is for the life of the body. Consequently, prayer is a vital need of the soul, as the need to breathe is vital to the body. Not a psychological need: many Christians, sad to say, live without prayer; they do not feel the need to pray, and, if they pray, it is formalism or legalism. The need for prayer is on a supernatural level. No one can say to God: "Father," except by the action of the Holy Spirit. Prayer is an exigency of faith, hope and charity, which in the face of their object who is God cannot but affect those who live by these virtues.

Having made this remark, I say that there is a great resemblance between prayer and breathing. The latter, itself, is the symbol of the former because that breath, the air that is inhaled and exhaled is the symbol of the Holy Spirit to which he has given his name. The Latin word for "breath" is *spiritus*. I recall that Jesus affirmed this symbolism in an active way when, appearing to His disciples after His resurrection, He breathed on them saying: "Receive the Holy Spirit" (Jn 20:22).

Now, breathing involves two movements. The first is to inhale air. The aspirated air then, vivifies the entire body because, by penetrating into the lungs, it oxygizes the blood which flows through all the members, especially the brain. Thus, it is truly the entire body that is revitalized. The second is to exhale air, sending back the air that was inhaled.

The same is true for praying. The first step is to inhale the Holy Spirit, that is, the Breath of the Father's love; it is bringing Him into oneself, or more precisely welcoming Him. In fact, it is not I who, by the movement of my thorax, draws the air into my lungs; it is not I who exercises an attraction on the air in which I am suffused. On the contrary, it is the one that presses on my lungs,—that is the atmospheric pressure—and which presses on them so that I dilate my thoracic cage.

In the same way, when I pray, when my soul breathes, it is not my soul that draws the Breath of the Father's love, the Holy Spirit, but it is the Holy Spirit, of whom it is said that fills the entire universe, who places a pressure on my heart, since He is the love with which the Father loves us, and since the Father who loves us from all eternity "has loved us first" (1Jn 4:9-10, 19). I have only to open my Heart to this Breath of love; I have only to welcome the Father's love, according to the psalmist: "I open my mouth wide and I inhale" (Ps 118:131). Also, when we call the Holy Spirit, saying: *"Veni, Creator Spiritus,"* or again all the *"Veni's"* of the *Veni, Creator Spiritus,* it is necessary to understand the meaning of this invocation.Our purpose is not to beg Him to come: He asks nothing better, He to whom can be applied, in all truth, the words of the Apocalypse: "I stand at the door and knock. If someone opens to me, I shall enter his home." If he does not, the reason is that love does not impose itself, it offers itself. By invoking the Holy Spirit, our intention is to tell Him exactly that we are opening the door of our heart to Him, that we accept His offer, and, thus, he can enter.

Consequently prayer consists in receiving, in inhaling the Holy Spirit, the Spirit of the Father, paternal love; then exhaling, giving Him back to the Father in a spirit of filial love.

Indeed, thanks to our constant begetting as sons in His beloved Son, Jesus Christ, the Father loves us in this Son as He loves this Son, and with the same love who is, no one else, but the Holy Spirit. He communicates to us His Breath of love by the risen Christ living in us. We love the Father in His Son alike, as His Son loves Him, and with the same love who is the Holy Spirit. We do so by exhaling this same Spirit, this same Breath of love, exhaling Him in filial love, co-jointly with the Son, with Jesus Christ living in us, since the Spirit of the Father is, also, the Spirit of the Son. Let us recall these words of St. Paul: "The proof that you are sons is that God has sent into your hearts the Spirit of His Son who cries 'Abba, Father!' "Another: "You have received a Spirit of adopted son which causes us to cry out 'Abba, Father!' The Spirit, as person, unites Himself to our spirit in order to attest to our being God's children."

This inhaling and exhaling, is the breath of love which constitutes prayer. It is recommended to pray to the rhythm of bodily breathing, and, preferably, seated, which contributes to making one's entire being, body and soul, to participate in prayer, and to cause the body to profit from the benefits procured for the soul.

This breathing will be that much more profound as we are more united and more identified with Christ the Beloved and all loving Son of the Father, since it will coincide as much with Christ's very own breathing. Thus, the need to let the Holy Spirit cause us to know and to love Christ in order to be identified more and more with Him.

Now Christ's breathing consists of inhaling the Breath of love in whom the Father says to Him: "You are my Son; I have begotten you today." "You are my Son in whom I am pleased." Then, to exhale this same breath of love in whom He recognizes Himself as Son, and expresses to Him His gratitude as Son saying: "Abba, beloved Father!"

Our breathing should then, imitate Christ's breathing, better still, it ought to blend into Christ's respiration. It will consist, therefore, of breathing the Spirit, the breath of the Father's love, by listening to the Father say to us, because we are sons in His Son: "You are my beloved son; you are my beloved daughter, in whom I am pleased." Then, it will consist of inhaling this same Breath of the Son's love, in whom we recognize ourselves sons, and express to Him our love of a son like Him exclaiming: "Abba, beloved Father!"

This exhaling of love can be explained in various ways. According to the different reactions which the words will arouse in us by means of which, in order to express His love for us, God reveals to us such and such an aspect of His mystery, giving us a glimpse of such and such perfection, or recalling to us such and such wondrous work of His love.

This exhaling will express itself in the following ways:

At the thought of the transcendency of the Father, of the Creator as such; of the Father, principle and source of all, as well as, of the essentially relative and dependent nature of our being before His absolute being—"I am He who is; you are the one who is not"—it will be expressed in the love of adoration, of glorification, of complacency.

Before one or another of God's perfections glimpsed in His creatures, or manifested by His interventions in the history of humanity, such as His beauty, transcendency, power, holiness, justice, mercy, fidelity, goodness, it will be expressed in the love of praise.

At the remembrance of the miracles that He performed on behalf of mankind in general: Creation, Incarnation, Redemption, the Eucharist, filial adoption, etc. and those which He has performed for each one of us, in particular, it will be expressed in the love of admiration, of gratitude and of thanksgiving.

At the recollection of our sins; it will be expressed in a repentant and contrite love, begging for forgiveness.

At the thought of our deficiencies, of our needs or those of others, it will be expressed in the love of desire, petition and intercession.

In this silent heart to heart when the Father begets us, at each moment, as sons in His Son, by His vivifying breath of love, and gives us, in this Son rest, peace, joy, strength, light, purification, consolation, love, we can only repeat: Father, beloved Father!

Of course, during this breathing, nothing prevents us quite the contrary, from expressing these same sentiments to the One in whom we breathe: Jesus Christ, as well as to the One by whom we breathe: the Holy Spirit; both of whom possess the same nature and the same perfections as the Father, and accomplish—although differently—the same actions as He.

I shall make a few remarks about the first of the four elements which enter, as we have seen, into the definition of all life: the principle, itself, of life.

What is the immanent principle, the internal cause of the Christian spiritual life?

Speaking to Nicodemus about our rebirth of water and of the Spirit, of our new spiritual birth which gives us access to God's Kingdom, Christ said to him: "He who is born of the flesh is flesh; He who is born of the Spirit is spirit. Do not be astonished if I say to you: 'You must be born again on high' " (Jn 3:6). From that remark, we ought to conclude that our soul which is the principle in us of our "carnal" life, that is, of our natural life, is not, cannot be by itself, the principle of our spiritual life, in other words, of our supernatural life. It needs, in order to become so, to be supernaturalized, elevated above its nature, and essentially transformed. From *psysche* it must become *pneuma*; it must be seized and penetrated by the Spirit. Such is the proper role of what is called habitual, sanctifying, or even, created grace, about which I have already spoken briefly. The latter is a spiritual, permanent reality which transforms us in our being, communicates to us a "new life" (Rm 6:4), and makes each of us a "new creature." "If someone is in Christ," St. Paul writes, "he is a new creature; the old being has disappeared, a new one is there" (2Cor 5:17; Gal 6:15). Created grace is, then, a principle of being and of life in us. It transforms our soul not its faculties. It is an internal and permanent cause which makes us "participants in the divine nature" (2P 1:4), more precisely, in the divine nature in so far as it is possessed by the Son: a participation which makes us temples of the Blessed Trinity by making us become sons of God in His only Son. However, it is the formal, and not the efficient cause, of this renewal, this supernatural birth, this divine sonship, of God's dwelling in us.

Indeed, the first and efficient principle of our supernatural life is the grace that we call uncreated, and which was discussed earlier. It is God present in us personally, who "having life in His very self," as St. John says, communicates this life to us in His Son Jesus Christ who possesses it in its fullness, and has merited its possession for us. Now, Christ communicates this life to us by the Holy Spirit. It is the Holy

Spirit in fact, who, by uniting us to Christ, allows us to receive His fullness, to be animated by the very life with which He is animated, being Himself the breath of the life of the Father and of the Son. Consequently, although our supernatural vivification is the common work of the three divine Persons, and although it can be attributed impartially to each of them, it is appropriate to the Holy Spirit. The reason is: appropriation, by virtue of which a work, besides being common to the three divine Persons, is especially attributed to one, is based on the affinity which exists between this work and the specific nature of the person to whom it is attributed. Now, our supernatural vivification is the act which by causing us to participate in Christ's filial life, causes us to live by the life of the divine Persons through communion in the very knowledge and love with which they know and love each other. Being, on the one hand, Christ's filial spirit, it is the Holy Spirit who is responsible for the realization of this participation in us. On the other hand, because He is likewise the Spirit of truth, that is, the Spirit of the One who is Truth, in other words, of Christ Who, indeed, declared Himself to be the Truth, the Holy Spirit has, as mission to make us probe into all the truth revealed by Jesus Christ, especially to make us know the Father and the Son, with this knowledge which implies a vital experience, and, thus, love. Consequently, it belongs to Him to make us share in the knowledge and love of the divine Persons, a union in which consists, to repeat once again, the Christian spiritual life. Thus, it is He who is the principle of this life. Also, St. Paul can affirm that "the Holy Spirit is our life" (Gal 5:25), and the Credo can proclaim our faith in "the Holy Spirit who gives life." Accordingly, this life is called spiritual. It is the life of our spirit animated and vivified by the Holy Spirit.

Now it is easier to understand St. John's words, so full of exultation and so overwhelming, which I quoted in part, and which I quote here in their entirety: "What was from the beginning, what we have understood, what we have seen with our eyes, what we have contemplated, what our hands have touched of the Word of life—because Life manifested itself: we have seen it, we give testimony and we announce it to you this eternal life, who was next to the Father, and who appeared to us—what we have seen and understood, we announce it to you, that you, also, might be in communion with us. As for our communion, it is with the Father and His Son, Jesus Christ. We write this to you so that you might rejoice, and that your joy might be complete" (1 Jn 1:4).

Such is the life to which God, from the beginning, had invited man to share, a life which they lost through the first sin, which, then, subjected them to death, a life that Christ gave back to them by freeing them from this death, thanks to His own death and resurrection. Several of the new prefaces of the mass, vying with each other, speak about this life; among them, that of the second Sunday after Pentecost: "By His passion and cross, Christ delivered us from eternal death; by His resurrection from the dead, He gave us eternal life."

Footnotes

1. M. Cl. Tresmontant, *Lettre*, Sept.-Oct., 1962 (Teilhard de Chardin and theology).
2. *In Joann. Evang.* 11, 2 P.G., 74, 553.
3. *Thesaurus*, 34, P.G. 75, 609-612.
4. *Epis. 3 ad Sarapronom.*, 5, P.G. 26, 628.
5. *In 1 Cor.*, ch. 3, reading 3.
6. Letter to Mme G. de G., 1906.
7. St. Ireneaus, *Adv. Hoeres*, 1. III, c. 19., P.G. vii, 939.
8. *De incarnatione Verbi*, no. 13-14, P.G. XXV, 120.
9. *Contra Gentes*, no. 34, P.G. XXV, 68-69. Cf. Jn 14:9; Mt. 11:27.
10. L. Lochet, *Fils de Dieu*, Cerf, Paris, 1963, p. 191.
11. *Contra arianos*, 2, 59. P.G. 26, 273.
12. *In Joann. Evang.* 2, 1. P.G. 73, 213
13. *De recta fide*, no. 30, P.G. LXXVI, 1 177.
14. *Traité de l'Amour de Dieu*, IV, 1.

Chapter 7

LIBERATION OF THE HUMAN PERSON

By making us share, through participation in His filial life, in the very life of the Blessed Trinity, Christ does not free us only from spiritual death. The divine life that He has communicated to us brings about a transformation in our entire person and in our relationship to the world. This transformation consists in other liberations, which will be analyzed in the following chapters.

Indeed, our participation, through grace, in the divine sonship of Christ, which makes us adopted sons of God, is not sufficient to make us live fully in the trinitarian life. As St. John Chrysostom says: "it is not enough to be God's children through the grace that He has given to us, we must be so by our actions."[1] Actually, just as the adopted child in order to be truly part of the adopted family, ought to try to acquire the manners of his new parents, their language, way of life, thoughts, feelings, so, we, introduced into God's family as sons, must strive to lead the life of sons. We must be "imitators of God," as St. Paul says, "as is appropriate of beloved children," (Ep 5:1) striving to imitate our older brother Who is His Son by nature and His perfect image, in which He makes Himself visible: Jesus Christ. We must become more and more like Christ, by allowing the Holy Spirit — the Spirit, of the divine family — to make us think, love, act, feel, and speak as our oldest brother, the Son of the family, into which the Father has adopted us as sons. St. Paul addresses us: "Those who are sons of God are the ones led by the Spirit" (Rm 8:14). In a w rd, we must let ourselves be transformed by the Holy Spirit into the likeness of Jesus Christ (Cf. Rm 8:29).

As is seen, the transformation, in question here, is no longer the "physical," essential, ontological transformation which was the subject of the preceding chapter. This latter is effected by means of the sanctifying grace received in baptism. It consists, as we recall, in the renovation of the very substance of our soul, in the stripping off of the old man, in the restricted sense of original sin, and in the putting on of the new man created in God's image, in other words, in the initial act of our divinization by means of our incorporation i.ito Christ, the Son of God, then by our adoption as God's children. Here it is a question of another transformation, no longer that of the soul and its faculties but of their activity: a moral transformation. St. Augustine speaks of both transformations when he writes: "Certainly, this renewal (moral transformation) of the soul is not accomplished at the very moment of his conversion, like his renewal ("physical" transformation), which is accomplished suddenly in baptism through the remission of all of his sins . . . Yet, just as, no longer having a fever, is different from recovering from the weakness due to the fever, just as, extracting a spear embedded in the body is totally different from the comforting care which heals the wound; so, the first degree of healing for the soul consists in removing from it what is a cause of apathy: it is done by the remission of sins. The second degree is to cure this apathy: it is accomplished little by little by the progress accomplished in the renewal of the divine image."[2] Thus, this renewal consists in becoming what we are, that is, sons of God.

The spiritual life and human development

So, the Christian spiritual life comprises and procures, at

least it ought to, the unfolding of our life as God's sons—
and, thus, of our human personality—thanks to our
progressive resemblance to Christ and, in Him, to the Father,
realized by their mutual Spirit of love. Indeed, there is no
opposition between our spiritual development and that of
our personality, as man or woman. Better still, the spiritual
life tends, by its very nature, to the real development not only
of our supernatural, but also, of our entire human life.

On this subject, there exists a sad misunderstanding
which is so important to dispel; it is really very serious,
being, in great part, at the root of contemporary atheism.
This is it. There are millions of individuals who believe,
often in good faith, that God is a constraint to man. They are
convinced God's grandeur is made up of the insignificance,
and even of, indeed, the annihilation of man. Thus, they
think, if one is for God, one is against man: it is the thesis of
all Marxists and of all atheistic existentialists. "The more
religious man is," writes Marx, "the less he is a man."
According to Sartre, "If God exists, man is nothing."[3] They
have, also, succeeded in placing man's grandeur, and, even,
his existence in the negation of God. Marx says, "Atheism is
a negation of God, and, by this negation, he admits the
obviousness of man." For Sartre, "atheism is a humanism,"
in this sense, that the non-existence of God is a condition of
man's reality and of his involvement in earthly life.
Paraphrasing Nietzsche's famous remark: "God is dead,"
Malraux wrote: "God is dead, therefore, man is born."
Modern man believes that he can exist and grow only to the
exact extent that he discards the very idea of God. For that
reason, many of our contemporaries have believed that they
must cease being Christians, or they refuse to become so, in
order to safeguard man's dignity, and, thus, his intelligence,
liberty, creative power, and consequently the esteem and love
of the world, human values and temporal activities.

Certainly, these are aberrations due to a misunderstanding about who God truly is, and hence, what is Christianity. God, the God of Jesus Christ, in any case, is not that God
who is considered by the majority of the moderns as an attack

on man's dignity, a constraint to his intelligence, a limitation on his liberty, a threat to his grandeur. Does that mean that Christians—and I do not mean only lay people—have no part in responsibility for this misunderstanding? Sad to say! If the Christian religion, to speak only of it, was able to give to our contemporaries the impression of having devaluated and having continued to devaluate man in order to magnify God more, would it not be because there has existed and still exists theoretical or practical presentations of the Christian message which deform the true face of the God of Jesus Christ, and can only cause him to be denied?

Indeed, a certain expression of Christian spirituality inspired, be it by Jansenism, or by a deformed monastic spirituality either poorly understood or taught, and, thus, inappropriate, to married couples or to the unmarried preached hatred and escape from the world considered as bad and condemned by God, which led, consequently, to a disinterestedness of the common good, in a word, a spirituality of "separation" or of "non-involvement," an ethics of interdicts and penalties, which was suspicious of the body and of sexual life, a way of preaching and of practicing resignation to inhuman conditions of existence within a certain social class, a defensive attitude against the disturbing statements of scientists of the nineteenth century, as so many indications which manifest, without justification, the basis of distrust, not to say, contempt, among a great number of Christians yesterday, and, even, today, with regard to all that concerns man and his world.

Thus, it is understandable that so many men, among them eminently educated and remarkably intelligent people, sometimes geniuses who reject God and religion, or who turn to the absurd and despair, are constrained by a religion where God is presented as a limit, a menace and a constraint.

To repeat, such is not the God of Jesus Christ. This God is not against man but for him. He only desires man's happiness, and, thus, his success, liberation, and development by means of a communion of love with him. Instructed by God's Word, the Catholic Church has always taught—

and Vatican II recalled it solemnly in the Constitution *Gaudium et Spes*—that God created, in an admirable manner, the dignity of human nature, and restored it, in a still more admirable one. Holy Scripture, indeed, teaches us that God created man to His image and likeness, capable of knowing and loving Him; that He has made him master of all earthly creatures, in order to dominate them and to use them, while glorifying Him; that He has made him "a little less than divine, the consummation of glory and of magnificence" (Ps 8:5-7). It teaches us, also, that, even after the sin of the first man, God did not stop loving man, that He, even, loved him so much that He, Himself, became man in His Son Jesus Christ. If Jesus Christ is, indeed, truly God and truly man, He is the true God and the true man. He is not only a man but the Man. For that reason, "renewing man in man, according to St. Leo's beautiful expression, He restored to man God's image." Speaking of it, the Council says: "Image of the invisible God (Col 1:15), it is the perfect Man who restored, in Adam's descendants, the divine resemblance, altered since the original sin. Because in him human nature has been assumed, not absorbed, by the fact, itself, this nature was, also, elevated in us to an unequalled dignity."[4] By that very fact, the Church teaches us that the spiritual life is not an abstract activity which would be exercised independently of all human substratum; that it does not imply the destruction of our human nature under the pretext that it was corrupted by original sin; and that it is, above all, in Christ's teaching, a question of the necessity of "losing his life," of "renouncing self," of "carrying one's cross," of "mortifying oneself," of "dying like the grain of wheat cast on the ground." The Catholic Church has never taught that human nature was totally corrupt, but only injured, not that it was necessary to understand the Lord's word that I have just quoted, in the sense of an annihilation of this nature, but of asceticism which term is not death but the development of life.[5] In fact, the Church states that grace does not suppress nature, but implies and utilizes it in order to liberate and to complete nature. The role of nature is to animate with God's life our entire person, injured as it is. Precisely because it has to deal with a sick organism, its function is, also, to work constantly to heal it by making it recover its natural forces, by raising it completely to the supernatural order, that is, by divinizing it entirely. In the Constitution quoted above, Vatican II recalled:

"The Church, by pursuing the salvific end proper to her, does not communicate to man divine life only; it spreads, also, and in a certain way over the entire world, the light which this divine life radiates, especially by healing and by raising the dignity of the human person."[6] Because the matter which grace uses, accomplishes and divinizes is our human personality, our spiritual life will be expanded that much more as our personality will be corrected, healed, liberated, transformed. The same way that a statue will be all the more finished, provided that its material will be cleaned and purified of all defects.

However, a word of caution. Let us not imagine such a liberation and an expansion that would make all the defects of nature disappear. We all have our limits which are irreducible due to our human condition and to its inevitable imperfection, limits which, in addition, we ought not to determine in advance and permanently. The spiritual life is entirely compatible with the defects of nature. It is, also, compatible with the insufficiencies and deficiencies of mental health, understanding by the latter not the maladies of reasonable intelligence, but the psychosomatic conditions which escape, at least indirectly, free will. Undoubtedly, these are obstacles to the spiritual life, which can disturb the complete development and expansion of everyone, but they can, also, be for him a means of gaining in depth what they cause him to lose in extent. Some psychologically ill individuals can have a sufficiently profound spiritual life which allows them to develop a vibrant personality without causing their deficiencies to disappear. As Father Louis Beinaert says, "One must not expect grace to perform more miracles in the psychical order than in the material order, and that she transform immediately injured personalities.

God is, without doubt, master of His gifts, but, in the customary ordering of His providence, He does not heal more psychological maladies than bodily infirmities. His action is more intimate; it is the heart that it transforms. What happens, then, is that, beyond even the psychological difficulties that remain, a peace, a presence is manifested that succeeds in breaking through the clouds and in shining upon faces that know how to open themselves. We have all encountered these individuals still haunted by difficulties; we know that it will never be possible to offer them officially as examples, but who give the sense of the divine presence and the impression of this heroism which makes saints. . . . Paradoxically, it is by accepting a wounded humanity that their efforts can transform; it is by recognizing that that is the way God asks them to walk towards Him, that something in their very humanity continues to manifest the grace which dwells in them. Never completely transformed, and yet revealing the essential transformation that is affected in them, they, themselves, are, indeed, saints, also, in the making."[7]

So, then, the fundamental truth which Christianity teaches is to believe in God dwelling in man, to believe that God loved man to the extent of making him like Himself in order to make him become what He is. However, it is, also to believe that, in order to realize this fact, He pushed this love to the extent of dying for him in this God made man. "God proves His love for us," says St. Paul, "in that while we were still sinners, Christ died for us" (Rm 5:8).

Because the mystery of the redemptive Incarnation explains the passion in the two-fold sense of the word, of God for man, for every man, we are not permitted to love God without loving men, all men. How could we be disinterested in man if we love that God? How sad and tragic is the contempt of those who, in order to love man, believe they have to deny God who has treated and treats man with so much respect and love! For that reason, we will never protest enough against this contempt on which, I repeat, rests, in great part, today's atheism, appearing in History as man's revolt in his effort to attain the fullness of his stature. With all our hearts we ought to agree with this admirable statement made some time ago by the Christian Cameroons: "We want for ourselves supporters of man and of the total man. Not man amputated of his religious dimension as in the secular ideology. Not man amputated of his value as a person for the profit, presumably, of the masses, as in the Marxist ideology. Not man reduced to the state of consumer or of producer, as in the capitalistic hypothesis. Not man considered *in aeternam* as an irresponsible ward, as in the colonial system. Not man giving to woman the right only to be beautiful and to be silent. Not man evaluated only because of the glitter of his decorations or because of his wealth. Not man clothed, helmeted, armored, in his race, caste, class, civilization, frontiers, or in his culture. . . . But man complete, body and soul, come from God's Hands, and destined to return to Him with his brothers. Of that man, we are, we want to be, supporters with all our heart."

Consequently, before the interrogations of contemporary man, which all have as center man himself "on the move towards a more complete development of his personality, towards a discovery and a constantly increasing affirmation of his rights,"[8] the Church had to remove solemnly the misunderstanding that makes God and man irreducible antagonists, one of which cannot exist without denying the existence of the other. The Church removed it through the second Vatican Council, by recallng its doctrine on the dignity of the human person in a magisterial way, that Pope Paul VI was pleased to emphasize in his vibrant address of December 7, 1965. Here are some excerpts. After having insisted on the theo-centric concept of man and of the universe, which the Council was not afraid to present to today's world, too prone to be concerned only about man, Paul VI declares: "The Church of the Council is not content to reflect on her own nature and on the relationships which unite her to God. She is, also, very concerned about man as he is really presented in our time: the living man, entirely concerned about himself, the man who makes himself not only the center of all that interests him, but who dares to consider himself the principle and the last end of all reality. The entire phenomenal man, that is, with the veneer of his countless appearances, has, as it were, risen up before the assembly of the Council Fathers, men, too, and all, attentive and loving pastors and brothers.

"Secular and profane humanism has appeared in its dreadful aspect, and has, in a certain sense, defied the Council. The religion of God Who became man was confronted with the religion (because it is one) of man who made himself God. What happened? A shock, a struggle, an anathema? Such could have happened, but did not. The old story of the Samaritan has been the model of the spirituality of the Council. A limitless sympathy engulfed it entirely. The discovery of human needs (and they are so much the greater as the child of the earth becomes greater) absorbed the attention of the Synod. Recognize at last this merit, you modern humanists, who renounce the transcendency of supreme things, and know how to recognize our new humanism: we, also, more than anyone, possess the cult of man." A bit further on: "A current of affection and admiration flowed from the Council over the modern, human world. Errors have been denounced, it is true, demanded by charity as well as by truth, but, directed to persons, there was only a reminder, respect and love. Instead of depressing diagnoses, encouraging solutions; instead of funereal predictions, confident messages came from the Council to contemporary society: its values have not only been respected, but honored; its efforts supported, its aspirations refined and praised. For example, the countless languages spoken by people today have been accepted for expressing liturgically the word of men to God and God's word to men; as man, man's basic vocation to a fullness of rights and a transcendency of destinies have been recognized; his highest yearnings for existence, for human dignity, for honest liberty, for culture, for the renewal of the social order, for justice and peace have been recognized and encouraged."

After having noted that the Council "has spoken to man

of today, such as he is," Paul VI continues: "There is still another point that we ought to raise: all this doctrinal wealth exists only for one thing, to serve man. Of course, it is a question of every man, whatever his condition, his distress and his needs. The Church has proclaimed herself, so to speak, the servant of humanity, just at the moment when her ecclesiastical authority and her pastoral government have, by reason of the solemnity of the Council, put on a greater splendor and greater force; the idea of service has occupied a central place in the Church."

Then, Paul VI recalled that "the dominant interest sustained by the Council in human and temporal values . . . was never separated from the most genuine religious preoccupations, be it prompted by charity which alone arouses this interest (and where charity is found, God is there), be it by reason of the bond . . . existing between human and temporal values, and those, appropriately, spiritual, religious and eternal." Relying on this fact, the Holy Father did not hesitate to affirm: "The modern mentality, accustomed to judge all things according to their value, that is, their utility, will be willing to admit that the value of the Council is great, at least, because of this motive: all has been directed to what is useful to man. Let no one then ever declare useless a religion, like the Catholic religion, which, in its most conscious and most efficacious form, like that of the Council, proclaims itself entirely in favor of, and at, the service of man. The Catholic religion and human life, thus, reaffirm their alliance, their convergence towards a single human reality: the Catholic religion is for humanity; in a certain sense, it is the life of humanity. It is the life because of the explanation that our religion gives of man, the only exact and sublime explanation in the end (isn't man left to himself a mystery before his very own eyes?). The Catholic religion gives this explanation precisely by virtue of its knowledge of God: in order to know man, the true and complete man, one must know God.

"However, to repeat, if we remind you that, on every man's face—especially when tears and sufferings make it more transparent—we can and ought to recognize the face of Christ, the Son of man (Cf. Mt. 25:40), and if then, in Christ's face we can and ought to recognize the face of the Heavenly Father: 'He who sees me,' says Christ, 'sees also the Father,' (Jn 14:9) our humanism becomes Christianity and our Christianity becomes theocentric, so that we can, also, state in order to know God, one must know man."

I must explain by what means the Holy Spirit realizes our resemblance to Christ, the cause of our spiritual and human development, according to the admirable words of the Council: "Whoever follows Christ, the perfect man, becomes himself more of a man."[9]

First of all, let us note that this resemblance ought not to be a reproduction, impossible, actually, of the historical Christ feature for feature. The Christ, like whom the Spirit wishes to make us, is the Christ such as He wishes to live in us now, in the twentieth century and in such a country, starting with what we are, and whatever is our physical, psychological or moral condition. Our resemblance to Christ ought to be, under the inspiration and action of the Spirit, an original reproduction peculiar to each, in our unique existence, of the continually better known life of Christ.

The spiritual combat

Having said that, how ought we to let the Holy Spirit realize this resemblance in us? By struggling and causing to die within us what St. Paul calls "the carnal man," in other words, by freeing ourselves and by assuring the growth of grace of "the spiritual man," as described by the same apostle.

Before saying in what this struggle consists, it is indispensable to present two adversaries: carnal man and the spiritual man, and, thus, ask ourselves first of all: briefly, what is man?

Man is a synthesis of two principles: a spiritual principle

called "the soul," and a material principle called "the body." These two realities are not complete in themselves, nor united one to the other accidentally; on the contrary, they are of necessity relative to each other, one of whom, the soul, can exist by itself and gives its existence to the human being.

The concept of man, or anthropology, to which Christians have been accustomed, and which is still current, is that which has been influenced by Descartes' philosophy. It is described thus: "Man is a creature composed of a soul and of a body," whose union is compared to that of a rider with his horse: their union is, then, an accidental one.

Biblical anthropology is different. The Bible is unaware of any dualism, that is, any doctrine that divides the human person into body and soul, that it juxtaposes when it does not put them in opposition one to the other. It considers the soul a spirit, originally, good and immortal—because created by the Source of good—but prisoner of the body into which it has fallen and which, itself, is considered heavy and opaque, unworthy of the soul's nobility, truly, basically bad, created by the Source of evil, and from whom the soul ought to escape and to liberate itself.

The biblical concept of man does not rest on abstract or philosophical ideas. It rests on God's word; it trusts, essentially, the account of creation: "God said: 'Let us make man to our image and likeness'" (Gn 1:26). "Then God Yaweh formed man with the clay of the earth; he breathed into his nostrils life and man became a living being" (Gn 2:7). We must come back to this anthropology which, better than any other, can help us to know man since it comes from Him who created man.

According to these quotations, it seems that, in a human being, there can be distinguished three elements: body, soul and spirit. Such are, in any case, the elements which St. Paul enumerates in his letter to the Thessalonians: "May the God of peace, Himself, sanctify you entirely, and may your entire being, spirit, soul and body, be preserved without reproach until the coming of our Lord Jesus Christ (1 Th 5:23).

These elements are like three more profound zones or

levels of the human person, in which he is constantly being divided yet remaining truly one. This three-fold division has been admitted by several ancient and modern philosophers, without, however, their having succeeded in agreeing on the terminology. I shall adopt St. Paul's.

The first level, the "body," includes the flesh (in Hebrew: *bachar*, in Greek: *sarx*). It exists only inasmuch as it is animated by the vital breath. As soon as it is deprived of this breath, the body ceases to be a body; it becomes a corpse. It is nothing more than flesh doomed to decomposition: "dust which returns to dust."

This first level includes, then, the vital breath itself (in Hebrew: *nephess*, in Greek: *psyche*, in Latin: *anima*). It is the vital principle which animates the flesh and makes it a "living being," as expressed in Genesis, the principle which unites us to our body, resides in it for a lifetime, and regulates its functions with a wisdom which escapes our will.

The element "body" includes also the external senses (hearing, sight, smell, taste, touch) and the internal senses: memory and imagination.

Finally, it includes instinct, that is, the sensible conscience which perceives by means of the external and internal senses, not only the body and the realities of the exterior world, but also the realities of the interior world: desires which shape the human person like the desire to eat, drink, sleep, to mate, as well as the sentiments which affect it: joy, sadness, sympathy, antipathy, jealousy, hatred, anger, anxiety.

Such is the first level of the human person. Some people call it *anima*: the living soul. Man possesses the soul, thus understood, in common with animals.

However, man possesses this soul in a completely characteristic manner which distinguishes him from the animal by making him a rational animal. That is the second level of the human person designated by the term "soul," and which certain authors call in Greek: *nous*; in Latin: *animus, ratio, spiritus*; in French: *raison, entendement, esprit*. Indeed, this level is composed of an immaterial and immortal principle by which man is aware of himself, how he thinks, reasons and performs voluntary acts. The soul is, thus, endowed with two faculties which form our dignity as man: intelligence and free will. The intelligence, in question, is discursive and reasonable; it is reason which allows us to reflect on ourselves, as well as on sensible realities, to deduce concepts in order to work out philosophy and sciences, and to make applications from them.

However, the intelligence with which the soul is endowed is not only discursive intelligence, but, also, intuitive intelligence which is, not a second faculty, but another facet of the same faculty. It constitutes what is called the "center," or the "basis," or the "summit" or the "fine point" of the soul by which man participates in the very life of God, which life is called in the Bible *rouah*, in Greek *pneuma*: "Spirit," and which, thus shared by man, becomes also the "spirit" in him. St. Paul says: "The Spirit, as a person, is joined to our spirit in order to testify that we are children of God!"[10] The spirit designates, then, the third level, the most profound of our being, the basis of our personality, our most profound self, which is essentially a fundamental impetus toward the Beautiful, the True, the absolute Good—that is, God—thus, towards that which is a reflection of Him which participates in Him; a basic thrust which, all in all, is a certain ability to love these values, a love which comes from God, and which tends toward Him. This love constitutes the fundamental will about which the mystics speak, which is not, in the modern sense of the word, the power to bind its forces and to move with a certain interior tension, a more or less violent energy, towards an object to be conquered, no, but the aptitude of our most profound self to direct freely towards the Good, the True and the Beautiful: which is more in conformity with the Hebrew sense of the word "will" which means: desire, aspiration, love.

Our spirit, then, is the capacity of our soul to attain God and to attain Him through love, for our spirit is but our profound self inasmuch as it participates in the Holy Spirit.

Now the Holy Spirit, as we know, is love, and the "love of God," says St. Paul, "has been poured into our hearts by the Holy Spirit who has been given to us" (Rm 5:5).

St. Paul's use of the word "heart" allows me to complete the structure of the human person according to Christian anthropology.

In context, the word "heart" designates, as most often with St. Paul, the same reality as the word "spirit." Furthermore, it is the meaning which this term has, in general, in biblical language which, as is known, scarcely knows abstraction. In order to express spiritual realities, the sacred writers use words which designate material realities. In particular, such is the use, which they make of the word "heart," as does St. Paul and, likewise, all the tradition of the Fathers of the Church, such as St. Augustine a tradition steeped in Scripture, especially in the writings of the apostles and collected, for example, by Pascal. It is, in fact, in the Pauline sense of "spirit" that Pascal uses the word "heart" which, consequently, has not for him the meaning of sensible affectivity, still less of sentimentality, as is so often thought. That is the case in the following well-known maxims: "Noble thoughts come from the heart." "It is the heart that feels God, not reason." "We know truth not only through reason, but also, through the heart; it is from this last source that we know the first principles." For Pascal, the heart, then, is the highest intellectual faculty: intuitive intelligence transfigured by the Holy Spirit. It is the spirit.

Sacred writers distinguish rightly, in the human person, a body and a soul, but they do not separate them, still less, place them in opposition to the other. For them, man is truly "one"; he is a living body or a soul incarnate. The body and the soul are united, not accidentally, but essentially. Consequently, there is no contempt of the body, no tendency toward manicheism or angelism.

In such a concept of man, it is understood that, for the Sacred writers, the term "body" and "flesh" can mean rather often all of man in his concrete reality as a living person, whose basis these terms designate—the physical body—and they underline the visible, perceptible aspect, as in this passage from St. John: "And the Word was made flesh," which the authors of the Credo or the creed of Nicaea, have rendered, appropriately, by "He became man."

The same is true of St. Paul with this difference however, that, for him, as we shall see, if the words "body," "flesh" designate sometimes all of man—body and soul intimately united, with the accent on the flesh—it is most often man, insomuch as he is fallen and contaminated by original sin. Likewise, the word "spirit" means for him all of man equally—body and soul, with the accent on the spiritual principle of the thinking soul—but penetrated and sanctified by the Holy Spirit.

Such is man in a general definition. Now we can define more precisely carnal and spiritual man.

First of all, what is carnal man?

Let us begin by discarding a possible misinterpretation that is still rather often made. In present usage, the word "flesh" means "the senses"; a carnal man is a sensual man; the sins of the flesh signify the sins against purity to which is generally opposed the sin of the spirit which is pride.

It is not like that with St. Paul. For him, the "flesh" is not usually identified with the "senses," nor with the "body" either; it is identified with human nature, as the Bible, in general, understands it, especially St. John when he says: "And the Word became flesh," but, as I just said, identified with fallen human nature, deprived of divine life. The expression "the works of the flesh" does not mean sins of impurity, but, precisely, man's sins, the result of original sin, and, understood, the sin of the spirit, that is pride.

"Carnal man," whom St. Paul, also, calls the "old man," designates the man deprived of God, left to the sole resources of his fallen and unregenerated nature: to his own thoughts, his own forces and his own instincts.

Now to consider what is the spiritual man. Here, too, I begin by eliminating a possible and rather frequent misunderstanding. In current usage, spirit usually means the superior part of human nature, the soul insofar as living in and for itself, with its two faculties: intelligence and will, and contrary to the body. When a spiritual man does not mean someone with spirit, humor, nerve, he is a man whose life resides in the exercise of his highest faculties, in the activity of this spiritual substance which is the human soul, and who often neglects, is unaware of, and, even despises his body and material things. The spirit is, then, opposed to the body and to matter.

It is not in that sense that St. Paul uses the term spirit when he speaks of the spiritual man. By this word, as has been seen, the apostle does not understand soul in opposition to the corporal and material being. He means human nature complete—body and soul—but regenerated, renewed, divinized and animated by the Holy Spirit. The "spiritual man," whom St. Paul calls, also, "the new man" designates, then, the man animated by the spirit of God, more precisely, by the spirit of the Son of God, the Spirit of Christ, Who is born in each of us mystically and spiritually at baptism.

Now baptism frees us completely from the carnal man only on the level of being. On the level of acting, the carnal man continues to rule in us, even though with more difficulty, to oppose the good desires of our nature, regenerated and animated by the Holy Spirit and to fight against the spiritual man. The carnal man, the old man, against whom we must fight, is, then, the man such as original sin made him, and such as he remains after the disappearance of this sin, thanks to baptism. It is the man inhabited and dominated by the perverse law of which St. Paul speaks, and who struggles against the law of his spirit (Cf. Rm 7:22-23). It is the man obsessed and dominated by evil desires, by his inclinations toward evil, which stem from original sin and which are called concupiscence.

It is true that concupiscence is basically good; it became evil only as a consequence of original sin. It existed before it; it did not proceed from it, but from the very nature of man such as God made him.

Indeed, concupiscence (from the Latin *concupiscere*—to

desire, from which comes its name, also, of covetousness from the Latin *cupio*—I desire) is a force, a power which is in us and which makes us desire a being in its concrete reality, which supports us, makes us sensitive, inclines us, makes us tend toward this being so that we incorporate it unto ourselves, or we are incorporated into it. Thus, it designates all of the appetites, tendencies, inclinations, or leanings of our nature. It makes me want such a fruit, draws me toward it and impels me to eat it. Thanks to it, man and woman mutually desire each other, and are impelled to be united in the flesh for their own fulfillment and for the propagation of the human race. By the intermediation of our senses, it, also, draws our intelligence to know beauty and truth, and finally, it draws our will to search for and to do good. All these things are good. Therefore, concupiscence, too, is good and useful, even necessary. Without it, we would not be drawn to preserve and to develop our physical life, nor to develop our nature, nor to propagate the human race, nor to know beauty and truth, nor to practice the good.

As is seen, this concupiscence is multiform. It is cloaked in as many forms as there are objects which solicit it. By placing these objects into three categories, three forms of concupiscence can be distinguished, according to this text of St. John where the Apostle speaks, it is true, of disordered concupiscence, but which can serve us as a guide, since disordered concupiscence is only the good concupiscence become bad as a result of original sin: "If someone loves the world, the Father's love is not in him, because all that is in the world: the concupiscence of the flesh, the concupiscence of the eyes and the pride of life, is not of the Father but of the world" (1 Jn 2:15-16).

The following is a description of this triple concupiscence, in fact, inspired by that of St. Augustine in his interpretation of St. John's text. The renowned Doctor of Hippo speaks, of course, of concupiscence disordered by sin; yet, what he says applies equally, with some changes, to the original concupiscence.

Concupiscence of the flesh consists in the regulated

satisfaction of the bodily senses: touch, taste, smell, hearing, sight. There is sexual concupiscence, the concupiscence of drinking and of eating, the seduction of perfumes, the charm of a "pleasant and well-modulated voice" which sings beautiful melodies, the love of beautiful and varied forms, of brilliant and lively colors, and, above all, "light, the queen of colors"; then, all "the countless seductions that men have known how to add to what fascinated the eyes, by means of art under all its diverse forms."

Concupiscence of the eyes is more subtle than concupiscence of the flesh. It passes through the same bodily senses but aims not so much at a carnal pleasure as at an experience of which the body is the instrument: a healthy curiosity which pushes the intelligence to know beauty and truth. As it is essentially the appetite of knowing and, since, among the senses, the eyes are of primary importance for knowledge, St. John called it "the concupiscence of the eyes."

The third kind of concupiscence consists in wanting to be first, to become lord and master, not in order to satisfy his pride by dominating and by being waited upon, but in order to work for the good of those whose leader he is, by making himself their servant (Cf. Jn 13:13-14; Mt 20:25-28; Lk 22:25-27). It consists, also, in wanting to be loved, not in order to satisfy his egoism, but, in order to procure better the good of those by whom he is loved, by making them accept more easily, thanks to this love, the demands that the pursuit of this good involves.[11]

Such is the concupiscence which Adam and Eve would have enjoyed if they had not sinned. Such is the concupiscence that Jesus and Mary possessed. He, thanks to the union of His human nature to the person of the Word; she, thanks to an entirely gratuitous privilege.

However, as a result of original sin, these tendencies or inclinations, designated by the term concupiscence, have been degraded and have degenerated into disordered desires, unregulated passions, desires or evil inclinations. Concupiscence has been disturbed; it has become the source of sins. St. James affirms: "Each one is tempted by his own concupiscence which entices and seduces him; then, having conceived, concupiscence gives birth to sin" (Jm 1:13-15). Further on: "From whence do the struggles and quarrels among us come? From your lusts which battle in your members, don't they?" (Jm 4:1). Man's soul and body have become their slaves.

Christ liberates man from this dual slavery through the power of His Spirit. For the moment, I will speak only of the soul's liberation. In the baptized, this concupiscence is not definitively conquered but only weakened. Sin can still rule over us by enslaving us to it. In other words, if the old man received at baptism a mortal blow, he is not, however, definitively dead: it is necessary to get rid of him continually. Otherwise, certain statements of St. Paul made when addressing the baptized, would not be understood. After having said to the Christians of Rome: "You are no longer in the flesh, but in the spirit, since the Spirit of God dwells in you," he adds further on: "We are no longer tributaries of the flesh in order to be obliged to live according to the flesh. If you live according to the flesh, you will die; but, if by the Spirit you cause the works of the flesh to die, you will live" (Rm 8:9,12-13). Again: "Do not let sin rule any longer in your mortal body, in order to make you obey its lusts" (Rm 6:12). To the Ephesians, he writes: "You have been instructed to strip yourself, in what concerns your past life, of the old man corrupted by deceptive lusts, in order to renew yourself, in your spirit and in your thoughts, and to put on the new man, created in the image of God in a genuine justice and true sanctity" (Ep 4:21-24). To the Galatians he says: "Let yourself be led by the Spirit and do not satisfy the desires of the flesh; there is an antagonism among them, so that you do not do what you would like to do." A little further on: "Those who belong to Christ have crucified the flesh with its passions and lusts" (Gal 5:16-17, 24). Likewise, to the Colossians he writes: "You have stripped yourself of the old man with his ways, in order to put on the new man who will not cease to renew himself in the image of Him Who has created him" (Col 3:9-10).

Commenting on another passage of the same apostle, St. Augustine makes the following observation: "If baptism caused immediately man's complete and eternal renewal, St. Paul would not have written that our interior being is renewed from day to day."[12] For his part, Origen wrote in his commentary on the Epistle to the Romans: "Do not think that it is enough to renew our life only once: we must always and each day renew the newness itself so to speak."[13] Besides, our personal experience is there to prove to us that the carnal man lives always in us, and tries to enslave us to him by making us produce his works which we all know, sad to say, more or less, and which St. Paul enumerates to the Christians of Galatia: "It is well known all that the flesh produces: fornication, impurity, debauchery, idolatry, magic, hatred, discord, jealousy, passions, disputes, dissensions, divisions, feelings of envy, orgies, gluttony and similar things" (Gal 5:19-21).

Life according to the flesh, life according to the spirit. As long as we are in this world, we are then necessarily torn between these two lives, even though we have chosen the second. Indeed, it is not in one day that God's sons and daughters are formed. Ordinarily, much time and patience are necessary. If God permits us to continue to be tempted by the lusts of the carnal man, the reason is that, having created us free, He wants us freely to make ours the victory that His Son effected over the flesh. Just as God could not prevent man from experiencing evil, out of respect for his liberty, so, He cannot, without destroying this liberty, force him to accept his liberation in spite of himself. God offers each one the means to become free because of one's own choice, but each is free to consent to using the means. We give our consent precisely through the effective struggle against carnal man. Also, we can, sad to say, "practice" our Christianity; we can even have what we will continue to call a "spiritual life" and to reason, to live according to the flesh, in an entire sector of our activity. I repeat: flesh and spirit continue to coexist in us and there is no hope that they coexist in peace, because St. Paul has told us: "there is between them an antagonism," and that carnal man will die definitively only at our death, and, even, after. For that reason, also, if carnal man is already dead mystically (on the level of being) on the cross and at baptism, we must make him die, on the psychological and moral level, every day, until our last breath. He will lose ground to the extent of our fidelity to Christ's Spirit that animates and leads us; he will, even, be able, from one minute to the other, to appear conquered. However, the spiritual man will always have to fear his sudden leaps. That is the spiritual battle. As has been seen, it consists in the mortification of the carnal man, which will allow the spiritual man to replace him progressively on the level of action, after he has been substituted for him suddenly at baptism on the level of existence. Thus, it is, thanks to mortification, that the Holy Spirit makes us like unto Christ, and that He develops, by that very fact, our life as God's children, and, thus, our personality as man or woman.

The word "mortification" has, for our modern ears, some kind of infantile resonance: it evokes the child who is deprived of chocolate or of jam, unless it evokes the hair-shirt and the discipline, or a pessimistic view of life, a distrustful and somber vision of man and of the world, which transforms religion "into a withering enterprise," truly an enterprise destructive of the human person, and mistrust, a priori with regard to temporal values. However, if this word is taken in its etymological sense which is its first meaning, it is an extremely Christian, and, at the same time, Pauline term, (it goes back to the beginning of Christianity): "to mortify oneself" is not so much imposing upon oneself "a small sacrifice," nor wasting away, nor repressing oneself; rather, it is making carnal man die in himself so that the spiritual man might develop. Such is the meaning of St. Paul's words which I have already quoted, and which support Our Lord's teaching: "If the grain of wheat does not die in the earth, it remains alone; if, on the contrary, it dies, it will bear much fruit" (Jn 12:24).

However, if the word "mortification" sounds disagreeable to the ears of our contemporaries, if it risks their rejection and depreciation of the spiritual life, let us change it. Why insist on it! The Christian vocabulary possesses others that are, also, as old and as Pauline: we can present the spiritual conflict in terms, for example, of liberation. This word, in fact, has the wherewithal to seduce our modern mentality smitten by liberty. Thus, I shall say that the spiritual combat consists in liberating, or better still, in letting the Holy Spirit liberate in us the spiritual man, the new man, captive of the carnal man, of the old man, and thus letting Him renew us in Christ's image. For that, we must allow the Holy Spirit to free our soul—more precisely, its faculties, especially, our intelligence, liberty and our love— as well as, our body and all creation, of all the enslavements to which they have been subjected because of sin. The following chapters are devoted to the study of all these aspects, of the liberation brought about by Christ.

Footnotes

1. 19° *Hom. sur Math.*, vol. VII, p. 165.
2. St. Augustine, *De Trinitate*, XIV, 17, 23.
3. Sartre, *Le Diable et le Bon Dieu*, p. 267.
4. *Gaudium et Spes*, no. 22, par. 2.
5. "I am the true vine-stock, and my Father is the wine-grower . . . He prunes every vine-branch that bears fruit so that it bears more" (Jn 15:1-2).
6. *Gaudium et Spes*, no. 40, par. 3.
7. "Saintete et santé mentale," in *Echanges*, no. 52: "Santé mentale et Vie spirituelle," p. 3.
8. *Gaudium et Spes*, no. 41, par. 1.
9. *Gaudium et Spes*, no. 41, par. 1.
10. Rm 8:16 For that reason, St. Ireneaus wrote that the Christian is made up of soul, body and the Holy Spirit (*Contre les hérésies*, v. 3).
11. "Let the Abbot be concerned more about being loved than being feared" (St. Benedict, *Rule*, ch. 64).
12. *De baptismo parvulorum*, Bk. II, no. 9, P.L., XLIV, pp. 156-157.
13 *Epist. ad Rom.*, Bk. V, no. 8, P.G., xiv, 1 042.

Chapter 8

LIBERATION OF INTELLIGENCE AND OF LIBERTY

Many men, today, have ceased being Christians, or refuse to become so because, thus, they think to safeguard the dignity of man by protecting the liberty of his intelligence and the independence of his will: "We cannot allow," they say, "that a doctrine be imposed on man's intelligence or that laws succeed in impeding and constraining his liberty." Because the spiritual life, rests precisely on this doctrine, and relies on these commandments, it seems to be opposed to the development of this intelligence and to the full exercise of this liberty. What is it, in fact? We will see that, in reality, far from shackling these two eminent faculties of man, the spiritual life frees them, on the contrary, from the slavery into which original sin had reduced them.

Liberation of the intelligence

It cannot be denied that in comparison to temporal realities, human intelligence is powerful, penetrating, admirable. It is capable of knowing the truth about things and of acquiring this knowledge of which man has the right to be proud. Even in comparison to its own object which is spiritual and moral truth, intelligence is, likewise, capable of attaining it. It can know God independent of the

Christian faith, thanks to visible creatures: it can, also, know the rules that God has written in man's conscience in order to guide his conduct and to direct his will in the pursuit of good.

In the search for truth, above all spiritual and moral truth, that does not prevent intelligence from suffering, because of original sin, an injury that has deprived it of its supernatural life, weakened its exercise and subjected it to ignorance, doubt and error. It needs to be rescued. It can be by means of the spiritual life and thanks to the virtue of faith which, with the virtues of hope and charity, as well as the infused moral virtues and the gifts of the Holy Spirit, forms part of the fourth constitutive element of this life, that is, of the faculties necessary for the exercise of activity according to the Spirit.

The spiritual man, whose spirit lives by God's Spirit, is endowed with a supernatural intelligence which perfects by healing and transforming his natural reason. This superior faculty of knowledge and of discernment, is, precisely, faith. Faith is, indeed, an interior illumination, or better still, an impregnation of the human spirit by the divine Spirit. "Christ, truth itself," says St. Gregory of Nyssa, "is the revealer of Truth, exteriorly, by His person and His doctrine, interiorly by the communication to the human spirit of a divine light which fortifies and enlightens it." "It is only by being enlightened beforehand by the glory of the Spirit can one enter into the intelligence and the glory of the Father and of the Son." Thus, faith supplies in man what is lacking in his natural intelligence. It obtains for the latter a dual supplement: a supplement of extension and a supplement of certitude, and, thus, of security. Thanks to the dual supplement procured by faith, in other words, by the light of the Holy Spirit, Christ liberates human intelligence from ignorance, uncertainty and error.

First of all, let us discuss the liberation by a supplement of extension. The spiritual man knows, through his faith, truths that only God knows. Such is the meaning of these words of St. Paul: "What we are talking about . . . is God's wisdom, mysterious, hidden, which, from before the beginning of time, God destined beforehand for our glory, which none of the leaders of this world has known. . . Yet, as it is written, we announce that the eye has not seen, that the ear has not heard, that it has not entered into man's heart, all that God has prepared for those who love Him. God has revealed it to us by the Spirit; actually, the Spirit examines every thing, even in the innermost, divine depths. Who, then, among men, knows man's secrets, if not the spirit of man who is in him? Likewise, no one knows God's secrets if not the Spirit of God. Now, we have not received the spirit of the world, but the Spirit Who comes from God in order to know the gifts that God has designed for us. We speak of them not in a language taught by human wisdom but in one taught by the Spirit, expressing spiritual realities in terms of the spirit. The psychical man does not welcome what is of the Spirit of God; it is foolishness to him, and he cannot know it because it is by means of the spirit that one judges it. The spiritual man, on the contrary, judges everything, and he, himself, does not rely on the judgment of anyone. Who then, has known the Lord's thought in order to teach him? We ourselves possess Christ's thought" (1Cor 2:7-16).

Thus, then, the spiritual man knows God's intimate life and his thinking about men, thanks to faith whose role is to make him who is moved by His Spirit, to think as God, by causing him to participate in divine wisdom, itself, placed at his reach through Jesus Christ. He knows that God's life is an exchange of love among three Persons: the Father, the Son and the Holy Spirit. He knows that, in order to have men participate in this life, the Son became man in the Virgin's womb, died on the cross, arose the third day, and that, as man, He entered, body and soul into the intimacy of the Father. He knows that Jesus Christ, who is this Son made man, realizes this participation by means of certain material things, called sacraments, in which through the church's ministry, His deified action or even His person is made mysteriously present: so many truths which human intelligence is incapable of discovering by itself, and which faith alone gives the possibility of knowing. It implies that these mysterious truths are not, as is still too often thought, in contradiction with reason.

In fact, the mysteries of faith, that is precisely, those truths that faith proposes to reason are not "like certain well-defined absurdities, proposed to the faithful in order to test their faith, or to break their independent spirit, to bring them under subjection, with hands and feet tied, to the Church"; they do not have "as mission to confront the Spirit, to fight Him and to subjugate Him." It would be necessary to deny God, if the mysteries of faith could contradict reason. Intelligence has for its object what is, and truth is the conformity between what is and the idea that intelligence has of it. Consequently, what contradicts reason is not and cannot be a truth. The mysteries of faith could be above reason; they could not be opposed to it. One thing is what surpasses reason; another what contradicts it. "To tell a child that it is daytime in the middle of the night is an absurdity that he has the right to discard with contempt. For him, to formulate one of those innumerable scientific truths, of which he has not the slightest notion, is to speak a language which is not within the realm of his reason, but of which he could not justly deny the truth. The blind man is unaware of light; it would be ridiculous if he denied its existence."[1]

The mysteries of faith are not, then, contrary to reason. Neither are they incomprehensible to it, by essence and in totality. The Christian mystery is, indeed, something secret, something hidden, but which has been revealed, and so, could be, and which has been revealed not only to some initiates but to everyone. We find that definition in Scripture, especially in St. Paul. We read in the gospel: "Jesus spoke to the crowd only in parables." Thus, He fulfilled the words of the prophet who said: "My mouth will speak in parables; I shall reveal things hidden since the beginning of the world" (Mt 13:34). In St. Paul's epistle to the Ephesians, he says: "It is to me, the least of all the saints, who has been accorded this grace of announcing among the pagans Christ's unfathomable riches, and to reveal to the eyes of all, the plan of this mystery, which, from all eternity, was kept hidden in God, the Creator of all things" (Ep 3:8-9; Cf. 1:9-10). In his letter to the Romans, the Apostle speaks, also, of "the mystery which remained hidden for many centuries, but which has just been manifested, and, according to the order of the eternal God, carried by means of the writings of the prophets to the knowledge of all nations" (Rm 16:25-26). He affirms the same thing to the Colossians (Col 1:26).

The Christian mystery is a secret of God, a truth, at first, hidden and now manifested and announced to all. Consequently, it is a truth accessible to the intelligence. God has not spoken to men in order to tell them nothing, and to present to their mind something absolutely unintelligible. We have the right to demand that our faith not be contradicted by faith, itself. Now, it teaches us that our reason comes from this same God Who reveals the mysteries: God would not demand that one deny reason and shut one's eyes to it. The definition ordinarily given of mysteries several years ago has probably contributed to twisting the question. It was said: "They are truths that we ought to believe, even though we cannot understand them." Since then, a more felicitous definition has been given of mystery: "A divine mystery is a truth that we cannot understand perfectly, and that we could not know if God had not revealed it to us." By saying that we cannot understand it *perfectly*, it is inferred that the mystery does not completely escape our comprehension. This definition is more in conformity with the Church's official teaching which declares that the rational study of mysteries is not only possible but also very enrichening. Let us recall the statement of the first Vatican Council: "When reason, enlightened by faith, searches with care, piety and moderation, it acquires, through God's gift, some very profitable knowledge of mysteries, as much by analogy of things that it knows naturally, as by the bond of the mysteries between them and man's ultimate end."[2] This rational search, as imperfect as it may be, nevertheless, helps human reason greatly not to prove the mystery but its "credibility," that is, the grounds there are for accepting it and for saying: "it is conceivable; it is reasonable." Now St. Thomas says that no one would believe if he did not *see* what he must believe: "*Nemo crederet, nisi videret esse credendum.*"[3] Furthermore, reason permits him, even, to acquire a certain knowledge of the most useful, even of the most necessary for the observance of the Christian life.

It is no less true that we cannot understand perfectly the Christian mysteries: they surpass not only human, but all created intelligence. No man, if he has some idea of who God is and who he himself is, will be surprised not to be able to sound their depths; the claim to penetrate them completely would even be the surest proof of a purely human doctrine. Those are the "depths of God" of which St. Paul writes and which, according to him, only the Spirit of God can penetrate (Cf. 1Cor 2:10-11). For us, these mysteries remain unfathomable once again, not, in this sense that we cannot enter into them, but in the sense that we will never reach or exhaust their innermost recesses: we will never exhaust them: we will never cease probing into their infinity. If, then, we talk about obscurity with regard to the Christian mysteries, this obscurity is not to be compared with that of night; rather, it resembles what produces, in our eyes, a too bright light which is completely blinding.

Far from demanding an abdication of reason, the mysteries of faith confer upon this latter a preferment, an ennobling; they free it from its powerlessness and ignorance by extending admirably the scope of its knowledge.

More than liberation by a supplement of extension, Christ, through the power of the Spirit, liberates human intelligence, thanks to a supplement of certitude, security, clarity and facility. Indeed, it is only thanks to Christ's teaching that certain fundamental truths about Christ and man, accessible, however, to, even, limited human nature, can be easily recognized by all, with a firm certitude, without any admixture of error. Such is the case of God's existence, of His oneness, of His principal attributes, creation and rule over the world. Such is, also, the case concerning the soul's spirituality and immortality, of the essential obligations to God, neighbor and self. In fact, history teaches us that these truths have been and still are, on the whole, unknown by people and by those who have remained strangers to Christian Revelation. In ancient times, great minds, themselves, such as, a Plato, an Aristotle, a Seneca, and those, also, who lived or are living in the Christian era, and who have consequently breathed or are breathing an atmosphere totally impregnated by Christianity, but who have not believed or do not believe in Christ, all of these have fallen into the worst errors.

The same can be said about many other problems which are posed from one day to the other to every man. Human intelligence, reduced to its proper lights, is incapable of solving them with clarity and certitude: such problems as evil, suffering, human destiny, love, death, the hereafter. Men have received ideas on all these questions, in great part, if not totally, from their education, their environment, their social class, their newspaper, etc. Their intelligence is prisoner of these ideas which are, rather, word for word, prejudices, and they do not furnish the real solutions to the above-mentioned problems. In all these areas, faith, also, brings to reason a supplement of light. By lifting it above itself, faith allows reason to judge everything with the eyes of God Who is Truth; faith enlightens it with the light of the Spirit whose mission is "to teach all things and to recall all that Christ said, and to lead all towards complete truth." (Jn 14:26;16:13). It opens to reflection perspectives scarcely imagined by reason. I shall give two examples.

The revelation of the mystery of the Blessed Trinity allows us to have a more exact concept of the human person. It invites us, in fact, to define the latter, like the divine person, by means of its essential, and not accidental, relationship to the community. The human person should not be considered as composed of self, independently of its necessary reference to the community. It is by opening oneself, by giving oneself to others that the person finds himself, affirms himself, matures and develops.

This same revelation of the mystery of the Blessed Trinity and the example of the Son of God made man, by making us know what love in God is, throw a new light on human love. They make us discover — at least, grasp with more certainty — its most essential form: its oblatory form. It is known that, for Plato and the other Greek philosophers who were inspired by him, love is essentially, covetousness, the desire for oneself, the aspiration of the one who has not, toward the one who has, the tendency of the inferior, toward the superior: *eros*. They do not admit the possibility of a gratuitous love which would be only a gift: agape, a love by which one loves the other not because of his value but in order to give him one. "Also, among men, all the relationships of love, marriage, friendship, etc., include the distinction of "lover" and "beloved"; the beloved being always more noble and more perfect, being like the exemplar of the being, of the will of the action of the lover . . . . The perfect Being no longer requires this tendency or need."[4] For that reason, for them, God is a stranger to love, or more precisely, He is the object of love, but He is not a loving object. He is the immobile and eternal end, who attracts all beings "as the beloved attracts the lover," without being attracted by them. He is the one whom one loves, but he would not love, since to love is to desire, to long for the one who has, and, being perfect, God is necessarily without desire and without need. The mystery of trinitarian Love and the example of Love incarnate in Jesus Christ teaches us that love is, also, above all, the gift of self to another, a disinterested love which sees in the one whom he loves, not an object to possess but a person to cause to blossom.

After all that has just been said about the importance of faith in the liberation and promotion of human intelligence, this thought of Pascal is understood; "Not only do we know God except through Jesus Christ, but we do not know ourselves except through Jesus Christ . . . outside of Christ, we do not know what is our life, our death, God, or our very selves."[5]

So, contrary to what certain ones think, in order not to speak too much about our contemporaries, it is not to have the faith that enslaves and humiliates the intelligence: rather, it is to believe in their newspaper, in the average thinking, in the philosophical system in style, in all the small talk found on the radio, TV, in the movies and in the theater; it is to accept without discernment the ideas of men deprived of all competency and, thus, of all authority. To commune by means of faith in the thought of God Who is Truth itself, can only free our intelligence from its enslavements and its limitations, by extending and perfecting our information by means of the growth in knowledge and certainty about what we have spoken. If our contradictors mean that, from the moment one opts for union in everything with God's thought, there are matters on the subject about which no further disagreement is possible, no further doubt is authorized, no further hesitation is permitted, we will reply that it is exactly the same for all knowledge acquired in a firm and sure manner. It is evident, in fact that, if one wants to preserve liberty of thought with regard to everything, it would be necessary to resign oneself to know nothing since all intellectual acquisition involves, of necessity, a limitation of this liberty. Each one is free to consider the truth acquired, like slavery, or even, if he is eager to keep this liberty for himself forever, to think the contrary about what he knows or doubts, to continue to search for what he has already found; he can, even, question truth indefinitely, and remain perpetually in ignorance of what is and what he can maintain as true or false; however, these are pure games or eccentricities of the mind. If, on the contrary, one judges, with the majority of man, that all knowledge, even though it be a limitation of thought — in this sense only that it removes from him the liberty of remaining in ignorance or uncertainty — is, in reality, a perfection, it will prove very difficult to maintain that the fact of knowing, by means of faith, truths which express God's thought, could constitute an injury to the liberty of our intelligence, a limitation and, thus, a humiliation. Indeed, we accept, on the testimony of those who have seen or of those who have studied, facts whose experience it is impossible for us to realize, affirmations that we do not always verify directly. Would we refuse, thus, this increase of knowledge under the pretext that we ourselves did not secure it? Or would knowledge become unacceptable to us, and would we complain of being frustrated about our so-called liberty of thought when, for our intelligence, it is a question of accepting the truths of faith?

To think like God on the subject of God Himself and of all things about which God has told us His thoughts, to conform our thinking to His, to love by the truth revealed by Him, is, then, not to subjugate our intelligence, but to free it and make it like Christ's.

However, how to arrive at this point practically? Is it necessary to question everything and to start right from the beginning? This is a perilous and furthermore, impossible undertaking. Yet, what is possible for us is to rethink events and problems in the light of faith, and, gradually, as they are presented, to evaluate ideas received, new or old opinions accepted as truths but which sometimes are not. As St. Paul says, it is "to verify everything" (1Th 5:21), even what could seem out of the ordinary or surprising, even scandalous, to us. Let us recall the words of the same Apostle quoted earlier: "The spiritual man judges everything and does not rely on the judgment of anyone! Who, then, has known the Savior's thinking in order to draw a lesson from it? We, ourselves, have Christ's thought." St. Paul adds: "Do you know that we will judge the angels themselves?" How after that, to dare maintain that the Christian faith enslaves human intelligence? It is, also, necessary for the spiritual man to know the truths of faith and to live them.

That is not all. It is not from this very faith itself, that spiritual man ought to free himself. No, let him also, question dogmas such as they have been taught to us through the Church. However, as we will see, just as I can obey as a slave and obey as a son, to be "under the Law" or to be freed from all law because I observe the law naturally, by virtue of an internal demand, so I can believe all the articles of the Creed through duty and exterior obligation, or, on the contrary, through internal necessity, because the Holy Spirit has made me assimilate them in such a way that my act of faith has become natural for me. That last way of believing is the only free faith.

Also, I ought not to be content to believe in dogmas only because the Church teaches them. I must try to fill myself in such a way with that teaching that I succeed in accepting it, not only because the Church gives it to me, but because I can no longer not believe it, the Holy Spirit having conceived this belief in me. That action implies a certain personal experience of God, a certain encounter with Christ Himself, analogous to that of those people of Samaria of whom St. John has spoken in the gospel. At first they had believed in Christ "because the woman had testified: 'He told me all that I have done.' However, after having heard him, they believed "because of His own word. They said to this woman: 'it is no longer because of your words that we believe; we have heard him ourselves, and we know that He is truly the Savior of the world.' "(Jn 4:39—42). Our faith is not adult as long as we are not able to say to those who have instructed us in religion: It is no longer because of what you have taught me that I believe. I have heard Jesus Himself in the intimacy of my heart. Then, but only then, I will have access to liberty of faith. I will live by and in the faith, and more, uniquely, according to faith. The liberty which the spiritual life obtains for human intelligence goes that far.

Liberation of Liberty

Just as intelligence has been impaired by original sin in its tendency toward truth — above all, in the moral and spiritual order — by an impediment which has subjected it to ignorance, uncertainty and error, so, too, the will has been impaired in its tendency to good by an impediment which, by weakening its forces has subjected it to a certain inclination toward evil. Liberty, that power of the will to choose good has become captive: it has been won over by the threefold lust of which St. John speaks: "the lust of the flesh" or immoderate search for bodily pleasures, "the lust of the eyes" or disordered search for satisfactions of the intelligence, and "the pride of life," or unruly search for independence and for domination. Other chains, likewise, impede its exercise. There are, first of all, those which fetter. Now, we have just seen that the intelligence of fallen man has been impaired as a result of his sin; for that reason, when liberty sins, it is often through lack of insight about the good to be chosen or through lack of uprightness which makes it look for incomplete or false goods. There is, also, sickness, environment and heredity. They constitute impediments, not in themselves, but because they can act in an unfortunate way on the weaknesses of intelligence and liberty.

Like intelligence, liberty, too, needs to be liberated. It is by obeying God's commandments that, without any paradox, it obtains liberation.

By purifying man of original sin, baptism frees his liberty on the level of existence. The divinizing grace by this sacrament transforms the roots of this faculty; it heals intelligence, will and love of their weakness. However, this liberation ought to be followed by another on the level of acts. Baptism effects this latter only as strength. It gives liberty the possibility of a full, personal liberation by submitting it to the action of the Holy Spirit, and by conferring on it the graces necessary to correspond to the action.

Now the Holy Spirit's action consists in freely making man's will God's will. Practically then, this liberation on the level of acts is realized by obedience to the Father, in the example of our eldest brother, Jesus Christ. Before proving it, we must respond to an objection that comes immediately to mind. Indeed, in order to be able to speak of a liberation of liberty by means of obedience to God, it is, first of all, necessary to prove this obedience reconcilable with this liberty. Also, doesn't obedience constitute a restraint to my liberty and, thus, an offense to my dignity as man, an obstacle to the development of my personality, if not, even a curtailment of its development? Not at all. In the preceding chapter, I have shown that the God of Jesus Christ is not against, but for man. He desires only man's good and, thus, his success and achievement by means of a communion of love with Him. If He created him free, the reason is that liberty confers on man an incomparable grandeur and dignity, since it allows him to realize his human and eternal destiny himself by consenting freely to loving communion with Him.

There is, in fact, in man a need, a deprivation, an incompletion, an indication of a positive good that he lacks. This good is nothing else than the end for which man is made, whose possession alone can procure for him his completion and, thus, his happiness. He would not have possessed it from his birth, because if possessed, thus, without having been chosen or merited, this end would not have been truly his, and such a possession would deprive him of liberty, that faculty which provides his grandeur and which gives him direction.

God is this end which, alone can give to a human being his completion. He is alone and at the same time, outside of us because He is transcendent, that is, distinct from us and infinitely above us. He is in us because He is immanent, that is, more intimately present to us than we ourselves, without, nevertheless, being lost in us. God, alone, is capable of completing our nature with his double tendency, that is, of gratifying forever our need of the infinite and our need of an interior and permanent presence which is expressed by an unlimited exchange of love. That is what caused Pascal to say: "One must love a being who is in us and who is not ourselves, and that is true of every single man. Now, only the universal Being is such a being."[6]

Thus, man can only be fulfilled by going out of himself in order to direct himself toward God Who is his end, and to communicate with Him: like the acorn that can find its fulfillment only by attaining its end, by becoming an oak.

However, am I not dispossessed of my being at the very moment when I think that I have attained its fulfillment? Because I must pay for this latter by means of the recognition of an absolute dependence with regard to God, I realize my fulfillment only by recognizing that I possess it from another. Doesn't God take from me that very thing that He seems to give me? No, because by being independent of other persons, I cannot not depend on God without alienating myself. Indeed, God is not someone else: He is more inside my being than my very being; He is the very source of my personality. My existence as a creature has not its prinicple in itself. For me, to exist is to belong only to and for God. My person is entirely relative to Him, and it affirms itself so much the more as it receives more and better from Him, as it is, consequently, more dependent upon Him. A river exists only because of the water that it receives from the source upon which it depends, and the more it receives from the source, thanks to this very dependence, it grows and accomplishes more: if it ceases to depend upon it, before long it dries up.

My relationship to God, my dependence upon God is, then, constitutive to my nature. Consequently, I have nothing to fear from Him concerning my fulfillment since it is its *sine qua non* condition.

Every fear, however, is not dispelled. Even so won't this dependence hinder the fulfillment of my person by suppressing my liberty? Actually, isn't this realization of myself that I find in God imposed without my liberty having to express its opinion? Not at all. I keep the power of accepting or rejecting it. Once again, God does not create me in possession of my being: I myself must conquer it by an intense stuggle. Yet, I can only succeed by recognizing and accepting my dependence in relation to God, thus, by obeying Him: like the acorn which cannot attain its end to become an oak, and cannot fulfill itself except by obeying the law inscribed in its being, with this difference that the acorn obeys blindly, while I do so freely. It is, then, obedience that directs the going out of self and the communion with God of which I just spoke, and realizes the fulfillment of my person.

However, how can I obey God and continue to be free? Doesn't obedience suppress liberty? Absolutely not. Not only does God cause me to be, but He, also, makes me be free; He wants me free. We read in the Bible: "In the beginning, the Lord created man, and He left him to the guidance of his free will: if you wish, you will keep the commandments; to be faithful depends on your pleasure . . . . Life and death, good and evil are before man; what he will choose will be given to him." (Ec 15:14-17). Yet, the liberty with which God has endowed man is not license to do evil. The sacred text continues: "(The Lord) has not commanded anyone to do evil. He has not given anyone permission to sin." (Ec 15:21). Liberty is not, contrary to what is often believed, the power to do good or evil indifferently and equally. Its object is the good, the same as intelligence has truth for its object. Liberty is not the power to sin, just as intelligence is not the power to be mistaken, or to walk is not the power to fall. If it includes the possibility of doing wrong, through a shortcoming or deviation of nature, liberty is essentially the power of the will to choose and to follow the good, just as intelligence, if it can happen to be mistaken, is essentially the ability to know the true; or as walking is essentially the power to stand erect and to advance, even though it could happen that the person walking might fall. Liberty has been given to men only in order to make him capable of being inclined spontaneously towards good, by being attracted to it from within, without being compelled to it, otherwise, except by the good, itself, for which liberty was made. Thus, the moral obligation that he has to avoid evil does, in no way, destroy his liberty; rather it realizes his liberty since it inclines him to choose what is good, and the nature of liberty is, precisely, to choose good. So it is God Who has given a meaning to liberty. Not only did He give it a meaning, He Himself is its meaning and end. In fact, because it participates in the nature of the person, and because the person can fulfill himself only by communion with the absolute Good which is its end, liberty, itself, is only an aspiration, an outburst toward the absolute

Good. This orientation of liberty toward God is constitutive of its being. God is, then, not only the source of my liberty but also its end. Consequently, He is its fulfillment. In Him, that is, by adhering to Him and obeying Him, it is fulfilled since in Him, alone, it finds that to which it aspires. Far from suppressing man's liberty and from being a hindrance to his person, obedience to God gives to liberty its complete plenitude, and to the person his perfect fulfillment since it makes the person commune with the absolute Good for which he is made. Vatican II explained all that I have just said by declaring: "Man always turns freely toward good. Our contemporaries esteem this liberty highly, and they pursue it ardently. They are right. Often, however, they cherish it in a way that is not right, like the license to do anything, even evil, provided that it gives pleasure. Yet true liberty is a privileged sign of the divine image in man. God wanted to 'leave him to his own counsel,' so that he of himself could search for his Creator, and by attaching himself freely to Him, he could fulfill himself, thus, in a blessed plenitude."[7]

Obedience consists in recognizing — in the twofold sense of the word — our dependence in relationship to God, that is, to acknowledge it, to accept it, and, at the same time, to thank God for it, since it permits us to be all that we are. It consists, in other words, of welcoming God's gift, His love which makes us what we are, and of thanking Him by making a return to Him of the gift received. For that reason, obedience is integrated with love: it is an expression and a proof of it; consequently, it is another name for it. "If you love me," says the Lord, "keep my commandments. He who keeps my commandments, loves me." Again: "If you keep my commandments, you will remain in my love, as I myself have kept my Father's commandments and remain in His love."

Such is the profound meaning of obedience. In its etymological sense: to obey, *ob audire*, is to listen, to be attentive, to be open in order to give and in order to receive, the act, even, of gift, the plenitude of personality.

Obedience to God's commandments, well understood, far from binding, constraining or limiting man's liberty, procures for it its fulfillment, to the extent that, practised in Christ's spirit, it affects its liberation.

Jesus Christ has recast and perfected God's commandments which He, thus, made His own. This perfecting consisted in ridding them of all that men had added to them, but, also, and above all of interiorizing them. He gave us order and the possibility of observing them, not in an exterior, formalistic way, out of fear of punishment or of the law, but like Him, out of love. In fact, after having responded to the Pharisee who asked Him about the greatest commandment of the law: "You will love the Lord your God with all your heart, with all your soul and with all your spirit. That is the greatest and the first commandment, but a second is like it: You will love your neighbor as yourself," Jesus added: "On these two commandments depend all the law and the prophets." St. Paul was careful to make the Lord's thought explicit when writing to the Romans: "He who loves others has accomplished the law. Indeed, the commandments: 'Thou shall not commit adultery; thou shall not kill; thou shall not steal; thou shall not covet;' and all the others are summarized in these words: 'Thou shall love thy neighbor as thyself.' Love is not doing wrong to one's neighbor. Love is, thus, the accomplishmnet of the law."

So, by connecting them to love as their only principle, Christ has interiorized the commandments. Actually, thanks to Christ, the Law, whose expression the commandments are, became the new law. Now the latter is nothing else than the Law that God had promised in the Old Alliance to put one day into man's intimate being, to write in their hearts and that, in the New Alliance, He has, effectively, written in the hearts of Christians with His Spirit of Love. It is nothing else but sanctifying grace, that is, an interior dynamism, "the dynamism of faith operating by means of charity." It is "divine love poured into our hearts by the Holy Spirit Who has been given to us," as St. Paul used to say. In short, it is none other than the Holy Spirit. Consequently, the new Law is love.

While remaining entirely, as we shall see, exterior precepts expressing exteriorly this Law, the commandments of the new Law proceed from the interior, since they are, precisely, the exterior, multiple and varied expression of this interior Law which is nothing else but love: they flow from our life as children of God Who is a life of love; they have, as source, the grace of the filial Spirit Who is the Spirit of love. If we do not observe them in this spirit, if we practise them without being animated, interiorly, by love, we remain under the old Law. Such a practice, as St. Paul tells us, serves us as nothing. St. John of the Cross, also, warns us that, at the end of our life, we shall be judged on love.

However, if the new Law consists in love, it ought to be a law of liberty, because love is essentially free. In fact, liberty is the word the apostles use constantly to qualify the new Law, the life of grace, the presence of the Holy Spirit in us. St. Paul talks to the Galations about "the liberty that we possess in Christ Jesus" (Gal 2:4); he tells them that "we are not children of the slave but of the free woman," (Gal 4:31) and that "it is in order to be free that Christ has given us liberty," (Gal 5:1) that he has called us to liberty (Cf. Gal 5:13). To the Corinthians, he says that "liberty is there, where the Spirit of the savior is" (2Col 3:17; cf. 1 Col 9:1; 10:29). St. James states that "he who relies on the perfect law, that of liberty, and in a way continues . . . he will find happines in his works" (Jm 1:25). Further on he says: "Speak and act as men who must be judged according to the law of liberty" (Jm 2:12).

So then, the commandments, which express exteriorly the new Law, the law of liberty, can only be instruments of liberation itself. What liberation?

First of all, liberation from the slavery of fear. Interiorized, thanks to their attachment to love, the commandments free us from the fear of punishment and of what they themselves inspire, since the new Law demands that we obey them out of love. St. Thomas writes, "Children of God are led by the Holy Spirit, freely, under the impulse of love, and not at all as slaves out of fear . . . . He who refrains, solely, out of fear of the law, from doing what he wants, acts as a slave."[8] St. John, also, tells us, "fear cannot coexist with love: perfect love banishes fear because fear implies punishment; he who fears does not have a perfect love." (1 Jn 4:18).

Finally, this liberation, not from original sin, as was seen, is procured for us by the new Law itself, since this Law is identified with the divinizing grace received at baptism. This is the liberation from the enslavements of original sin, that is, of the old man, of our proud and egotistical self, as well as, of all our bad tendencies which enslave our liberty and from which the commandments free us little by little, by submitting us more and more to love, which is their soul. Thanks to them, the spiritual liberation of our liberty by means of love is effected.

We are now far from the concept which many of our non-Christian friends and even a good number of our Catholic associates, have of the commandments. Theirs is the same rebellious and scoffing outcry of Andre Gide:

Commandments of God, you have saddened my soul.
Commandments of God, will you be ten or twenty.
How far will you narrow your limits?
Will you teach that there are
    always more things forbidden?
New punishments promised to my thirst for all
    that I will have found beautiful on earth?
Commandments of God, you have made my soul ill,
You have surrounded with walls the only waters
    to refresh me.[9]

Envisaged as the law of love, far from being pure defenses that bully us, constraints that demand of us acts comformable to an abstract law, far, indeed, from being prescriptions imposed under the forbidding and withering form of repression, these commandments appear to us as means directed at nothing else but to develop us, to procure the liberation of our captive souls from themselves, not by means of the mutilation of our nature, but by means of the rectification of its unregulated tendencies, sources of all sins, by means of the mortification of self which closes the entrance of our heart, and by means of the infinite opening of the latter to Love.

Besides, by becoming, thanks to Christ, the interior principle of the commandments, love, in a certain way, frees us of these very commandments, since what is important, basically is not obedience to the commandments themselves, but love which animates this obedience.

Indeed, because the Holy Spirit is the new Law, because He vivifies us interiorly with the love that He is, it is by means of love that we are drawn to do good and to avoid evil, without needing the commandments to draw us to one and to protect us from the other. For that reason, St. Paul ventures to state to the Galatians: "The fruits of the spirit — that is, of man regenerated by grace and animated by the Spirit of love — are: charity, joy, peace, patience, benignity, goodness, fidelity, docility and temperance. For those who live in this way, there is no law" (Gal 5:22-23). To his disciple Timothy, he said: "The Law has not been made for the just" (1 Tm 1:9). Actually, the just man, is he who practises inevitably the commandment of love. Now, as St. Paul has told us, "Love is the accomplishment of the Law."

That is what we call, as St. Paul does, "the liberty of God's children," which caused St. Augustine to say: *"Dilige, et quod vis fac:* Love and do what you wish." Yet, it is obvious in what sense this famous maxim of the bishop of Hippo must be understood. Some people resort to this sentence in order to allow themselves the worst behavior. These words ought to be understood in the light of St. Paul's affirmation quoted earlier: "Love does no harm to one's neighbor." Love does not dispense us from observing the other commandments, and our neighbor ought to be able to say to us: If you truly love me, you will not commit an offense against conjugal fidelity; you will not strike me, you will not steal from me; you will not bear false witness against me; you will not be envious of me; you will not covet my goods, etc.

Truly love me, and you will be free to do what you want, because then your love for me will prevent your harming me since love does no harm to one's neighbor.

By placing love as the principle of moral life, we do not move toward the abolition of morality, that is, toward the abolition of the commandments to the profit of an individual. No, love does not eliminate the commandments.

In reality, because it is difficult, not to say impossible, for us to become here below an interior man, a completely spiritual man, entirely submissive to the interior law of love, totally possessed by the Holy Spirit, because we remain capable of sinning due to the inclination to evil, and to the threefold concupiscence of which St. John speaks and which is always within us, we can mistake for inspirations of love the impulses and caprices of our self-love. We need to be guided by a direction outside of ourselves, in order not to be mistaken in the choice of means leading to God. That is the role of the Lord's commandments.

Christ came not to abolish the Law, but to perfect it. The commandments exist, nevertheless, to serve as a landmark, as a guide in the choice of our liberty. We are not liberated from them. However, if we are not liberated from the commandments, we are from their literalness, from the letter that kills, when it is not vivified by means of the Spirit, through love. It is the primary role given to love which assures our liberation with regard to the commandments. Without love, we are their slaves, and thus we are not free men. With love, we accept the commandments in order to go to God freely but surely. "He who avoids evil," writes St. Thomas, "not because it is an evil but because of a commandment of God, is not free. However, he who avoids evil because it is an evil, is free. Now such is what the Holy Spirit accomplishes; it perfects the soul interiorly, by communicating to it a new dynamism, in such a way, that it has, by means of love, the same concern about avoiding evil as if the divine law commanded it. For that reason, it is called free, not that it is not submissive to the divine law but because its interior dynamism brings it to do what the divine law commands."[10]

Obedience to God must be viewed thus. It has value only if it is inspired by love, and expresses love.

In these conditions obedience becomes docility to the Spirit of Christ, and constitutes the true liberty of God's children. Furthermore, this latter, far from destroying human liberty, realizes it insofar as this latter consists, for the will, in determining itself by means of itself. Liberty, let us repeat, is not the possibility of doing anything whatsoever, it is the power to do good or evil indifferently. It is the power of the will to choose good, and to act spontaneously without being forced by anything else except by the good itself for which liberty was made. Now it is Christ's Spirit which inclines the will by means of the power of love, to be thus directed spontaneously toward good. Thus, understandably, St. Thérese of the Child Jesus could say: "I do always my will." What matter if the commandments remain necessary, the primacy belongs to love. Let us observe them and cause to be observed around us, not a morality of obligation which says: "it is forbidden," but an evangelical morality which proclaims: "love and do what you wish."

Such is the wonderful condition of man animated by the Holy Spirit. He enjoys a liberty of thought and action comparable to those of the Son of God, Jesus Christ, Our Lord.

Footnotes

1. Abbot F. Vernet.
2. Const. *De Fide catholica*, ch. iv, Denz. 1976.
3. St. Thomas, II, II, q. 1, a. 4, ad. 2.
4. A.J. Festugiere, *L'Enfant d'Agrigente*, Cerf, Paris, 1941, p. 112.
5. *Pensées*, no. 729.
6. *Pensées*, no. 485.
7. *Gaudium et Spes*, no. 17.
8. *Contra Gent.*, 4, ch. 22.
9. A. Gide, *Les Nourritures terrestres*, p. 125.
10. *Comment. sur II Cor.*, ch. III, read. 3.

Chapter 9

LIBERATION OF LOVE

Jesus Christ accomplishes the liberation of our intelligence, the liberation of our liberty, as well as the liberation of our love, by pouring into our hearts divine love through his Holy Spirit.

Corruption of Love

The slavery of love is a fact. Original sin put love into slavery, the slavery of corruption.

When creating the human person — man and woman — God, recounts Holy Scripture, made them to His image and likeness. This likeness, being a certain participation in the divine nature, which we know to be living Love itself, the human person can only be, also, love. There is no better commentary on this remark in Genesis than Our Lord's words to St. Catherine of Siena: "You — listen, humanity — you were made of nothing else but love." Or those verses of Ibn al Farid, the greatest Moslem poet of the Arabic language who died in 1235: "If my body were unfolded, one would see there its entire essence, total love."

Made of love, Adam and Eve were made for love, that is, not only for loving God, but, also, for loving one another, or, more precisely, for loving the God of Love by loving each other; so true it is that love was unique in its object as in its source. If after having told the story of the creation of woman, the sacred writer ends by saying that "they were naked both of them, the man and the woman, without being ashamed," it is, thus, to indicate the divine character of human love, even in what this love possessed of the sensitive and the sensual. Obviously, human love was moving from exterior attraction and from physical qualities to the profound subject, to the person who, being deified by being created to the image and likeness of God, transfigured and divinized everything, even the flesh.

Thus then, the two first beings of creation were given to each other to love with a love that went as far as the mutual penetration of one by the other, the fusion, without confusion, of one in the other, each keeping one's personality, one's self, in the image of the Blessed Trinity. In the Trinity, all is only love, and the most perfect unity reigns, there: yet the Person embraces the Person without ceasing to be his own person, realizing, on the contrary, completely who he is by means of this very embrace.

We know that the first man and woman did not love each other thus, as ordered. Instead of loving each other in and for God Who is the source and end of all love, they loved each other for themselves. They disobeyed God, and turned away from Him by their disobedience: not having believed in His love, they refused to offer Him theirs in thanksgiving. Having cut off their mutual love from its origin and its end, it was, thus, corrupted, no longer being lived as ordered.

Yet conjugal love did not remain long the only form of human love. Other kinds appeared successively to the extent that humanity developed: paternal and maternal love, brotherly and filial love, and friendship. If marriage is presented to us as the most complete form of human love, others are, likewise, reflections of the trinitarian love which is its source and exemplar.

However, all these forms of love never existed in the pure state. Human nature was already corrupted when they appeared on the earth, and it is known that Cain soon hated and killed his brother Abel. Indeed, from the day that human nature, because of the sin of the first man, was deprived of the participation which God wanted to give it in His own life, other men instead of being born with this life, fashioned in the likeness of divine Love, began their existence without God's love in them without resemblance to Him, because their birth made them participate in a fallen human nature.

So, since the drama of the earthly paradise, humanity continued to corrupt itself more and more: "And God looked upon the earth," recalls Sacred Scripture, "and saw that it was depraved because every human being had corrupted his life on earth" (Gn 6:12). Human love became more and more corrupt and corrupting. Long before St. Paul, the author of the Book of Wisdom painted a picture of these most sinister disorders: "Celebrating ceremonies of infanticides or of clandestine secrets, and giving themselves up to unrestrained debaucheries of strange rites, men, no longer, observed decency in their lives or in their marriages. One kills the other through treason, or satisfies outrage through adultery. Everywhere there is blood and murder, robbery and deception, corruption and infidelity, revolt and perjury, persecution of those with wealth, forgetfulness of good deeds, defilement of souls, crimes against nature, instability in marriages, adultery and shamelessness" (Ws 14:23-26). As for St. Paul, the following is his descriptive account to the Romans of the lamentable state into which human love had fallen in ancient times: "What can be known about God is visible to them," he says speaking of the pagans. "God, indeed, manifested this knowledge to them. In fact, after the creation of the world, His invisible perfections, above all, His eternal power and His divinity, revealed themselves to their intelligence through His works, so that they are inexcusable. Having known God, they did not give Him as God either glory or thanksgiving, but they lost the meaning of God in their rationalizations, and their unintelligent heart was darkened. In their pretension to wisdom, they became fools, and changed the glory of the incorruptible God for a representation, the simple likeness of corruptible men, birds quadrupeds, reptiles. God, also, left them, according to the lusts of their heart, to an impurity where they themselves debased their own bodies; they who exchanged God's truth for a lie, adored and served a creature in preference to the Creator Who is blessed eternally. So may it be. God, also, left them to degrading passions: their women exchanged their natural relationships for those contrary to nature; likewise, men, putting aside their normal relations with a woman, burned with desire for each other, and perpetrated homosexual infamy, receiving in their person the inevitable recompense for their disorder. Since they did not consider it good to preserve the true knowledge of God, God left them with their minds lacking judgment, to do what was improper: filled with every injustice, perversity, cupidity, malice, breathing only envy, murder, contention, deceit, wickedness, defamations, detractors, enemies of God, revilers, the haughty, braggards, ingenious as to evil, rebellious against their parents, mad, disloyal, heartless, without pity, knowing well, however, the verdict of God Who declares the authors of such actions worthy of death, not only those who perform them, but those who approve of what others do" (Rm 1:20-32).

So, by sinning, by disobeying God, by refusing to love Him, man ceased to cling to Love; he fell, and by that very fact, he ceased to be a harmonious entity. He remains made in God's image, but this image has been sullied by a "stain" that has tarnished and confused his traits, thus making the design blurred and indefinite: it is no longer a resemblance. In other words, man remains always love since he remains made in the image of God who is love, but this love is a corrupted one because the image no longer resembles God. Man remains made to love and to be loved, but the love that he gives or receives is distorted or depraved.

Instead of being a reciprocal gift, distorted love becomes possession; instead of giving in order to receive, it wants to receive, to possess and to enjoy without giving. Distorted love is called egoism, that is, disordered self-love because, in reality, by loving in this way, it is not even the other that is possessed. One cannot love him. Not being free of self by means of the gift of self, he has not freed a place within himself for another; there is no place free for another. He is completely full of himself; it is himself that he possesses.

Depraved love is mistaken about the object; it mistakes the creature for the Creator. He is disappointed because the creature who is finite and limited, cannot satisfy his capacity which is infinite. He is, likewise, disappointed because he stops instead of going past the creature to Him who is infinite and who is in the creature. Depraved love is called "passion," in the etymological sense of the word, that is suffering, because it ends in disappointment or deception.

Thus distorted and depraved, human love becomes the source of all disorders. Our Lord pointed out very well this unique source from which they proceed when He said: "From men's heart come evil thoughts, adulteries, shamelessness, fornications, murders, thefts, false witnesses, injurious words, avarice, fraud, profligacy, slyness, calumny, pride and foolishness" (Mt. 15:19).

In his letter to the Galatians, St. Paul enumerated some of these disorders that he attributed to the flesh, by which he designates carnal man, that is, precisely, the man whose love is no longer animated and ordered by the Holy Spirit. He says: "It is known what the flesh produces: fornication, impurity, debauchery, idolatry, magic, hatreds, discord, jealousy, fits of passion, disputes, divisions, feelings of envy, orgies, gluttony and similar things" (Gal 5:19-21).

It is not only in the individual that perverted love engenders disorders but also in society.

Humanity's vocation is to love. Men are called to love, to love God, but also to love each other, and to be united with one another, love being essentially unifying. Such was, at least, God's original plan for them. They were to build a community in the image and likeness of the community of love, formed by the Persons of the Blessed Trinity. Wasn't Christ going to say one day when speaking to men: "Father, that they may be one, as you and I are one?" Already, in ancient times, wasn't Seneca going to declare: We are members of a large body. Nature has produced us from the same stock: she has put in us a mutual love; she has formed us sociable?"[1] So then, God wanted all men to love each other in Him like brothers.

However, the sin of the first parents, their refusal to love God, corrupted the mutual love that God had placed in them, and it introduced disunion. Brothers were separated from each other; they became enemies. By constructing the Tower of Babel, men renewed, on the collective level, the personal sin of Adam and Eve. Like the latter, indeed, they attempted to deify themselves by trying to accomplish the unity of the world by themselves alone, and according to their idea, consequently, without God and with no reference to His design. "Come," they said, "let us build for ourselves a city and a tower whose top penetrates the heavens! Let us make a name for ourselves, and let us not be dispersed all over the earth" (Gn 2:4). Now, according to Sacred Scripture, God's design was indeed man's unity, but in His name and within the diversity of languages and of peoples, because it is this diversity in unity which ought to produce the richness and the beauty of humanity. This diversity could only be produced through the dispersion of man. The sin of the Tower of Babel, symbol of pride and of revolt, did not have, as consequence and punishment, the diversity of languages and the dispersion of men among some peoples, but the transformation of this diversity into confusion and of dispersion unto disunity.

By cutting themselves from God's love, men delivered themselves to their collective lusts, which engendered the worst disorders: within the nation, the struggle of classes, dissensions, oppressions, violence, revolutions; among nations, competitions, hatreds, wars, dominations.

That is not all. Self-love, itself has, also, been corrupted by sin, and has, likewise, brought about all kinds of disorders. Yes, I tell you: self-love. In fact, love which we know to be man's vocation has not only God and neighbor, as object, but, also, man, himself. Man is called to love his own person.

To love oneself! But I used to think, that, on the contrary, you had to hate yourself! St. Augustine used to say, "Lord Jesus, make me know you, and make me know myself, so that I might hate myself and might love you." Has not Christ Himself said: "He who comes to me and does not hate . . . even his own self, cannot be my disciples?" (Lk 14:26). Again: "He who loves himself will be lost, and he who hates himself in this life will be preserved for eternal life" (Jn 12:25). However, if Christ wants us to base love of neighbor on love of ourselves — the second commandment is "You will love your neighbor as yourself" — it is, indeed, necessary for us, first of all, to love ourselves, because, finally, how could he love his neighbor as himself if he does not love himself? Consequently, love of self is included in the commandment that the Lord calls "the second," even though this commandment refers directly to love of neighbor. Likewise, no precept was necessary for this love that we ought to have for ourselves: it is a spontaneous act of our nature.

There exists then, a love of self which is not only legitimate but necessary, even obligatory.

However, it seems that hardly any preachers speak about this love of self in their sermons; nor do moralists and spiritual writers discuss it in their books on spirituality. If they do speak of it, they are condemnatory since they all see in it only a self love: egoism.

Actually, it is sin that corrupted love of self, and made it degenerate into disordered love of self, into a love for oneself. Self-love has become another name for egoism. By loving himself, man retreats and closes in on himself. "He considers himself as the center around which everything gravitates, the universe becoming himself; he sees everything as a function of his own interests. Such an attitude develops normally into narcissism, into introspection, that is, into this propensity to look at oneself without growing tired, to regard oneself with complacency in his innermost being, because of the pleasure that he finds there, to analyze carefully the least movements, sentiments and experiences of which it (his inner being) is the stage. One becomes preoccupied with self to the highest degree. One is satisfied with self, aware of one's value and merits."[2] Yet, by, thus, withdrawing in on self, one is impoverished and, furthermore, enriches us no one.

Without a doubt, because it can be a disordered self-love, a number of Christians, to speak only of them, do not practise a well-understood love of self. Believing that they are fighting against egoism, they fall into the opposite excess: hatred or contempt of self — not the hatred and contempt of self discussed in the Gospels, and which is reconciled with true love of self, but a hatred and contempt of self bordering on morbidity. In fact, when you have a little contact with people, you are astonished to find many who do not even have, I don't say any love but any self-esteem. How many times haven't we heard words like these: "I hate myself," "I despise myself," "I'm disgusted with myself," etc.? By speaking in this way, perhaps, they think that they have acted correctly: they think that they are practising a true hatred of self. In reality, there are in these reactions more egotistical scrutiny of self than true self-contempt, more pride than authentic humility. They detest themselves because they do not want to accept humbly their own person, origins, condition, environment, position. A person has contempt of self because he is not satisfied with his being a man or a woman, with his height, color of hair, age, because he refuses to accept himself as he is, with his deficiencies and defects. He is disgusted with himself because he does not accept the fact that it is possible to rise above failure, to sin, etc. These reasons are, most of the time, subconscious; they are no less real, however, and the self-contempt that they engender is often the cause of physiological and psychological problems, of complexes of all kinds, and even of mental unbalance. In an article entitled, "Science confronting love," an American doctor writes: "By discovering love, the intellectuals have, also, discovered the value of self-love, in other words: we ought to love ourselves in order to be able to love others . . . . The biblical injunction: 'You will love your neighbor as yourself,' implies self-love." He remarks further that self-hatred is an indication of a psychological illness, and he quotes this statement of a psychiatrist in support of his remark: "The more we study the situation, the more we affirm that mental illnesses are due to a lack of self-love. If people loved each other with a healthy love, instead of dragging unconsciously the weight of their own contempt, our task, as psychiatrists, would be cut in half."

Such is the state of slavery and of corruption into which human love has fallen.

Divinization of Love

However, Christ came to liberate love, the love of self as well as the love of others.

By His redemptive incarnation, the Son of God made human nature like new by returning to it, through the gift of grace, its natural forces. By the same act, he healed and liberated the love within it, by giving it the means of fighting efficaciously against the germs of sickness and of the dissolution that original sin placed in it, and which, at every instant, run the risk of weakening or of corrupting it if love does not use or uses badly these remedies. This last remark explains why human love, after twenty centuries of Christianity, is almost as depraved as in the times that preceed Pentecost, that is, the spreading of divine love over the earth. Why do the mores of contemporary society, of even that which is called Christian, resemble so strangely corrupted mores and the disorders of human love in the ancient world, such as described in the Book of Wisdom and by St. Paul in his letter to the Christians of Rome.

Christ did more than heal human nature: He elevated it again to the supernatural plane, to the divine plane. By that deed, He renewed and divinized human love by means of His Spirit. He liberated it from that which had caused him to cease belonging "to God" and for God, by uniting man again to God in the person of the God-man. Indeed, our union with Christ, or our incorporation with Him, to speak like St. Paul, caused human love to become unique in its object and its source. The Holy Spirit unified, on the one hand, the objects of human love, by identifying them with God in the Word Incarnate, Jesus Christ. On the other hand, He unified the love of ourselves and of others, as well as our love for God, by identifying these loves with the love by which God is loved and loves us in His Son.

As is seen, this marvelous truth is founded on the doctrine of the Mystical Body of which it is one of the most beautiful consequences.

As soon as we lean towards Christ, and as we unite ourselves to Him by faith and love, we are, in a certain way, grafted on Him, joined to Him, incorporated with Him. St. Paul expresses it very clearly. When writing to the Romans, he says that we have been "grafted," that we have been cut "from a wild olive tree in order to be grafted, joined, contrary to our nature, on to a fresh olive tree, and rendered participants in its sap" (Rm 11:17-24). In many of his letters, the same Apostle states that, through baptism, we are incorporated into Christ. We become parts of His very self: "Participes enim Cristi effecti sumus" (Heb 3:14); members of His body: "You are Christ's body, and you are His members, each one as far as he is concerned" (1Cor 12:27); "we are members of His body, formed by His flesh and bones" (Ep 5:30; 1Cor 12:13; Rm 12:5).

Thus united to Christ, like vine branches to the vine, like the members to the body, we are vivified by Him. Dead as we were, we are revivified in Him, and reborn to a new life: "We were by nature children of wrath, like the others," writes again St. Paul, "but God who is rich in mercy, prompted by the excessive love with which He has loved us, and so even though we were dead because of our faults, He gave us life with Christ . . . . He revivified us with Him" (Ep 3:3-6). To the Colossians, he says: "You who were dead because of your sins . . . God has caused you to be revivified with Christ" (Col 2:13). St. Peter blesses "God, the Father of Our Lord Jesus Christ Who, through His great mercy has regenerated us by Jesus' Resurrection from the dead" (1P 1:3).

Like a cell which is born in a human body, the Christian is born in Christ's mystical body. As St. Paul says, he is "created in Jesus Christ," (Ep 2:10) and, as a result, he is "a new creature" (2Cor 5:17; Gal 6:15); he lives with a new life (Cf. Rm 6:4).

This new life is Christ's own life. It vivifies us and circulates from then on in us, since it is the same sap that circulates in the trunk and in the branches of the same vine; it is the same blood that circulates in the head and in the members of one same body. Our Lord affirmed it Himself: "As the Father Who sent me is living and, as I live by the Father, so he who eats me will also live by me" (Jn 6:5-7). That is the reason St. Paul can state — and all baptized can justly do so, even if not to the same degree — : "I have been crucified, that is, the old man, the man according to his fallen nature, has been crucified in me with Christ, and if I live, it is no longer I that lives, it is Christ who lives in Me" (Gal 2:19-20). Evidently, the above supposes a certain identity between Christ and the Christian, real, "physical," that is, essential transformation of the regenerated soul. St. Paul explains it when he says that, at the moment of baptism, we put on Christ (Cf. Gal 3:27; Rm 13:14). If, indeed, we put on Christ, that is, if our soul, naked as it was because of the first fall, is clothed again with this metaphysical apparel that is sanctifying grace, or to use St. Paul's words once more, if we put on the new man who has been created in God's image, in a true justice and sanctity, (Ep 4:24) and who is precisely none other than Christ, then we take Christ's form, we are really transformed into Him, and consequently, we enter into communion with the Word, with the Son. St. Paul writes: "He is faithful, this God who has called you to union with His Son, Jesus Christ Our Lord" (1Cor 1:9). For his own part, St. John says: "Our communion is with the Father and with His Son Jesus Christ" (1Jn 1:3). We are, as St. Peter affirms, "rendered participants in the divine nature" (2P 1:24).

By incorporating us in Him, Jesus Christ identifies Himself, so to speak, with each of us; He substitutes Himself, in a sense, for each of us, like at Mass where He substitutes Himself in the bread and wine. Just as He said: "This is my body; this is my blood," He, also, said: "He who receives one of these little ones, receives *me*" (Mt 18:5). Again: "I tell you, truly, all that you have done to the least of my brothers, you have done it to *me*" (Mt 25:40). To Paul, thrown to the ground on the way to Damascus where he was going in order to persecute the Christians, he said: "Saul, Saul, why do you persecute *me*?" (Ac 9:4), words that St. Augustine explained thus: "Christ is not in the head only, without being in the body, but the whole Christ is in the head and in the body . . . If His disciples were not His members, He would not have said to Saul: 'why do you persecute *me*'? It is not Christ Himself, actually, but His faithful whom Saul was persecuting on earth. However, He did not want to say my holy ones, my servants, nor even, what is nobler, my brothers, but *me*, that is, my members whose head I am."[3]

Let us note that this identification of Christ and of the Christian is not the privilege of only the baptized in the state of grace and of all those who are comparable to them, that is, all those, even non-Christians, who do God's will such as they know it and are in good faith. If all of these are pre-eminently members of the mystical Body of Christ, they are not, however, the only ones to be incorporated with Him. Other men are also members of Christ, virtually at least, thanks to the vocation common to all to be part of His mystical body. One can, in this way, extend to all living persons the benefit of belonging to Christ in a certain way. There is no distinction to be made between love of God or of men incorporated into the Son of God. If their object is not the same (there is God, our neighbor and we, ourselves), our reasons for loving God, and for loving our person, and that of our neighbor are identical. There is only one sole motive for charity, one sole reason for loving supernaturally; it is the all-loving nature of God Who is Love. Because of it we love God, our person and that of our neighbor according to the communication that God made to us about it in His Son Jesus Christ. Since there is only one reason for loving, there is, also, only one love, although there are three objects to love: God, ourselves and others. The unity of the motive of supernatural love involves the unity of this love of charity. With this same love, we love God, our neighbor and ourselves because it is the same nature, the same divine "goodness" that I love, here in God, there in myself and in my neighbor. That is what the Catechism means when it tells me to love my neighbor as myself for the love of God. Let us note, by way of conclusion, that it is not necessary to always be conscious of this unique reason for loving. It is sufficient that God dwells in our heart.

Unity of love does not flow only from the unity of its object; it results, furthermore, from the unity of its source which is the love with which the Father loves His Son eternally, and that the Son gives back to the Father eternally; the same, also, as that with which God loves us and with which we love God: it is the Holy Spirit. The Holy Spirit is, indeed, the mutual and unique love of the Father and of the Son, the personal love that unites, in the indivisible unity of the divine nature, the trinity of the Persons.

Now, by coming to dwell in us, thanks to our incorporation in Him, Christ brings with Him this Spirit of love. Let us recall these words of Our Lord: "If I do not go," He said to His disciples, "the Holy Spirit will not come to you, but if I go, I will send Him" (Jn 16:7). "If you love me, you will keep my commandments, and I shall pray to the Father, and He will give you another Consoler so that He will dwell always with you: the Spirit of truth, whom the world cannot receive because it does not see nor know Him. However you will know Him because He will dwell with you and He will be in you" (Jn 14:15-17). "Righteous Father, the world has not known you, but I have known you, and those have recognized that it is you who have sent me. I have revealed your name to them, and I will reveal it to them so that the love with which you have loved me may be in them and I in them" (Jn 17:25-26).

This coming of the Holy Spirit in His disciples took place on Pentecost. They had believed in Christ after His resurrection, and the glorious Christ had come mystically in them, making possible the coming of the Holy Spirit, of the Love with which He is always loved by the Father, and that He gives back to the Father unceasingly. This love took possession of their hearts, effectively, fifty days after Easter. Then they were filled with it to the point of being intoxicated by it. Now this same Spirit, this same love, is always ready to come into all those who, by their faith in Christ, become, like Him and in Him, sons of the Father, and consequently, the object of His infinite complacency. Jesus Christ Himself affirms it: "He who believes in me, from his heart, as Scripture says, will flow rivers of living water. He said that, explains St. John, of the Spirit whom those who would believe in Him would receive" (Jn 7:37-39). Thus, Jesus Christ communicates to us the one who, in the Blessed Trinity, as we have seen, is personal love; like the word of love written by the lover to the beloved, by penetrating into the heart of the beloved, love communicates to him what it (the word of love) carries within it.

Now the Holy Spirit, the Spirit of love coming into us, creates there the new heart promised by God in this passage of the prophet Ezekiel who announces the future baptism in the water and the Spirit: "I will bless you with pure water," says God, "and you will be pure; I will purify you of all stains and of all abominations. I will give you a new heart, and I will put into you a new spirit; I will remove from your body the heart of stone, and I will give you a heart of flesh" (Ezk 36:25-27). The Holy Spirit grafts, so to speak, our heart onto the heart of Christ Who is the very heart of God. By that very fact, He renews, He divinizes our love since He communicates to this new heart the love of the Father and of the Son Who He Himself is: he illumines the fire of His love which renews the face of the earth, by beginning with our heart. St. Paul tells us: "God's love has been diffused into our hearts through the Holy Spirit Who has been given to us" (Rm 5:5). St. Augustine also writes: "When the Holy Spirit Who proceeds from God is given to man, He enkindles in him the love of God and of his neighbor, and He is Himself this love."[4]

This new, supernatural and divine love which the Holy Spirit diffuses into our hearts by means of His presence, and which proceeds from them insofar as they are grafted on the heart of Christ Who is the heart of God, is the love of charity, in the most beautiful and most profound sense of this word, often diverted from its theological meaning. Thus, it is with this same love that we love God, our neighbor, and our very selves. Let us note, also, that, in order to love with this love of charity, it is not indispensible to be continually conscious that we love with a supernatural love. It suffices to be in the state of grace, that is, in communion with God.

Thus, then, in its source as in its expression, love is unique. There is only one love: divine love. Human love, at least the love of charity, that is, the one which is inhabited by means of grace, through the Holy Spirit, is only the sensible but real image, the participant in God's love — like the image of the sun, since it participates in its light and warmth. Human love is only the expression, within man's reach, of divine love. The different forms of human love (conjugal, paternal, maternal, filial and fraternal, of engaged couples and of friends) are only "reflections in which the human prism breaks up the unique Love of the Father."

This theological explanation is perhaps a bit difficult. Yet, because the very important consequences that flow from it are so awesome, so surprising that we might be tempted not to believe, this doctrinal study was necessary in order to establish the reality and the stability of their principle. In fact, this study has proved to us that human love possesses a divine dimension. By bursting forth from man's heart in a communion of love with God, it is from God's own heart that it springs, and it is God Whom it attains in the person loved. It allows us to say truthfully, of human love what Pascal used to say about man: "Love infinitely surpasses love," a statement about which I add my comments to those of Paul VI: "In love, there is infinitely more than love. We mean that in human love there is divine love."[5]

In these vistas that the mystery of our incorporation, of our union with Christ, opens to us, love of self ceases to be love for oneself. The Holy Spirit has liberated it from the egoism into which it had degenerated: He caused it to rediscover its source and its true object. Love of ourselves is blended with the love we have for God; it is a modality of God's love, since it is, also, with the same love that we love God and ourselves, and that, what we love in us is the child of God; it is God's image in us, rendered a participant in God's very nature by our union with the God-Man Jesus Christ. Furthermore, by loving ourselves not only is God present in us in the Christ Whom we love, but it is also God Who loves us by means of us. Indeed, our incorporation with Christ makes our good acts be attributed to His person as the Son of God: it is He Who lives in me, Who acts, prays, suffers and loves in me. So, when I really love myself, it is Christ, it is God Who, in and by me, loves me and loves Himself. So it is, then, divine to love oneself.

However, how demanding this is too! The reason is that since, by loving myself, it is Christ Who loves me, I am obliged to love myself as He loves me; I must wish for myself the good that He wishes for me, to ask of myself what He expects of me. Now what He wishes for and of me, is that I allow His Spirit to fashion me in His image, to form in me the new man, the child of God that I became in baptism. It is there that hatred of self intervenes, a hatred spoken of in the Gospel. Actually, so that the new man might grow in me, I must hate myself and cause to die all that is opposed to this growth within me; I must, to use St. Paul's words, "kill the limbs of earthly man: fornication, impurity, passions, evil desires, lust . . . ; I must banish anger, pride, wickedness, slander, dishonest remarks, lies," (Col 3:5, 8, 9) in a word liberate myself of the old man.

This hatred of self put aside, this hatred which is conciliated perfectly with authentic self-love, which is, even, love of self, since one only hates self for one's own good, the spiritual life, far from demanding me to depreciate and to hate myself, asks me to love and to develop all that I am: my soul and my body, to the extent that they contribute to the development of my life as a child of God.

Thus, it is necessary and so urgent to remind Christians that self-love is a commandment of God, that, thus, they not only have the right but the obligation to love themselves. It stems from their natural equilibrium and from their supernatural development.

In these same perspectives, love of neighbor becomes again what it ought to have been from the beginning; it also, finds again its divine dimension which gives us, with the exercise of this love, a new, expanding and exalting intelligence: to love one another is to love God and to be loved by God and with the same love that He loves Himself.

From whence flows several consequences.

All love of neighbor, whatever it is, and not only the love of those with whom we would not have natural and legitimate ties — such as, conjugal, paternal, maternal, filial, fraternal, love of sweethearts and of friends — far from being a danger, a screen between God and those who love each other, brings them to the love of God. It is love for God since those who love each other with this love of charity penetrate, through their exterior being, to that which causes the goodness and beauty of their bodies and souls, grace, in the supernatural sense of the word, that is, Christ present in them. There is no longer, as St. Augustine says so well: "but Christ loving Himself,"[6] because there are, then, of the two sides only Christ joined into two beings, through two beings, the loving Christ giving Himself to the Christ loved, in order to reintegrate Himself into God-Love.

The reason that He reintegrates Himself into God-Love is that Christ, the Son of God, is one with His Father. He who loves Christ loves the Father. The love of neighbor encompasses, therefore, the love of God since it encompasss the love of Christ, and love of Christ includes love of God. "The Sons of God," says St. Augustine, "are the body of the only Son of God; since He is the head, we the members, there is only one Son of God. So he who loves the sons of God, loves the Son of God, and he who loves the Son of God, loves the Father."[7] Again: ". . . by loving your brother, do you perhaps love him alone, without loving Christ? How is this, since these are then members of Christ whom you love? By loving Christ's members, you love Christ; by loving Christ, you love the Son of God; by loving the Son of God, you love the Father. It is impossible, then, to divide love."[8] So, our love, by encountering Christ's love in our neighbor, encounters, by that very fact, God's love. This fact ought to reassure those who ask themselves anxiously how to reconcile the love of the beloved with God's love, and those who, entirely absorbed by the necessities of their family life, or the inevitable attachments which absorb their days, are sad because they believe themselves excluded from divine union!

Another consequence concerns the meaning in which it is necessary to extend the expression "to love his neighbor for the love of God." To love for the love of God does not at all mean that it is necessary to avoid loving one's neighbor in and for himself. Unbelievers make this objection to us, and they are not always wrong. Indeed many Christians believe and make others believe that to love for the love of God (even and, especially, it seems, persons who are naturally dear to us) means that it is a question of loving a person whom one ought at first, in some way, disincarnate, an impersonal being without a face, a person that one would have emptied of his substance, so to speak, a vision, a shadow of a person, behind which one would be forced to recognize, often in vain, the gentle face of Him who is, as St. Paul says, the image of God. A sick person used to say of a religious who cared for him: "She has a faultless devotion, but I have a strong impression that she is not at all interested in me. Without a doubt, to her, I am like a stepladder for mounting to heaven. She is interested in the stepladder, she uses it." No, it is not necessary to resort to such mental gymnastics in order to love one's neighbor for the love of God. Thanks to incorporation into Christ, God and neighbor become one; to love the neighbor for the love of God, or, as is said, through Christian charity, is to love him, also, in and for himself.

Thus, to love his neighbor with a love of charity, is, at the same time, to love him in and for God, and to love him in and for himself, since these actions are but one. Likewise, indeed, to love a member of my body for the love of my body is to love it because it forms part of my body, but it is, also, to love it for love of itself, because my body and it, by completely being one, are, however, distinct. So, by loving my neighbor for the love of God, I love him, indeed, because he is a member of Christ, but I love him also, him and in himself because if Christ and he are but one Christ, it is one Christ in two persons. The person of my neighbor remains, and it is his person that I love when I love him, his person, because of the communication that God made for him of his own nature in the person of His Son Jesus Christ.

We must never lead our neighbor to believe that we love him for a motive other than for himself, out of Christian charity, in the current sense of a beautiful expression, muddled or misunderstood, which suggests only a last resort for loving when all others, human and normal, are impossible. We must not be stoical in his regard by reducing him to an abstraction or to a "stepladder," except in certain cases where, actually, neither human nor normal motives can operate, where love of neighbor, in and for itself, demands superheroic virtue of which we are not always capable. In other cases among which we must include those where it is a question of loved ones, it must be stated that to love one's neighbor for the love of God, is to love a person of flesh and blood, not an anonymous person, but a definite being with a definite name. Like Christ's love for us, our love of neighbor ought to be personal. Our neighbor must feel himself loved for himself, as if he were the only one in the world; we must be interested in him as in a unique mystery. Every person encountered must arouse my interest and love, as if he were a unique work of creation. Since it is the person of my neighbor that I love, it is his entire person that I love. I want his entire happiness, not only his eternal, but also his temporal happiness.

That having been said, it must be stated again that, if I

love my neighbor in and for himself, I ought to love him, also, and at the same time, in and for God. My neighbor has nothing to lose by being loved in this way. Quite the contrary! He will only be more and better loved. True love for men can only be, indeed, a love in and for God, a love inspired by God, Himself. I truly love my neighbor only by loving God. To refuse to be loved for the love of God is to refuse to be loved by means of God's love, that is, by the strongest of all possible loves, by God Himself, of which St. John said "that it is greater than our heart" (Jn 3:20). The divine way is the true way to love. What human love is more real, more authentic, more disinterested than the Father's creative love? What human love is more serious, more sincere, more complete than the Son's redemptive love? What human love is superior to Christian charity, since it consists in loving like the Father and the Son; better still, to love with the same love of the Father and of the Son, which, passing by means of the human heart of the Christian, attains the beloved? Man will not truly be loved unless he is loved as God loves him, and with the same love by which he loves God.

In these viewpoints, also, the detachment of creatures, "so often proposed, so rarely explained," finds its true meaning. To detach oneself is not to strangle one's heart, still less to choke it, to dry it up, to make it sterile: this would be to diminish man: now anything that lessens man is not Christian. Christ, our model, had a virile but very tender soul, a heart sensitive to all suffering, misery and joy. He knew shared affection and friendship; He suffered indifference and ingratitude. St. Paul's letters give witness to the tenderly loving heart of the Apostle. "You are in our hearts in life and in death," he writes to the Corinthians (2Cor 7:3). To the Philippians: "I carry you in my heart . . . . Yes, God is my witness; it is with tenderness that I love you in the bosom of Christ" (Ph 1:7-8). As for St. Peter, he practised, without any doubt, what he preached to his faithful: "Love each other ardently and from the bottom of your heart" (1P 1:22). "Have, above all, for each other an ardent love" (1P

4:8). Nothing is more contrary to authentic Christianity; nothing is more of a caricature of a truly christian man than the odious inhumanity of the "Master of Santiago" whom with all his horrible rigidity Montherlant has depicted for us. A Christian who draws from his supposedly spiritual life reasons for not loving with his human heart, is a monster who disfigures, at the same time, in his person man and the God-Man.

To detach oneself is not so much to leave creatures as to leave oneself in order to return to them again, for, then, we no longer return with the same heart; from, henceforth, we are going to them in another, and by means of another heart, in and through the heart of the God-Man. By freeing our heart of itself, that is, from egocentrism and egoism, the Holy Spirit transforms the bonds by which He is attached to creatures; He christianizes them; in a word, He makes us love, like St. Paul, "with Christ's inner being," that is, with Christ's own heart living within us. He makes us find again the unique source of love: God Who is in Jesus Christ. To love, thus, is no longer a danger because, when I love, it is no longer I who love, it is Christ who loves in me, and it is Christ Whom I love. However, before arriving at that point, it is necessary to pass through a good number of trials and ordeals since it is not easy to love in and through Christ.

However, we are not expected to be entirely liberated of ourselves in order to begin to love. Love is never prohibited because "love is from God" (1Jn 4:7), St. John tells us. However, we are asked to love indeed. For that reason, we never love too much: we love poorly or not enough. We must love, even if there is danger in loving. It is better to love than to renounce love because of its dangers, *on condition* that we truly love, that is, that we endeavor to love always more, always better, to love in God because it is not to love truly, nor well nor enough, to love outside of God; on condition, in other words, to act so that our love becomes more and more, a gift, God's gift in the gift of ourselves.

Also, by grafting, so to speak, man's heart on God's heart in Christ, and by communicating to him the love that He is, the Holy Spirit has made human love the visible, sensible expression, within our reach, of divine love.

We need to see, to hear, and to touch the person who loves us and whom we love. Now, here is one of the reasons for the difficulty of our love for God, and of our faith in His love. According to St. John, "No one has ever seen God," (Jn 1:18) and no one will see Him, because St. Paul tells us, "He dwells in an inaccessible light" (1Tm 6:16).

By becoming incarnate, the Son of God satisfied this need of our heart by giving God a human face, since Christ is infinite, invisible Love become visible, the divine Love endowed with our humanity. The reader can raise the following objection concerning this: "What you say is not true for us. It is true for Jesus' contemporaries, and also, for only those among them who lived like Him in Judea and in Galilee, but not for us living twenty centuries after Him."

This objection is well-founded. Actually, Jesus Christ, Love Incarnate, is no longer with us in His visible body. "His earthly life," as St. Paul remarks, ended almost two thousand years ago. He ascended into heaven, and He became for us, like His Father, an invisible object of faith.

However, that does not prevent us from believing in His love and from loving Him, without having ever seen Him (Cf. 1P 1:8). It is also, true that God is a spirit, and that we ought to know, love and unite ourselves to Him in a spiritual way. Yet, that does not happen at once, and it happens only to a small number. We cannot prevent our heart from wanting to see the person whom it loves, and by whom it is loved.

Undoubtedly, Love incarnate remains, indeed, with us in the Holy Sacrament of the Eucharist, but His eucharistic presence is a sacramental one, a presence under signs. We do not see with the eyes of our flesh; we do not hear with our ears; we do not touch with our hands, His humanity, which is hidden under the appearances of bread: *latet humanitas*.

The objection is, thus serious, and solid; I have heard it; I have anticipated it, or rather, God, Love, has foreseen it and He has responded to it.

It seems to me, that this response is formulated best by St. John, the Apostle of Love in the passage of his epistle where he says: "No one has ever seen God." He, also, states: "But if we love each other, God remains in us and his love is perfect in us . . . for God is love and he who remains in love remains in God and God remains in him" (1Jn 4:7, 12, 16). It is as if St. John wanted to say: "The love of God disconcerts you, perhaps, because God is invisible, but, by incarnating Himself in Christ, and, by the incorporation of all men in Christ, in us and in our brother, God placed Himself at the reach of our human heart, by allowing us to love Him and to be loved in and by persons of flesh and blood like us."

In fact, as we already know, when we love each other, it is Christ whom we love and Who loves us, and, when we love Christ and are loved by Him, it is God Himself Whom we love and Who gives us His love. It follows, then, that, by loving each other, we fulfill the desire that we have to see, to hear, to touch the person who, alone, can satisfy completely our need to love and to be loved: God Who is present in us in Jesus Christ. By our loving each other, it is Christ whose substitute we are, whom we reveal to each other. Consequently, we give God, in a certain way, a human aspect; we make Him become and feel through us. We do this insofar as we cease to be an opacity in order to become a transparency through which He can shine; in order to become a living and sensitive witness of His love; in order to become "witnesses of the amicable presence of God in humanity."[9]

Such is the awesome liberation that Jesus Christ procures for our love by means of the strength of His Spirit, by making us capable of loving in and through Him — here below, by means of charity, in heaven in the plenitude of this same charity — the Persons of the Blessed Trinity, ourselves and all persons, as they love themselves, and as they love and with the same love with which they love.

Footnotes

1. *Lettre a Lucillius*, no. 95.
2. Gérard Bélanger, *L'amour, chemin de la liberté*, Paris, Ed. Ouvrieres, 1965, pp. 56-57.
3. *Tract. 28 in Joann. Evang.* no. 1, P.L., 35, 1622.
4. *De Trinitate*, bk. 15, ch. XVII., no. 31, P.L., 42, 1082.
5. Quoted by Jean Guitton in *Dialogues avec Paul VI*, Fayard, Paris, 1967, p. 330.
6. St. Augustine, *In Epist. Jean ad Parthos*, P.L., 35, 2055.
7. *Ibid.*
8. *Op. cit.*, P.L. 35, 2055-2056.
9. De Grandmaison.

Chapter 10

LIBERATION OF THE BODY
FROM CONCUPISCENCE

The liberation that Christ accomplished by the power of the Holy Spirit concerns not only our soul and its faculties, but also our very body.

In itself, the human body is neither bad nor despicable, as a false, but apparently very pure and lofty spirituality would lead one to believe. Christian anthropology, that is, the Christian concept of man, is not the anthropology of dualistic doctrines. These latter divide the human person into body and soul, which they juxtapose or even put into opposition, one against the other. They consider the soul as a spirit, originally good and immortal, but prisoner of the body when it fell, and which is considered heavy and opaque, unworthy of the nobility of the soul, being, indeed, thoroughly bad. The soul must try to break loose from it, and to liberate itself as much as possible by the contemplation of ideas until death comes to deliver it completely and definitively.

Liberation from Corporal Inclinations

Such is not Christian anthropology, regardless of what certain Christians and certain spiritual books, inspired or influenced by the Greek dualism which infiltrated into the Church, lead one to believe. As has been seen, the Bible is unaware of this dualism. For the sacred writers, man is an incarnate soul or an animated body. Likewise, the words "body" and "flesh," often mean all of man, body and soul, with emphasis placed on its visible responsive, corporal aspect. St. Paul is of like mind. For him, they mean more precisely man insofar as he is fallen; the same as the word "spirit" means for him, all of man, body and soul, with the emphasis on the spiritual principle which animates him — but man inasmuch as vivified and sanctified by the Holy Spirit.

It is in the light of these explanations that the adjective "spiritual" in the expression "spiritual life" must be understood, which can indeed lead to confusion, if one is unaware of the Pauline sense of the word "spirit." Thus, the Christian spiritual life relates to the body as well as to the soul.

Likewise, the body forms part of the human condition. It is intimately associated with the soul which needs it in order to act, express itself and to communicate with another soul.

In fact, it is by means of the body that the soul produces all the actions that it realizes outside of itself. Furthermore, even the most spiritual acts need the body in order to exist, so that one must declare that the body is at the service of the soul, and that it is, consequently, necessary for the soul in order to act, especially in order to produce thought. "The soul is united to the body," writes St. Thomas, "for the act of intelligence which is its proper and principal act. For that reason, the body, united to the rational soul must be disposed, as best as it can, to serve the soul and what is necessary for thought."[1]

The body is, likewise, necessary for the soul so that it can express itself. Our human condition wants us, in fact, to accede to the realities of the spirit through sensible things, especially through the body. It is by means of the body that the soul manifests exteriorly its life and its interior activities, and, thus, makes them known. Thus, it is that persons communicate among themselves. The soul does so, thanks to this reality which we call a sign. A sign is a thing which, besides the image that it offers of itself to the senses, makes known to our spirit something other than itself. The signs which emanate from the body, such as spoken or written language, gesture, and attitude, express, in a sensible way, and, thus, make known the thoughts, wishes, and sentiments of the soul which, without them, would be unknown.

Finally, the body is necessary to the soul so that the latter can communicate with another soul. Here below, the direct communion of soul to soul is impossible. It can only be realized by means of the intermediary of a body which, because it is intimately united to the soul, manifests, offers and provides this union.

The body forms not only part of our human condition, but part of our divine vocation. The soul, in fact, is called to union with God, and the body is associated with the soul in this call, to such an extent that it is necessary for it (the soul) in order that it may realize this union. Thanks to the body, the soul can know, serve and love God.

Such is the grandeur of the human body. Likewise, the Son of God did not disdain to take on man's human body, and not only a body like that before original sin, but a body like that of Adam's other descendants, "flesh similar to the flesh of sin," (Rm 8:3) "a body of sin," (Rm 6:6) the body such as original sin made it, a "body pledged to death," (Rm 7:24) to quote St. Paul.

Indeed, the human body is, no longer, the body willed by God. It has become heavy, opaque and dangerous. It is a fallen body, like the soul itself, and because of it. In fact, the first man refused the human condition such as God had offered it to him. The Creator's intention was to give man a soul spiritualized by means of his entire dependence with regard to God Who is spirit, and body spiritualized by means of the full mastery of such a soul on it. By sinning, by preferring to be independent and his own master, man renounced this spiritualized state that God was offering him, and was content with a state that we must qualify as carnal or "animal." By ceasing to depend upon God, the soul lost its perfect mastery over his body, and is, no longer, capable of spiritualizing it. From then on, the body, left to its own law of matter, attracts the soul to animality. The soul is, no longer, capable, in particular, of mastering the instincts of the body, nor of defending it always against the forces of corruption, nor of having it live eternally. The human body has, thus, found itself subject to concupiscence, suffering and death. Such is the triple slavery from which Christ liberates our body.

In order to study the body's liberation from concupiscence, I shall consider the latter, first, in its general sense of evil instincts, then, in its particular sense, of disordered sexual instinct.

First of all, it is by the power of the Holy Spirit, operating in the sacraments, that Jesus Christ frees our body from its evil inclinations.

At baptism, Christ takes possession of our body, as well as of our soul, by pulling us away from our carnal condition inherited from Adam. Our body ceases to belong to us: from henceforth it belongs to the Lord, affirms St. Paul (1Cor 6:13): both the body and the soul become Christ's members. As St. Augustine says: "If Our Lord had united Himself only to a human soul, our souls, alone, would be His members; but He united Himself to a body in order to be our head, and, as we are composed of a soul and of a body, our bodies are, also, His members."[2] St. Paul had already stated this truth which supported his preaching on purity: "Do you not know," he writes to the faithful at Corinth, "that your bodies are members of Christ? Will I then take Christ's members in order to make them the members of a prostitute? Away with such a thought!" (1Cor 6:15-18).

Furthermore, baptism makes our body as well as our soul, and thanks to the latter, a temple of the Blessed Trinity, especially of the Holy Spirit. Again St. Augustine says, "The Holy Spirit dwells in and by means of the soul, and in the body." St. Paul had said to the same Corinthians, "Do you not know that you are a temple of God, and that the Spirit of

God dwells in you? . . . The temple of God is sacred, and the temple is you" (1Cor 3:16-17). A bit further on: "Do you not know that your body is a temple of the Holy Spirit Who is in you, Whom you have received from God?" (1Cor 6:19-20). To the Thessalonians: "God wants . . . you to avoid shamelessness and for each of you to know how to protect your body in all sanctity and respect, without abandoning it to unbridled passions, as do the pagans who do not know God; and without injuring his brother in such a matter by lewdness . . . . God did not call us to impurity but to sanctity. He, then, who despises this precept, does not despise a man, but God Who has placed in us His Holy Spirit" (1Th 4:3-8).

Thus, by liberating the body from original sin and by communicating to it the divine energies in order to free itself little by little from the results of this sin, baptism makes it worthy to minister to the glory and praise of God. So, St. Paul can write to the Christians of Rome: "I exhort, you, brothers, through God's tenderness, to offer your bodies as a living, holy host, pleasing to God: such is the spiritual devotion that you must render" (Rm 12:1). To the Corinthians: "Glorify God in your body" (1Cor 6:20).

Besides, through baptism, the Holy Spirit makes our body an integral part of the Church, the very body of Christ, according to these words of St. Paul: "Christ is the head of His body which is the Church," (Col 1:18) and, also: "The Father has given Christ, as supreme head, to the entire Church which is His Body" (Ep 1:22-23).

Finally, by making us participate in Christ's death and resurrection, baptism, as we will see in greater length in the next chapter, frees our body from eternal death.

Washed, anointed and marked with the sign of the cross, our body is consecrated to the service of our soul in order to allow it to live according to our new state as Christ's members and, thus, sons of God. Such is the meaning of the baptismal rite of the "signing." This latter consists in tracing the sign of the cross on several parts of the body, and finally, on the entire body, accompanying each sign with an appropriate prayer. At the same time, these prayers signify, precisely, the taking possession of the baptized, body and soul, by Christ, the placing of the body at the service of the soul. They are as follows:

I bless your forehead so that you may be Christian,
I bless your eyes so that you may see divine light,
I bless your ears so that you may hear the Lord's voice,
I bless your nostrils so that you may breathe Christ's
  gentleness,
I bless your lips so that you may speak the words of life,
I bless your chest so that you may believe
  in the inseparable Trinity,
I bless you entirely in the name of the Father and of the
  Son and of the Holy Spirit so that you may have
    eternal life and may live forever and ever![3]

At Confirmation, the Holy Spirit anoints, again, our body in order to help our soul give witness to Christ. The person confirmed receives the gift of strength which will allow him to be unafraid of those who kill the body because of Christ, but, rather will allow him to shed his blood for Him.

In the Sacrament of Reconciliation, the Holy Spirit gives back to the soul of the repentant sinner health or life, as the case may be. Thus, He allows the soul to take up the struggle against disordered inclinations of which the body is the center and instrument, so as to liberate it from them by bringing them under control and reforming them.

Through the Sacrament of the Eucharist, the Holy Spirit assimilates us into Christ by uniting us to Him in a vital union. Thus, He puts our soul in the position to be able to take possession progressively of our body, thanks to a greater and greater configuration of the body to Christ's by means of His transformation of the carnal body into a spiritual one, in which his liberation consists.

By means of the Sacrament of the sick, the Holy Spirit, according to the situation, liberates the body from the illness, fortifies it against suffering or prepares it for a more glorious resurrection, by purifying the sick one of sins committed through his body: seeing, hearing, smelling, tasting, speaking, touching and walking.

Through the Sacrament of Holy Orders, the Holy Spirit consecrates the priest, body and soul, as the representative of Christ-the Priest. Formed as "a mediator between God and men, that he should be for us: holy, innocent, stainless," (1Tm 2:5; Heb 7:26-27) the priest must resemble Him by the total and definitive giving of his body, as well as of his soul, to the service of God and of men and by means of a saintly life. Thus, the Holy Spirit disposes of graces destined to free his body of any impediment and of any evil inclination,[4] in order to allow him to realize this resemblance.

We will see further on the role that the Holy Spirit plays in the sacrament of marriage by means of His relationship to the liberation of the sexual instinct.

However, in spite, of the sacraments, our body can still be subject to its disordered desires because the sacraments only liberate it from them with our participation. They give us the graces necessary for this liberation. It is up to us to use them. Why is it thus? The answer is: having created us free, God wants us to achieve freely the victory that His Son won for us, over sin, the cause of the slavery of our body. We manifest our consent precisely by means of the effective struggle against the evil tendencies of our body, a struggle which confers upon us a high dignity since it makes us cooperate with the Holy Spirit in its progressive liberation.

This cooperation consists in that our spirit is used, under the action of the Holy Spirit, to master the constantly reborn strength of the evil inclinations of our body, which incline it toward indolence, carelessness, indifference, laziness, vanity, intemperance in eating and drinking; to renounce, as far as it is possible, unnatural and artificial needs which are not absolutely vital, but the fruit of tyrannical habits, such as the use of tobacco, and which can enslave our interior liberty and destroy our spiritual life; to use, with moderation, such things that are inherent to the human condition—such as, food, drink, sleep, rest—but also, prudence and moderation, when one must be restrained in striving for asceticism.

Christian asceticism, indeed, to be authentic, ought not to exhaust nor to break away from the body. "He who wants to act like an angel" . . . , you know the rest! As united as it may be to our soul, our body has its own life. To misunderstand its real needs, its legitimate demands and pleasures, is to destroy its development and, consequently, to harm the soul which, in order to develop, needs a normal, healthy and balanced organism: *"Mens sana in corpore sano."* Thus, he must love his body. The above is part of the duty of loving oneself of which I spoke earlier. St. Paul remarks: No one has ever hated his own body; on the contrary, each nourishes and cares for it, as Christ does for the Church"(Ep 5:29). The liberation of the body goes along, then, with the care which one must take of it: to see to its sleep, rest, nourishment, hygiene, sports and recreational activities. How many sins of act or omission in this area, which are never confessed! Asceticism ought to tend toward submitting the body to the spirit (Cf. 1 Cor 11:27), so as to dispose it to fulfilling its role and to making it free with regard to its, even vital, needs, according to St. Paul's statement: "I know how to deprive myself just as I know how to be relaxed" (Ph 4:12).

The monks, themselves, dedicated through their vocation to bodily mortification are not however authorized to ruin their health voluntarily. The entire Rule of St. Benedict, for example, is characterized, relative to the corporal life, by a striking concern for discretion, moderation and balance: *"Omnia mensurate fiant"*(let everything be done with moderation). "This statement, as has been said, flows like a refrain through the entire Benedictine rule. The entire Benedictine rule (sleep, alternation of manual labor, reading, silent meditation followed by chant) ought to tend to the perfection of the human balance by taking into account the temperament of those who are delicate, climate, places, work, summer, temperatures."[5] It is told that St. Francis of Assisi, after having begun by calling his body "my brother ass," and treating it, as such, ended by humbly begging its pardon.

Liberation from the Sexual Instinct

The Holy Spirit, also, helps those whom He animates with His breath, freeing their body of that particular aspect of concupiscence called the sexual instinct. In itself, the sexual instinct is good. It is willed by God; it is a gift from Him. Thanks to it man and woman desire each other mutually, and are drawn to unite themselves physically with a view to their personal growth and to the propagation of the human race.

Sexual union being willed by God, the act that establishes it and the carnal pleasure attached to this act are the same, and, thus, good. Consequently, a married couple has the right to perform this act and to enjoy its pleasure. This act and this pleasure are even holy and sanctifying when the married couple is in the state of grace. One can go, even, so far as to say that, provided that they take place within marriage and in conformity to nature, they are good in themselves and by their origin. They do not become good only by reason of the good use that is made of them, in other words, thanks to the ends of marriage. Their value is intrinsic because they are produced by an intrinsically good action. In fact, if the sexual aptitude, gives place to the worst deviations and disorders, the reason is not that it is a faculty that original sin would have essentially corrupted: sexual aptitude, as such, remains good. It has no reason to be exorcised in some way and made good by the ends of marriage, although its usage ought to be justified and recognized by these ends.

In itself, the flesh is not bad, and it is not from its intervention that evil flows, but from the domination that the spirit can confer upon it. When it remains in its place, the flesh plays an important role. Because we are, at the same time, spirit and flesh, we ought to use the flesh to lift ourselves to the spirit. The soul — consequently, also, — is expressed and perceived by the body. The true masters of the spiritual life are not at all unaware of the need of the human heart. "Love," says St. Bernard, "if it ends by means of the Spirit, begins by means of the flesh."

The reason for the deviations and disorders to which sexuality leads is to be found elsewhere: in man's heart and in his liberty which has been damaged by original sin. In fact, if original sin did not essentially corrupt the sexual instinct, it broke man's inner equilibrium, and this rupture had repercussions on the flesh, in the usual sense of the word. Man began to experience a feeling, unknown until then, of shame.[6] His senses became irritable. His reason, no longer, ruled in conjugal intimacy, sexual desire or carnal pleasure. Woman began to submit to the physical and often brutal mastery of her husband (Cf. Gn 3:16); man began to dissociate the conjugal act from the gift of personal love, an act which ought to have been the expressive sign of love. If the term concupiscence evokes most frequently the idea of sexual lust, the reason, it seems, is that, in no way does the disorder become more apparent than in the area of sexuality. The deviations to which it succumbs ends by terminating the soul's spiritual life, by dulling the spirit and by making it lose the meaning of the invisible realities and the taste for supernatural things. If it is the spirit that causes the flesh to sin it is the flesh, then, that takes revenge on the spirit. For that reason, it has become a dangerous and distrustful temptress, not in itself, to repeat, but because of the disorders of the sexual instinct due to the lack of balance within the innermost depths of the human person and of his free will. The disorder causes man to abuse this instinct, precisely, by making a profane and abusive use of it, either by performing the sexual act contrary to his nature, or by diverting it from its end.

Now, in the man who lives by the Spirit of God, the liberation of the sexual instinct of its disordered tendencies takes place by placing it in progressive order. The spiritual life does not necessarily demand that he choke his instinct through the renunciation of marriage, still less, that he repress it. Far from despising or mutilating it, the spiritual life disciplines, calms and develops it, thanks to true continency, enlightened by chastity, supported by the spiritual life, and which is something very different from repression. To repress, that is, to struggle subconsciously and incessantly against inclinations that are repulsed regretfully, is unhealthy, and makes one ill. Chastity, on the contrary, is less a struggle against the senses than a liberation of the sexual drive, not by disregard, nor by destruction, but by its integration into the building of personality, its domination and its orientation toward the highest ends, its use for spiritual realities. This disregard is infinitely frequent; many human beings are unaware of or refuse to know the role of sexuality as the substructure of most of our instinctive activities, of our organic psychological sensibility. Yet ignorance or refusal does not prevent things from being as they are; they expose us, on the contrary, to dangers, because nature takes vengeance on those who do not want to pay attention to its laws: we command it only by obeying it. Since, in fact, our personality is not independent of sexuality, we can be masters of ourselves only when we have put under control this instinct. The control here . . . is not in crushing, in annihilation, but in the orientation of these drives toward truly spiritual ends, whose instrument they are."[7]

These spiritual ends are all reduced to love, to charity, to the gift of self under all forms. Furthermore, this end is even that of all human sexuality. The usual way that tends to this end is conjugal love with all its physiological and genetic perspectives. However, there is another more direct way, that of chastity dedicated to the cause of the heavenly Kingdom, because it is not the destruction of love, but its most perfect form, because it is the most detached and the most spiritual. Yet, it must be based on humility, ruled by charity and accompanied by all of the other virtues.

The body ceases, then, to be dangerous. Impregnated by the divine, it is transfigured, spiritualized by the Holy Spirit, divinized. It is, so to speak, evangelized and converted by Christ; it is once again adorned with grace like Adam and Eve before their fall: it has put on Christ, the Christ Who lets

Himself be touched, and His feet kissed by a prostitute, and Whom the Church, without needing to be daring, shows us on the crucifixes in His chaste nakedness. The body finds again, without, from then on, any peril, its role: to explain, to prove, to encourage and to communicate love.

Putting the sexual instinct under control is, then, the work of love transformed by the Holy Spirit into charity, of the love-gift towards which Christian chastity orientates the spiritual man, and which liberates him from all carnal disorder and any neurotic problem.

Likewise, it liberates him from all sensual excitement and from every feeling of shame when viewing nakedness; certainly of itself, nudity is neither moral nor immoral. It is God's handiwork, and we deform Christian teaching by pretending that it condemns nudity as such. However, by losing, through his fault, divinizing grace, man lost his control over sensual appetites. It is this loss which is the deep reason for embarrassment and discomfort in the presence of nudity, as well as the carnal excitement that such a sight might provoke.

By restoring to the man who practices chastity under the movement of the Spirit, and who controls it with his senses, the spiritual life progresses little by little toward the state of original purity where man was unaware of all sexual problems because he was free from all interior disorder. It makes him capable of supporting the sight of nudity without any danger. To him can be applied St. Paul's words: "All is pure to the pure" (Tt 1:15).

In marriage, the liberation of the body consists in restoring the sexual instinct to the state of harmonious balance which it possessed in the original plan. "In the state of innocence," says St. Thomas when speaking of carnal pleasure and of the fire of concupiscence, "there would have been nothing that would not have been regulated perfectly by means of reason. The sensation of pleasure would not have been less in this state, as some say; sensible pleasure would have been, on the contrary, so much the greater as nature was purer and the body more endowed with regard to sensation. However, concupiscence would not have been the disordered pleasure that it now is because it would have been ruled by reason whose characteristic is not to cause less pleasure in the senses, but that concupiscence be not attached to this pleasure in an immoderate way, that is, more than reason prescribes . . . . This is the meaning of St. Augustine's words: "in the state of innocence, the intensity of pleasure would not have been diminished, but that the fire of the passion or the disorder of the spirit would have been forbidden."[8]

Marriage, in fact, does not authorize the gratification of all caprices and instincts. It does not legitimize all desires of enjoyment and possession. There is conjugal chastity to be observed that does not consist in disincarnating love, but consists in doing nothing contrary to nature or to the end of the sexual act, by allowing all that is done according to nature, and in the interpretation of this act before, during and directly after the union.

If marriage is not licensed to satisfy all desires, neither is it licensed to use, without control, legitimate carnal pleasures. Married couples are obliged to abstain from them under certain circumstances. It is necessary, then, that this continence is not endured as an angry and regrettable mutilation, but accepted and even desired through them as the means, among others, of learning how to master themselves, to dominate their passions, to liberate the sexual instinct by integrating it into their personality and by making the conjugal act more and more an act of love. It is a tedious and difficult task. In the discourse that Paul VI gave to the Notre Dame group on May 4, 1970, he said:

"Who doesn't know it? It is only little by little that a human being succeeds in hierarchizing and integrating his many tendencies to the point of controlling them harmoniously by this virtue of conjugal chastity where the couple finds its full human and Christian development.

"This work of liberation, for it truly is one, is the fruit of the true liberty of God's children whose conscience demands, at the same time, to be respected, educated and formed, in a climate of confidence and not of anguish, where moral laws, far from having the inhuman coldness of an abstract objectivity, are there in order to guide the couple. When spouses try their best, indeed, humbly and patiently, without becoming discouraged by failures, really, to live the profound demands of a sanctified love, with the moral laws to remind them, these are no longer rejected as an obstacle, but recognized as a powerful help.

"The path of spouses, like all human life, knows many stages, and difficult and sorrowful phases, also, have their place as, indeed, you will experience in the course of the years. Yet, it is necessary to say it openly: never should anguish or fear be found among those of good will, for after all, isn't the Gospel the good news, also, for families, and a message which, if it is demanding, is no less deeply liberating?

"To be aware that one has not yet conquered his interior liberty, that one is still subject to the impulse of his inclinations, to discover oneself almost incapable of respecting, in an instant, the moral law in so fundamental an area, raises, naturally, a disturbed reaction. However, it is the decisive moment when the Christian, in his confusion, instead of abandoning himself to sterile and destructive revolt, complies humbly with the overwhelming discovery of man before God, a sinner before the love of Christ the Savior.

"From this radical consciousness, begins all progress in the moral life; the couple finding each other thus 'evangelized' in depth, the spouses discover 'with fear and trembling' (Ph 2:12), but also with an amazing joy, that, in their marriage, as in the union of Christ and the Church, it is the paschal mystery of death and resurrection that is being accomplished.

"In the heart of the large Church, this small church knows itself, then, for what it truly is: a weak, sometimes sinful and penitent, but pardoned community, on the road to sanctity in the 'peace of God which surpasses all intelligence' (Ph 4:7).

"Far from being, for all that, sheltered from all failure — 'let him who flatters himself to be standing take heed lest he fall' (1Cor 10:12) — or dispensed of a persevering effort, at times under cruel conditions which only the thought of participating in Christ's passion can make supportable (Cf. Col 1:24), spouses know, at least, that the demands of the moral life of which the Church reminds them, are not intolerable or impractical laws, but a gift from God to help them have access to, by means of and in spite of their weakness, the riches of a fully human, Christian love. From then on, far from having the anguishing feeling of finding themselves caught in a dilemma, according to circumstances, of sinking perhaps into sensuality by abandoning the sacraments, truly, by revolting against a Church considered inhuman or of being inflexible in an impossible situation at the price of harmony and balance, truly at the price of the survival of the family, the married couple will open themselves to hope, in the certitude that all the resources of the Church's grace are there to help them on their way toward the perfection of their love."

The sacrament of marriage, especially, gives them a special grace whose attribute is to heal concupiscence, that is, to liberate the sensual instinct of all that it drags along with it of corruption and impurity, to discipline it by directing it towards its end. Thus, it helps the married couple to make the act of union, not an imperious and frenetic drive of instinct, but a human act, an act of a free person, in a word, to spiritualize this act, that is, not to strip their union of sensible pleasure, nor to take from it its character of free outpouring and spontaneity, but to accomplish it, in such a way that, ultimately, it is love that inspires it, that is expressed and is communicated by means of it. To achieve this end marriage is essential, an institutional, indissoluble and monogamous marriage; consequently, trial marriages, as well as sexual and preconjugal relations outside of marriage are condemned. Actually only marriage, as an institution excluding all claims and divisions, can give its completely true value to sensual union because it, alone, assures the conditions for the encounter of two persons in a relationship of love where is realized not only the meaning of this union which is, as has just been said, to express this relationship of love, but, also, its dual finality which is to develop it and to render it fruitful and where this same union acquires its social and religious dimensions that ought to characterize it.

In fact, the only encounter that procures for man and woman their true development is that which a love relationship realizes, uniting them one to the other by means of the total and reciprocal gift of their person because such a gift can only be irrevocable and without decision.

Actually, to refuse to commit oneself entirely for life, to think that one can be married only for a time, is the very negation of the gift because, in this case, one does not give himself, one only makes a loan of himself, continuing to belong to himself, since he retains the right to take himself back when he wants. Furthermore, by its nature, love is absolute. One loves forever. "When one loves," says Dom Delatte, "he does not foresee the day when he will cease to love. If concern like that occurs, it is a sign that one does not love, that one has never loved."

Besides, such a complete gift as that demanded by conjugal love is possible, only, between one man and one woman. He who loves, but without becoming involved to the point of renouncing the right of giving himself to another would make of his gift a refusal to give himself.

In addition, the only encounter that allows man and woman to procreate is that which the same relationship of love established by each other's commitment, also, realizes. Since procreation implies the education of children, based on love, no education impregnated with love is possible if there does not exist between the parents a relationship of stable and exclusive love.

Finally, the twofold involvement on which this stability and this exclusivity rest ought to be institutionalized; I mean it ought to be made before civil society and, in Christendom, before the religious society. The essentially social nature of man demands, indeed, that his dual promise integrates the married couple in their vocation as persons mutually responsible to their brothers, as mankind, so that, if they are baptized, in their vocation as Christians mutually responsible to their brothers in Christ, present in the Church. For such, it is necessary that their consent be recognized and guaranteed by society, and for Christians, that it be ratified and sacramentalized by the Church, that is, it becomes the visible sign of Christ's love for all men.

It is the absence of the twofold promise, or the absence of one of them that prevents admitting trial marriage, as well as sexual relations outside of marriage, even those between an engaged couple.

Indeed, in a trial marriage, the principal reason for refusing to commit oneself, a more or less conscious and acknowledged motive, is the refusal to have one's liberty limited by another, a refusal inspired by mistrust of another, or the fear of risk and of failure. In short, it is an egoism which does not respect the person by using it as an object, and which is, basically, a negation of love. It is necessary to say as much and more about relationships outside of marriage.

As for premarital relationships, what prohibits them is not the refusal to involve oneself; it is the fact that no promise is and can yet be made: the engaged couple is still single. Even though they have decided to marry, they remain free with regard to each other. Each is, thus, bound, during the engagement, to respect the liberty of the other under penalty of bringing harm to his person. Marriage is a love of choice; all that goes against this liberty of choice harms the love that establishes the marriage. Each one ought to love the other even as far as his legitimate right to take back his word, since the engaged couple surrender their mutual liberty the day of their marriage, not before, at the pronouncement of their consent before society, as well as before the Church, if they are Christians. It is then and only then that they will be able to unite themselves physically, having thus fulfilled the conditions upon which their sensual union can from henceforth realize its dual end: the couple's growing union and procreation, which implies effectively and legitimately sexual relations; likewise, the conditions upon which it will be able to realize its fullest meaning: to express themselves bodily, to support each other and to deepen the union of their hearts, which demands the total and irrevocable gift of their persons.

Thus, then, the total encounter between man and woman supposes that the relationship of love which demands it, be a stable, definitive, exclusive relationship established on a mutual gratitude and a reciprocal confidence. Only marriage, monogamous and indissoluble, can establish and maintain such a relationship.

As is seen, the sexual liberation which procures life in the Holy Spirit has nothing to do with that which is recommended, alas, everywhere. The latter is only a license to use sexuality at will, without constraint or restraint, with no concern for one's true good or that of the other. Such liberation, far from freeing the sexual instinct, ends up by alienating it, by subjecting it to eroticism, to those "debasing passions," source of such disorders and so many evils, of which St. Paul speaks (Rm 1:27).

The result of all that has just been said is that the liberation of the body consists in letting the Holy Spirit transform it from "the body of sin," (Rm 6:6) from "the flesh of sin," (Rm 8:3) from "the carnal body," (Col 2:11) into "the spiritual body," (1Cor 15:44-45) as St. Paul expresses it. It consists, in other words, in allowing grace to free our bodies, as much as it is possible on earth, from certain sensual conditions to which original sin has reduced it, and to have it participate in conditions proper to the spirit that animates it, and which is, itself, animated by the Holy Spirit.

This spiritualization of the body, far from dehumanizing it, makes it, on the contrary, more human. Man's body, in fact, because it is precisely man's body, that is, the body of a spiritual being and not a body of an animal, is not fully itself until it is transfigured by the spirit that dwells within it. It is so much more a body as it is more spiritual. If it is imperfect here on earth, the reason is that it is "an animal body," and if it is an animal body, the reason is that it is a "body of sin," a body marked by the sin which has removed it from the complete hold of the spirit. "If our body is heavy and dangerous," writes Canon Mouroux, "the reason is not that it is united, but because it is not united enough, to the soul, and that, consequently, it escapes it in part.Moreover, it happens that the soul does not possess itself completely, and must look for itself, conquer itself, lose itself in order to find itself."[9] Now the soul is made for God, and it will not find itself, and will possess itself only in the measure that it will be divinized. The more divinized it will be, the more it will possess itself, and will be capable of possessing its body. The more it possesses it, the more it will be capable of transforming it, of spiritualizing it, as much as it can, without ceasing to be itself and to fulfill its role.

Thus, then, Christ frees the human body not by the flight of the spirit, but by the taking possession of man's body, as well as of his spirit, through the Holy Spirit, in other words, by invasion of it by the Holy Spirit Who transfigures, sanctifies, divinizes and spiritualizes it to the image of the very body of Jesus Christ our Lord.

Footnotes

1. St. Thomas, *De Anima.*
2. *Sermon* 161, 1.
3. Roman ritual for the baptism of adults.
4. Cf. The Ritual of ordinations.
5. Riquet, *Conferences de N.-D. de Paris,* 1948.
6. "Their eyes were opened," he said of Adam and Eve, "and they knew that they were naked and, fastening fig-leaves together, they covered themselves" (Gn 3:7-10).
7. Dr. Biot, *Guide médical des vocations sacerdotales et religieuses,* ed. Spes, Paris, 1945, pp. 225-226.
8. *S. Th.,* 1 q, 98, a. 2, ad 3.
9. Canon Mouroux, *Sens chrétien de l'homme,* Aubier, Paris, 1945, p. 101.

Chapter 11

LIBERATION OF THE BODY FROM PHYSICAL DEATH

The human body needed to be liberated not only from its evil inclinations, but also from death and the suffering to which humanity had been subjected as a result of the sin of the first parents.

We recall the sentence of death pronounced by God against Adam and Eve immediately after their disobedience: "And God Yahweh said: Here man has become like one of us with his knowledge of good and evil. Now let him not raise his hand; let him not take, also, from the tree of life in order to eat of it and live eternally" (Gn 3:22).

We recall, also, that their disobedience was punished with another chastisement: "To the woman God Yahweh said: 'I will multiply the pains of your pregnancies, in pain you will give birth to children' . . . . To man He said: 'Because you have listened to your wife's voice and have eaten of the tree of which I had forbidden you to eat, cursed be the soil because of you! By dint of suffering you will draw subsistence from it all the days of your life' . . . . By the sweat of your brow you will eat your bread' " (Gn 3:16-19).

Death, a natural phenomenon

From these passages of Sacred Scripture, among others, the Church has concluded that death and suffering were consequences of original sin. The Council of Carthage (411) declared: "Whoever says that Adam, the first man, was created mortal so that, whether he sinned or not, he had to die corporeally, that is, leaving his body would not be a consequence of sin, but a necessity of nature, let him be anathema" (Canon 1). For its part, the Council of Trent (1546) stated: "If anyone does not admit that Adam, the first man, after having broken God's order in paradise, lost immediately the sanctity and justice in which he had been placed, and incurred . . . the death with which God had threatened him beforehand . . . and that . . . the whole Adam, body and soul, was changed into a worse state, let him be anathema" (Canon 1). Also: "If anyone states . . . that Adam only transmitted death and bodily pains to all of humanity, but not the sin which is the death of the soul, let him be anathema" (Canon 2).

It seems, then, that, according to the Church's teaching, supported by Scripture, death and suffering would not have existed if Adam and Eve had not disobeyed God. However, the Church, also, teaches that this exemption from death and suffering was due to special privileges called privileges of immortality and impassibility with which God had endowed Adam and Eve, and which they would have handed down to all their descendants, but which, as a result of their sin, they lost for themselves and for all of their posterity. The Church knows, in fact, that, by his earthly condition, man is, according to St. Paul's expression, "a being of flesh and blood," (1 Cor 15:50) "a corruptible and mortal being." (1 Cor 15:33) Suffering and death are part of the very nature of biological life common to man and to animal, which (nature) involves the same phenomena of birth, growth, reproduction, degeneration or decrepitude, and death. These conditions have existed in the animal kingdom before man's appearance, and, thus, before original sin. Consequently, they are, also, inherent in human nature. Because of the very structure of his organism, man's body must wear itself out. Through nature, man must suffer and die. Suffering and death would, thus, have existed for humanity, even if it had not fallen. If, before the fall, human nature was exempt of suffering and of death, it was solely because of the special privileges of impassibility and immortality which must accompany divinizing grace, but did not belong by right to even divinized human nature, elevated to the supernatural order. So, it is original sin that, in fact, subjugated man's body to suffering and death by causing it to lose, in the person of his first parents, the privileges in question.

Thanks to His death and resurrection, Jesus Christ freed man's body from this twofold slavery by means of the infusion of his Spirit into humanity. In this case, it is a question of amazement, of even scandal and rebellion to us to see them both survive, since how is it that, in spite of this restitution, men continue to die and to suffer? What must be understood by immortality and impassibility? By answering, first of all, this last question, it will be possible to talk about the body's liberation from death and suffering. I have done so in a previous work.[1] May I be permitted to transcribe this answer by summarizing it a little.

Meaning of the immortality of the body

Thanks to His resurrection, Jesus Christ liberated man's body from death, and He alone could do it. Man can suppress suffering, at least, certain kinds, but never death. He can struggle against it by delaying its due date, but not cause it to disappear. Even if, thanks to the progress of science and medicine, he could postpone it, he would only succeed in prolonging a dead life. In fact, it is obvious that immortality must not be thought of as an absence of death, which would consist of a continuous and indefinite prolongation of the present life. Such is inadmissible, not only from the point of view of science, as we have seen, but, also, from Christian

Revelation. Actually, if Adam would have continued, indefinitely, his existence in a carnal body, he would have continued to live, spiritually speaking, the simple life of faith which was his at that time. He would never have attained the vision of God face to face, still less, complete union with Him.

In fact, what St. Paul said about all men can be applied to the first man: "As long as we live in this body," he writes to the Corinthians, "we live exiled far from the Lord because we travel in faith, not with clear vision" (2Cor 5:6-7). Actually, the first man, except for an extraordinary grace which would have lifted him above his nature, was incapable of enduring this vision: his carnal body would not have been able to bear the extraordinary rapture that his soul would have experienced. He would have died ecstatic. It can be said that this response of God to Moses who asked Him to show His face? "Man cannot see me and continue to live," (Ex 33:20) applied first to Adam.

Still less, could Adam have been united completely to God because, given that his carnal body was subject to the laws of matter as well as to the corruption of death, he would have been unable to penetrate into the bosom of God Who, being spiritual and incorruptible, could not admit unto Himself anything material or mortal. As St. Paul states: "Body and blood cannot inherit the kingdom of God, nor corruption inherit incorruptibility. This corruptible being must be invested with immortality" (1Cor 15:50, 53). Such was equally true of Christ Himself. For that reason, on the eve of His death which was to be followed by His resurrection, and which would allow Him to enter body and soul into the bosom of the Father, He said to His apostles: "If you love me, you will rejoice that I am going to the Father" (Jn 14:28).

For Adam, then, there was not only a biological, but, also, a metaphysical and theological need for his animal and carnal life to die here below.

However, what does immortality, lost by the first human beings and restored by Christ, mean? What does death mean

— death with which God threatened Adam and Eve as a punishment for their disobedience, them and those who came into the world with their sin, causing them, thus, to lose this privilege? The death which they incurred is spiritual death, that is, the separation of their soul from God, and it is also its consequence: physical death, the only one that I have seen here. This death consists in the separation of the soul and of the body, but making it clear that, while the body ceases to live and decomposes, the soul, because it is spiritual, continues to live its personal life, even though, in a completely different state of existence. This having been said, I think immortality signifies not the absence of death in the present life, exemption from biological death, but a definitive resumption of the corporal life by means of the soul in the hereafter, with a body free from its earthly, carnal condition which subjected it to physical-chemical laws.

In fact, studied in the light of the texts from the New Testament relative to the resurrection of the body, the passages of the Old Testament, which I quoted earlier and on which is established the exemption from death, permit us to affirm that such is, indeed, the meaning of this exemption. When the author of the Book of Wisdom says "God created man for immortality," (Ws 2:23) it means God wanted to give Adam's body a life other than the one he had, which, I repeat, was mortal. In time, God would have caused Adam to pass into another sphere of existence where he would have enjoyed a new and completely different unending corporeal life: eternal or immortal life. This latter would have corresponded to the resurrection such as we know it through the New Testament, and which Christ already experienced as "first fruits," says St. Paul "of those who have fallen asleep" (1Cor 15:20). Actually, Christ's resurrection was not a resuscitation, a return to His first state, as was that which He effected in favor of Jairus' daughter or the son of the widow of Naim, or again of Lazarus, but a birth into a new life, freed from carnal conditions and completely spiritualized because it was totally penetrated with the Spirit of glory: an immortal life, according to these words of St. Paul:

"Christ risen from the dead dies no more; death no longer has power over Him. His death was a death to sin once and for all, but His life is a life for God" (Rm 6:9-10).

Without a doubt, it would have been thus for Adam, Eve and their descendants, if they had persevered in the state of innocence. The necessary transition from the mortal state to immortal life would have consisted in a last change or transformation — that is, the word that St. Paul uses with regard to the resurrection of the body (Cf. 1Cor 15:51-54) thanks to which their mortal being would have taken on immortality, as St. Paul expresses it (Cf. 1Cor 15:53). This change would have been effected without apprehension or anguish, but in a natural and peaceful way. It would have resembled sleep followed by an awakening. Adam would have "been asleep," — to use the expression of the same apostle (1Cor 15:53) and he would have awakened thus to eternal life. (The Eastern Church calls the Blessed Virgin's death her "sleep.") To the first man something would have happened analogous to what, according to St. Paul, will happen to the last men, to those who will find themselves alive at the end of the world, and who will be transformed, without passing through death and corruption, in order to enter immortal, eternal life (Cf. 2Cor 5:1-5).

That being so, cannot one think that the privilege of immortality had to consist in the reunion of the body with its soul in another world, after having been separated from it by death in this world, in other words, in the resurrection of the body to a new life, the incorruptible and immortal one? It is not that the resurrection is not solicited by human nature. On the contrary. Indeed, as St. Thomas teaches, considered in itself, insofar as reunion after the death of the human body and of the human soul, which death had separated, the resurrection is necessary; it cannot produce itself: it is natural, that is, it is demanded by the very nature of man who is a being composed substantially of body and soul. Being made, essentially, one for the other, the body and soul of every human being ought necessarily to be one day reunited again so that he might be formed in the perfection of his specific nature and in his individual integrity.[2]

However, St. Thomas teaches, at the same time, that, seen no longer in itself, but in the realization relative to its efficient cause, this reunion or resurrection is not natural. Nothing in man's nature could be an efficient cause of the resurrection: the soul cannot be reunited to its body by means of its natural power; the body cannot be rendered naturally suitable for this union except by means of generation. So, when one would admit the presence in the body of any kind of inclination tending toward its union with the soul, this inclination could not become a reality. Resurrection can only be the effect of a cause which surpasses all the forces of human nature, namely God acting miraculously. Consequently, positively speaking, the resurrection is a miracle.[3]

In this perspective, cannot one admit that the privilege of immortality would, then, have consisted in the possibility of the effective realization of the body's resurrection to eternal life, thanks to a special, miraculous act of God, without which this resurrection cannot be realized because it surpasses the forces of human nature? Consequently, cannot one maintain that it is that life of which God threatened to deprive Adam forever if he disobeyed His command, and which, in reality, He did deprive him? Did not the sacred writer quote God as saying: "Look, man has become like one of us with the knowledge of good and evil! Now let him not stretch out his hand; let him not take from the tree of life, in order to eat of it and to live forever?" (Gn 3:22). The death, with which God threatened Adam as punishment for his disobedience, is the *definitive* separation of his immortal soul from his body by the decomposition of the latter. Such is the meaning of "Morte morieris" (Gn 2:17). Actually, it seems more exact to translate this grammatical construction proper to Semitic language by saying, not: "you will certainly die," but "you will die a definitive death; you will return to nothingness, to dust."

Indeed, since, through Adam's disobedience, "sin entered into the world," as St. Paul says, (Rm 5) the natural passage of the human body from the present life to eternal, immortal life changed meaning. It became his passage from being to nothingness; it became eternal death, that is, the soul's definitive separation, which remains living, with the body, by means of the definitive annihilation of the latter, an annihilation so definitive that the resurrection, or return to life, restored later to man by God, is nothing less than a miracle, as St. Thomas tells us.

It is, indeed, this definitive character given to this separation of the soul and body, to which each corporeal being is of necessity subjected, which has transformed death as a punishment by making of the natural phenomenon that it was, a "contrary-to-nature phenomenon."

Also, by means of its nature, as St. Thomas, likewise, told us, the soul, separated from its body, tends to be reunited to it because to exist without the body is contrary to the soul's nature because its nature is to be united to the body. For that reason, to deprive the body of the privilege of immortality by refusing it a return to life by means of its reunion with the soul, in other words, by refusing it resurrection, was to deprive man of a good which was appropriate to his nature. Consequently, it was to punish him.

Here is another argument which proves that the privilege of immortality had to consist in the exemption, not of the body's death here on earth, but of its definitive death. I am taking it from this passage of the Epistle to the Hebrews: "During the days of his body—that is: the days of his mortal life—having, with a violent shout and tears, presented pleas and supplications to him who could save him from death, He (Christ) was listened to by reason of his filial devotion" (Heb 5:7). This text allows us to state Christ asked His Father to exempt Him not from temporal death—we know, in fact, that, in spite of the repugnancies of His body, He agreed to die—but from eternal, definitive death, by causing Him to come back to life, by his resurrection. Such is, indeed, the meaning of these words: "to save from death," because, otherwise, one cannot see how the sacred writer could state that Christ was listened to, the fact being, to repeat, He submitted to death. Actually, his resurrection was the object of Christ's prayer of supplication, and the Father's hearing of this prayer was related to it.

It is, also, by that very fact, ours. "Our Redeemer's resurrection," says St. Gregory, "gave us immortality."[4] In fact, thanks to His loving obedience to His Father, impelled even to death on the cross, Christ, the head of humanity that He came to save, made reparation for the disobedience of Adam who had caused us to lose this gift of immortality, according to these words of St. Paul: "Just as through the fault of one individual, it was decreed for all men to die, likewise, by means of the justice of one individual, there resulted for all men a justification which gives life. Indeed, just as, through the disobedience of one man, countless men were made sinners, so through the obedience of one man, countless men will be made just" (Rm 5:12-20). Again: "Christ rose from the dead; He is the first-fruit of those who have fallen asleep. Because death was the result of one man, it is also, by means of a man, that the resurrection of the dead comes about. Likewise, too, all who die in Adam will also live again in Christ" (1 Cor 15:20-22). Thus, Christ can say: "I am the resurrection and the life. He who believes in me, even if He is dead, will live again; and whoever lives and believes in me will not die eternally or forever" (Jn 2:25-26; cf. Jn 6:54) and not, according to an erroneous translation: will never die.

Immortality thus understood, let it be said in passing, there is no difficulty to affirm with the Council of Carthage that death is not a necessity of nature but a punishment of sin: if death, as a separation of the soul from the "animal," "earthly" body, that which has been "taken from dust," according to St. Paul's expression, (1 Cor 15:44, 47) is a naturally necessary phenomenon, as science wishes it; by contrast, it is not as a definitive separation: it is contrary to the nature of the soul because—St. Thomas told us—"the nature of the soul is to be united to the body." For that reason, it is a punishment for sin.

Immortality thus understood, there is no longer any difficulty to affirm with the Council of Trent that, through the loss of this privilege, "Adam in his entirety, body and soul, was changed into a worse state." This change, this deterioration does not contradict the evolutionist affirmation of a continuous development of human nature. In fact, the latter has only been changed in its metaphysical definition which does not consider science: it ceased to be composed of a soul and body. By contrast, it underwent no transformation in its physical definition, which alone is dependent upon science: no change is produced in its biology or in its anatomical structure.

The privilege of immortality is, then, perfectly compatible with the evolutionist concept of man's origin.

Christ killed death by his death

Lastly, I must show that Christ restored this privilege to humanity by His death, thus freeing men from death. As St. Augustine says so eloquently: "Christ died, but He killed death; He put an end to what we fear; He accepted this death, and he killed it." We will ask St. Paul to explain how.

In the Epistle to the Hebrews, one of Paul's disciples, reminds us that Christ's mission as leader was to guide toward salvation the children whom God had given to Him. In other words, He must lead them to divine glory, to give them access to God. However, it was impossible without a transformation, a perfecting of their corporeal being. Indeed, these children "had in common a person of flesh and blood" (2:14). Now "the flesh and blood," as St. Paul tells us, "can not inherit incorruptibility," (1Cor 15:50) that is, as I explained earlier, that the human body being subject to laws of matter, being subject to the corruption of death, cannot enter into the bosom of God. Nothing material or mortal, in fact, can enter into God, only a being essentially spiritual and immortal. For that reason, when speaking of this carnal body, St. Paul, as is recalled, adds a passage further on: "This corruptible body must take on incorruptibility and this mortal body must take on immortality" (1Cor 15:53). It was equally true, as I have already noted, of Christ Himself. Thus, on the eve of His death which would — because it would be followed by His resurrection — free Him from His corruptible and mortal body, and permit Him to unite Himself body and soul to God His Father, He said to His apostles: "If you love me, you would rejoice that I go to the Father" (Jn 14:28).

So, then in order to be able to lead His brothers into the bosom of God, Christ first had to make them incorruptible and immortal, to transform their body of flesh and blood into a spiritual being. Now, to do this, "He, Himself, also, took a completely similar body of flesh and blood so as to destroy by His death the one who had power over death, that is, the devil, and to deliver those whom the fear of death forced into servitude their entire life" (Heb 2:14-15). Having, thus, put on a body comparable to the "body of sin," (Rm 8:3) according to St. Paul's expression, that is, precisely — a body of flesh and blood, an infirm, mortal, feeble and perishable body, Christ was then imperfect in His corporeal being. For that reason, he needed to be consummated, to reach the same degree of perfection to which God wanted to raise His brothers from their state of flesh and blood to "the life of glory" (Heb 2:10). He succeeded by means of death.

Indeed, death detached Christ from "His body of flesh," (Col 1:22) and made Him die to the determinisms to which His body submitted Him, that is, to corruption and to mortality, as well as to the laws of space and time. In a word, death spiritualized His body. However, it did not do so by itself because death, the consequence of sin as well as definitive death, could not free from sin nor, consequently, from the "flesh of sin"; it could not free Christ from itself. The end of carnal existence, death was incapable of eliminating the distance which separated Christ from divine glory. If He only had to die, Christ would have just stopped living, and He would have been liberated from death by His death. If, then, Christ has, through His death, destroyed death; if His death killed death and rendered His body spiritual and, thus, incorruptible and immortal, it is due to the fact that His death was followed by His resurrection. This latter was, indeed, not Christ's return to His original state, but a birth to a new life, freed from bodily conditions, completely spiritualized because it was totally penetrated by "the Spirit of glory" (1P 4:14). Certainly, after His resurrection, Christ began to exist in a spiritual body. From then on, the vital principle, the breath of life which animated His body here below as it animates every human body, is no longer the carnal, corruptible and mortal breath, the *psyche*; it became spiritual through the participation of the Holy Spirit who changed it into the *pneuma*, into the breath of incorruptible and immortal life. The Holy Spirit communicated His own life to Christ's humanity, and transformed it into Himself by imprinting His form upon it: He spiritualized it. As iron is transformed into fire by heat and made as brilliant as it, while remaining completely iron, so Christ's body, by uniting itself again to His soul the morning of His resurrection, while remaining completely corporeal, has been penetrated by God's Spirit which possessed from henceforth this soul without being disturbed any longer by its carnal covering, and spiritualized by the Spirit, that is, He has been vivified, rendered alive with a new life: an incorruptible and immortal life. St. Paul tells us: "Christ risen from the dead, dies no more; death no longer has rule over Him. His death was a death to sin once for all; His life is a life for God" (Rm 6:9-10).[5] Because Christ died, because His death was swallowed up in the victory of His resurrection, (Cf. 1Cor 15:54) that is, in the definitive triumph of His life, He liberated us from death, accomplishing thus the words of the prophet: "O death, I shall be your death," (Ho 13:14) and causing St. Augustine to remark: "O life, the death of death."[6]

Likewise, because this life killed death, His humanity — which is ours — spiritualized by the Spirit of glory, entered into the bosom of the Blessed Trinity. Since Christ's resurrection, death has, likewise, become a good, because it allows us, too, to be delivered from our corruptible and mortal "body of flesh," to put on incorruptibility and immortality, and, thus, able to penetrate, like Christ and thanks to Him, into the bosom of the Father. St. Paul states effectively: "Death is for me a gain . . . I want to go away, to leave this body, in order to be with Christ," (Ph 1:23; 2Cor 5:6-9) because "our city," he says further on, "is found in the heavens, where we await anxiously the Lord Jesus Christ, as savior, who will transfigure our miserable body in order to make it conformable to His body of glory" (Ph 3:20-21).

While waiting to render effective the liberation of the body from death by raising it on the last day, Christ delivered us from the fear that death inspires, according to these words of the epistle to the Hebrews, which I have already quoted: "Christ freed all those who were held in slavery their entire life through fear of death." Actually, when "sin came into the world," death, as we have seen, changed meaning. It became the passage of the body from existence to nothingness; it became eternal death. From a natural and undoubtedly peaceful separation from the body in its earthly state, it became painful and anguishing, because, as has been said, "it is experienced, or rather, is dreaded subjectively, like a plunge into non-existence, a sliding towards the unknown, a necessity so much the more anguishing as the other world remains inaccessible to our grasp." The definitive nature of death has given to it the formidable aspect that it assumed as the result of sin. By freeing us from eternal and definitive death through the promise of a future resurrection, Christ delivered us from the fear that death inspires. The certainty of our own resurrection, that His resurrection gives us, whose cause and certain pledge His is, frees us from this fear by lifting from death its penal character of condemnation of the body to eternal death. The Fathers of the eastern, as well as the western Church liked to comment about this fact. The passages that I am about to quote corroborates by the fact itself, the meaning that I have just given to immortality. St. Athanasius writes: "Since the Savior rose from the dead, death is no longer frightening. All those who believe in Christ know truly that by dying they do not perish, but live, and that the resurrection will make them incorruptible." For his part, St. John Chrysostom says: "Today Jesus Christ Our Lord has broken the bronze doors, and has caused the horrors of death to disappear. What am I saying, the horrors of death? He has even changed its name. Death is no longer called death, but rest and sleep. Before Christ's birth and the grace of the cross, the only name for death was fearsome. However, since Jesus Christ Our Lord offered Himself for us in sacrifice, since He, Himself, rose from the dead, God, full of goodness, destroyed those names (death and hell); he introduced among men a new and extraordinary kind of life. Departure from this world is no longer called death but rest and sleep" (Cf. 1Th 4:12; 1Cor 15:18; 1Th 4:15).[7] "In those days" (which followed between Our Lord's Resurrection and Ascension), says St. Leo, "the fear of a formidable death was abolished, and immortality, not only of the soul, but also of the body, was proclaimed."[8] For St. Augustine, "Christ arose, indeed, in order to give us hope, since a mortal man arose. For fear that by dying we would despair, and that we, then, would only think that our life ends with death, He established us in a security. We were anxious about our very soul; by rising from the dead for us, He, also, gave us confidence in the resurrection of the body."[9]

In reality, death's persistent rule is deceptive and temporary-deceptive because death like sin, was truly conquered by Christ. He who has been regenerated by baptism, has conquered sin and death by the same Christ. Although God does not want to confer upon the just the full effect of victory over death before the end of time, although, for all men—with the exception, at least, of the Virgin Mary—bodily resurrection is delayed until Christ's final coming, the glorification of the body has already acquired substantially by means of Christ's resurrection and ascension. By Him, redeemed humanity whose head He is, has already entered soul and body into the glory of the Blessed Trinity.

This deceptive reign of death is temporary because the victory of those redeemed from death is really and definitively acquired through hope, according to those words of St. Paul in his letter to the Romans, which I summarize thus: "We await the perfect adopted sonship which will include, also, the redemption of our body" (Cf. Rm 8:21-25). "Have courage," says St. Augustine, "death will also die in you. What happens first to the Head will happen to the members: death will also die in you. But when? At the end of the world." Indeed, the day of the resurrection will come when those whom Christ redeemed with His blood will sing with St. Paul the hymn of final and definitive triumph: "Death has been swallowed up in Christ's victory. O death where is your victory? O death, where is your sting? . . . May thanksgiving be rendered to God Who gives us the victory through Jesus Christ Our Lord." That day, to quote the same apostle, "He who resurrected Jesus Christ from among the dead will, also, give life to your mortal bodies through His Spirit Who dwells in you" (Rm 8:11).

Footnotes

1. Cf. Charles Massabki, *Le péché originel, peut-on y croire encore?*
2. Cf. *Suppl.* S. Th., q. 75, a. 1.
3. Cf. *Suppl.* S. Th., q. 75, a. 3.
4. *Hom.* 21 *sur l'Evangile.*
5. Cf. St. Thomas, *S. Th.*, III, q. 55, a. 2.
6. *Sermon* 233, no. 5, P.L., 38, 1114.
7. P.G. 50. 417-432.
8. *Sermon* 73, 1.
9. *Sermon* 177: *De Ascensione Domini*, II, nos. 1 and 2; the new breviary attributes it to St. Césaire, *Sermon* 210, 1-3.

Chapter 12

LIBERATION OF THE BODY FROM PHYSICAL SUFFERING

Through the overflowing of His Spirit into redeemed humanity, Christ, also, liberated the suffering of the human body. In order to understand how He did it, we must first define, just as for immortality, what must be understood by impassibility, that privilege which God had given man and the lose of which reduced him to suffering.

Suffering, a Natural Phenomenon

Theologians are thinking more and more that we must not consider this privilege as being the permanent preservation from all physical suffering. The latter, I repeat, is, of necessity, part of biological life, as much for the human body as for the animal body, to such an extent that a corporal being which would be entirely and forever free from it would not be normal. It would not even be viable. In any case, such an exemption would be prejudicial to it. Suffering, in fact, teaches us about the presence of an evil in our body, and, thus, allows us to fight it. Consequently, it is not bad in itself, and should be considered the result of original sin. Yet, it has as cause the physical ill of which it is the perceptible manifestation. However, the physical ill is not a consequence of the first sin. Its cause is the ontological constitution of creation: it flows from the imperfection of creation, which, because God is perfect, could only be imperfect. In fact, the existence of two metaphysical absolutes is inconceivable because one can only question by opposition between the two, and by limiting one because of this opposition. Being limited, creation is thus, necessarily imperfect. This imperfection involves for the created being the possibility of deteriorating.

In a word, physical suffering depends on humanity's bodily condition. It would have belonged even to an innocent humanity if humanity had not been endowed with the privilege of impassibility.

Yet, how to conceive, under these conditions, a human nature forever exempt from all suffering, since a human nature so structured does not seem viable, and such a structure, far from being a privilege for man, would, on the contrary, be an anomaly, incompatible with his nature as man, with the functioning of his organism? It is possible to respond to this question by saying that this impassibility would only be concerned about the difficult nature of work and the painful character of childbirth. Indeed, it seems that the enumeration made by the sacred writer about the pains inflicted on the first man and woman ought to be considered as restrictive. The Council of Trent seemed to allude only to these two difficulties when it speaks of the "pains of the body."[1] As for St. Paul, he only mentions sin and death in the text relative to Adam's disobedience. This fact explains why, even some theologians, having remained attached to the classical doctrine, rejected purely and simply the privilege in question. Without going that far, I think that suffering would have existed, even in an innocent humanity as the inevitable consequence of his earthly condition. However, it would have been presented, undoubtedly, in an entirely different context which is somewhat possible for us to surmise.

Effectively, we can think that a great number of the causes which, in our present condition, provoke suffering, would not have existed. I wish to speak of ills which flow from man's present sins: illnesses due to intemperance and the crimes caused through jealousy, anger, envy, pride; wars provoked by pride, hatred, ambition, the desire for power, etc. Now, all these sins have concupiscence as source. St. James states: "Each one is tempted by his own concupiscence which wins him over and seduces him; so concupiscence, having conceived, gives birth to sin" (Jm 1:13-15). Yet, in itself, this concupiscence, as we have seen, is good: it designates the whole of man's natural tendencies which have as their object the beautiful, the true and the good. Original sin brought about disorder and transformed these tendencies into inordinate desires, these "lusts which fight in our members," (Jm 4:1) by causing man to lose the gift of integrity which would have brought them under control. If then, as I have said, suffering does not originate with the sin of Adam and Eve, it does, however, come from it indirectly: it is the consequence of evils due to man's sins which are engendered by concupiscence crippled through original sin and, consequently, called "the daughter of sin (of original sin) and the mother of sin (of actual sins)." Therefore, if man had remained united to God, he would have kept, with divine life, the gift of integrity which would have made him avoid so many of the causes of sufferings. Furthermore, this divine life would have allowed the soul, as well as the spirit, to animate more completely the body; it would have had it participate in conditions proper to the spirit animated by the Spirit of God; as much as possible here on earth, it would have transformed it from an animal body into a spiritual one. This relative spiritualization would, undoubtedly, have merited for man's organism a more harmonious functioning which would have preserved it from other causes of suffering.

However, participation in divine life and the gift of integrity would not have prevented biological death, nor the erosion of the organism of which death is the consequence, and which would probably have been accompanied by some pain.

Whatever these suppositions may be, what is certain is that it is not contrary to faith to admit that physical suffering has existed in humanity even before original sin. Let us repeat: it flows from man' carnal and earthly condition. It is necessary, however, to exclude the pain of work for man and the pains of childbirth for woman. Indeed, the painful and sorrowful character which has affected respectfully, by right of punishment, what normally constitutes man's natural vocation, work, and woman's motherhood, does not belong essentially to human nature; it is not necessary to it as automation and the organization of leisure, on the one hand, and painless or natural childbirth, on the other, are in the process of proving. Normally, work and childbirth should be an accomplishment and a joy.

Thus, then, of themselves, it seems that the struggle which accompanies man's work and the pain involved in childbirth for a woman are the consequences of original sin.

Consequently, the privilege of impassibility ought to consist only in the exemption from the difficulty of work and the pains of childbirth.

As for other sufferings, as has been seen, some result from the various evils due to men's present sins; others are inherent to human nature as it has been created.

To Struggle Against Suffering

By His death and resurrection, Christ gave man the means of being freed from these sufferings. Indeed, we shall see that by obliterating original sin, Christ procured for him the possibility of combating the first (sufferings) as being the direct or indirect consequences of this sin. He gave man, by that very fact, divine life which, thanks to the energies that it communicates to him, allows him to cure concupiscence of the injuries which have made it disordered, the source of men's sins and the cause of their ills. Then, we will see that Christ, by His power, liberated man of the sufferings which possess the very structure of his nature, by obtaining for him the grace of resurrection on the last day.

Christ conquered suffering, on the one hand, by abolishing original sin of which it is, more or less, the direct result, and, on the other hand, by transforming it interiorly: thus, the Christian's dual attitude concerning suffering is to fight against it or to use it.

Suffering does not exist in itself, anymore than the evil of which it is the psychological reflection. It exists only in a good person in proportion to the latter; far from being an evil, it is, as I have shown, a good. However, suffering is a positive evil since it affects the sensibility, corners it and prevents it from enjoying good. To say to a person with cancer that his illness is the sign of the existence of an evil in him, that is consuming him, does not cause the person to suffer less. His illness is positively an evil. Viewed in itself, suffering is then detestable, almost as detestable as the sin whose offspring it is, and the Christian ought not to have any affection for it; it contradicts our basic need for happiness. If, then, suffering is an evil, it is absolutely permissible, even commanded, to fight against it, precisely because it is, more or less, a direct consequence of original sin, and the latter, having been abolished by Christ's victory, no longer exists. The redemption intervened, and, in the plan of Redemption, given back to men were all the means by which they might free themselves from evil.

It is permitted then and recommeded — not to say, commanded — to struggle against the pains inflicted upon Adam and Eve as punishment for their disobedience, as it is commanded to fight against the other consequences derived from this sin, especially against Satan and the inclination to evil. We can and ought to try to ease, and even, to abolish the fatigue of work, to reduce, and even, to eliminate the sufferings of childbirth.

Likewise, it is permitted and recommended — if not commanded — to conquer sufferings that stem from the evils of men's present sins, because, as has been seen, they also stem from, although indirectly, original sin. These sins have as source the concupiscence which original sin disturbed and transformed into evil inclinations. These latter, often, incline the will to desire moral evil, and, among the consequences which stem from this evil, suffering, in particular, is to be found.

As for sufferings which belong to the human condition, we ought, likewise, to fight them because we are made for joy, and these sufferings contradict the aspiration that is in us toward happiness.

In this struggle against evil and suffering, Christ gave us an example. He cured the blind, the paralytics, the lepers, the deaf, the dumb and other kinds of sick and infirm. He gave His apostles the power to cure maladies, just as He gave them the power to chase out devils — what he would not have done if the malady and, consequently, the suffering were not an evil.

Heir to the thinking of her Spouse, the Church in her liturgy, as in the prayers of the Ritual, asks of God the healing of the sick, the end of evils, the suppression of all the causes of suffering. Suffice it for one to recall this beautiful prayer of Good Friday: "Beloved Brothers, let us pray to God the Almighty Father: that He purify the world of all error, that He banish maladies and repress famine, that He open prisons and release the captives, that He protect travelers, that He bring back home those who are far away, that He give health to the sick and salvation to the dying. God eternal and all-powerful, Consoler of the afflicted, strength of those who grieve, hear the prayers of men who call you, whatever their sufferings: may all have the joy of finding the help of your mercy in their distress."

As the most authoritative representative of Christ and His Church, Pope Piux XII, speaking to some Catholic doctors, said: "For many centuries — and, especially, in our times — the progress of medicine has been constantly apparent, an assuredly complex progress, whose object includes the most varied branches of theory and of practice. Development in the study of the body and of its organism, in all the physical, chemical and natural sciences, in the knowledge of remedies, of their properties and of the ways to use them; advances in therapeutic application, not only of physiology, but also of psychology, and of the reciprocal actions of the physical and the moral." He encouraged them to continue their research in order "to ease the pains and sufferings of men."

Christ's victory over suffering is shared with every man who accepts His message. We are invited to free ourselves from suffering with, through, and in Christ, by fighting it, by looking for ways to suppress it with all our strength, and by all the natural means which are not harmful to the moral order, as well as by supernatural means. It is necessary to direct toward this end scientific research, to use for this end the developments realized, to bring about discoveries in medicine, to use for cures even magnetic and hypnotic practices in the natural order, on condition that it is not mixed with superstition nor the mental derangement of the personality. It is necessary to work for this success by means of a better understanding of the laws of nature, whose conflicts provoke accidents generating suffering, as well as by a better observance of moral laws, whose violations are the source of all kinds of maladies. We ought, likewise, to try to obtain this victory through the use of the Sacrament of the Sick, as well as charismatic healing, the prayers of the ritual, which have a charismatic efficacy, through the imposition of the consecrated hands of the priest — "they will place their hands on the sick and these will be healed" — by prayers and novenas made in order to heal.

Making Use of Suffering

It is highly improbable that men will succeed in eliminating all sufferings. Undoubtedly, they will have to wait for the day of renewal of all things, announced in Sacred Scripture, when sorrow and death will be engulfed in Christ's victory. While awaiting this day, Christians — and here is one of the many parodoxes of Christianity — by trying like other men to conquer suffering by fighting against it, are invited to conquer it also by using it, thanks to Christ, like Him and with Him, as an instrument of redemption. Thanks to His having used it in order to save us, Christ conquered both physical and moral suffering by removing its venom, so to speak, and by giving it a meaning which constitutes the most profound and the only ultimate response to its haunting why. If it is, indeed, true that, as I shall show, one can find in human suffering one or more meanings which are legitimate and constitute so many responses to the many questions that it poses, only Christ's cross gives it its richest and most exalted meaning.

The evil that suffering is, can become a good, more exactly, the means of a good, even of several goods. I say that it can become so because it does not necessarily. It cannot procure a good except on condition that one adopts, in its presence, not a sterile attitude of revolt which changes nothing, which only increases the pain and suffering, but an attitude of generous acceptance. In this last case, the beneficence of the suffering is shown as much in the moral order as in the supernatural.

First, in the moral order. Suffering is the ruler of life:

> Man is an apprentice; suffering is its master,
> And no one knows himself unless he has suffered.

It teaches us what we are, what we are capable of, what we are worth; it reveals to us our patience, strength, endurance and weakness. This self-knowledge is a great good. It was the least concession of the ancient philosophy:

"Know yourself." It makes wise men of us.

Suffering has a very salutary influence on our will. It seasons and strengthens us. It makes of us strong beings.

It purifies the soul by raising it above the senses: it spiritualizes it, while pleasure animalizes it. It refines it as fire refines gold in the crucible. It hammers and brings it to perfection, making it more profound, more reflective and more interior.

It gives us an understanding of others. It makes our hearts

compassionate. All things being equal, the best nurses are those who have suffered themselves. They have a lighter touch and a softer voice for their patients.

Suffering reveals humanity in its best light. Our humanity, with its selfishness, its divisions and its hatreds, is often quite a sad and ugly sight. However, it holds within it hidden treasures. Now it is suffering that reveals them. Let an epidemic break out, and all hearts are moved and drawn into a great outburst of solidarity and commiseration.

There are, also, many virtues, such as pity, clemency, goodness and generosity, which beautify the human soul; they would not exist, or at least, would not have the opportunity to be practised, without suffering.

Yet, it is, above all, in the supernatural order that suffering appears beneficent. Suffering takes or brings one back to God. Our own existence, or that of our peers, has certainly taught us that suffering puts the one whom it touches into a state of readiness to encounter God.

Because it teaches us the vanity of creatures, the just appreciation and true value of things, the meaning and the seriousness of life, suffering detaches us from everything and from ourselves. We lean too much on the world, persons and things. Let suffering come, and we begin to detach ourselves from creatures who prevent us from turning to God because we love them badly. Or, else, we were too complacent with ourselves; we looked for too many comforts and for our well-being and happiness. By thinking too much about self, we neglected to think about God. Let suffering come, and it elicits in the one that it strikes a self-forgetfulness; it detaches the person from himself, and opens him to the thought of God.

Indeed, suffering brings about this twofold detachment only to open us to God. The person detached from others and from himself becomes "fit for God."

For the same reasons, suffering brings to God those who had broken away and were separated from Him.

In prosperity, we often forget God; we imitate the prodigal son. With the goods that we have from our father, with the patrimony of youth, health, beauty, intellectual or material riches that we owe him, we leave the paternal home, religion, in order to go and live far away in the dissolute life of the spirit and of the heart: "vivendo luxuriose." God calls us back to Him through the inspirations of His grace. Yet, most of the time, we reject Him. Then, suffering happens to strike the prodigal through humiliation, ruin, poverty and sickness. Very often, it causes him to make some salutary reflections: the sinner repents and returns, throwing himself into his father's arms. He even blesses the sad instrument that cured him of his blindness, and gave him back his true life.

However, suffering is much more than an educator, much more than, even, an introducer close to God: it is a means of redemption whose use allows us to triumph over it more completely, thanks to the One Who, by taking suffering upon Himself, in order to liberate us from it, gave it the most enrichening meaning.

Because He is love, God only wanted suffering which is the inseparable companion of every human being, as a consequence of his earthly state, aggravated by sins, to have meaning. He caused it to enter into His redemptive plan.

By becoming incarnate, the Son of God took a human nature, encumbered with all the consequences of sin in order to conquer them, as well as sin itself, and its instigator, the devil. Just as He conquered sin by making Himself sin, so, also, He conquered Satan by letting Himself be seemingly conquered by him; so, also, He conquered death by accepting to die, He conquered suffering by accepting to suffer, that is, by using it as an instrument of redemption, or rather as an expression of love, because what saved us definitively is not suffering but the love born from suffering.

Indeed, if God wanted redemption to be accomplished by suffering and death on the cross, it is not that He is cruel, He in Whom there is only love. He planned it thus to permit Christ to express to Him His complete love. In fact, it was a question of Christ's saving men, that is, not only of His making reparation for their sins, but, also and above all, in the last analysis—a truth that is too often forgotten—of restoring to them their dignity as sons of God, thus, of remaking them divinized beings, that is, persons who participate in God's very being, hence who love like Him, since He is love.

Through sin, men turned away from God's love by turning toward self-love: they preferred to follow their own judgment which decided for them to settle themselves in their particular good, instead of accepting, in the testing darkness of faith and in an act of faith, the order willed by God Who invited them to participate in His nature, and to union with His very own life.

In order to make reparation for the offense committed and to re-establish the disturbed order, man had to snatch himself from sin, and from self-love, and to give himself to God. Man was incapable of effecting this detachment, and gift; Christ did it for all by snatching Himself, not from sin — He was incapable of committing it — but from Himself, and by surrendering Himself completely to God. This gift of Christ to God consisted, concretely, in the free adherence of His will to the will of His Father through the free acceptance of the way chosen by His Father for the fulfillment of the redemptive act, namely: suffering and death on the cross. "My Father, if it is possible, let this chalice pass from me! However, may your will be done not mine!" Why did God choose such a violent way? In order to give Christ the possibility and the means of proving to God His entire obedience and of giving witness to Him, even in that way, of the truest and most perfect love. Man's love for God consists, among others, in the conformity of his will to God's. Now, on the one hand, no conformity is so difficult, and so demands more love, than conformity in the voluntary acceptance of suffering, above all, in a suffering which leads to death, to an ignominious death. To obey a loved one, to the extent of dying for him, is not that the proof of the most perfect love? On the other hand, even though Christ's human will could only be entirely submissive to His Father's will, in this sense, that it was incapable of choosing the bad, yet, He could always choose between two or more created goods. Thus, then, before the aversion of His nature and of His body, at the thought of suffering and of the death on the cross decreed by the divine will to save the world, Christ would have wanted to effect salvation by another way than that chosen by His Father. However, knowing that He would not then have given witness to God of a perfect obedience, nor, consequently, the sign of the greatest love, He accepted, in spite of the reluctance of His nature and of His body, the sufferings and infamous death on the cross. "Instead of the joy which was proposed to Him," we read in the Epistle to the Hebrews, "Christ endured the cross whose infamy He despised" (Heb 12:2). By accepting the chalice that His Father gave Him to drink, Christ conformed His will perfectly to His Father's; He stripped Himself completely of self, and gave Himself entirely to God, by offering Himself, as a sign of the invisible gift of His love, His earthly life, His carnal being: His body and blood. This perfect obedience in the sacrifice that He made of Himself merited for Him the Father's love: "If the Father loves me, the reason is that I give my life in order to take it up again. No one takes it from me; I give it of myself" (Jn 10:17-18).

The necessary conclusion is that it is not Christ's sufferings which made reparation for the sins of the world, it is His obedience to His Father, pushed to the extremes of the cross, which is the supreme obedience: or better, it is His love for His Father, the love which He expressed through His suffering and ignominious death, more exactly, by the absolute conformity of His will to the Father's in the acceptance of the cross: love which was, for this reason, the most effective, the most sincere, the strongest, the most disinterested, the freest and the most authentic of loves. It is what caused St. John of the Cross to say: "I looked at your cross, Christ, and I read in it the song of your love." It was Christ's song of love for God, but also for all men whom He made His brothers, His friends: "There is no greater love than to give one's life for those whom one loves!"

From this fact, a new and more satisfactory answer is

given to the question asked by human suffering. Suffering has been radically changed, transformed, and returned, as it were. It has acquired a new meaning, its true meaning. As a direct or indirect consequence of sin, it became a means of reparation for sin and of reconciliation of man with God. From the pain inflicted by the refusal to love, on account of the injury caused by this refusal in the plan of love, it became the proof of the greatest love, and, consequently, the instrument of the restoration of the disturbed order.

Such is the meaning of Christ's suffering. Such will be, henceforth, the meaning of all human suffering, provided that it is united, through faith and charity, to Christ's redemptive act, because it is then a participation in His suffering. If Christ made reparation for our faults by means of His Cross, it was not to dispense us from all reparation: it is so that our reparation might be made possible and valid, thanks to His redeeming act, and that, aided by his example, we might obtain from this act the grace to accomplish it. God does not pardon us without demanding His Son's reparation, but He pardons us without demanding our personal reparation. He causes us, although pardoned, to be purified, or rather lets us be purified from sin, to destroy in us even its last traces. It is demanded through God's holiness and through His love for us, as well as through our love for Him. Now, it is by means of suffering that our purification is best effected. Indeed, purification consists, by means of authentic testimonies of love, in compensating for the refusals to love, which are our sins. Moreover, no love, I repeat, is purer, truer, more disinterested, more real, thus, more authentic, than the love that comes from suffering, because love is drawn from the conformity of our will to the divine will, and no conformity is more painful and demands more love, than the conformity in the acceptance of suffering.

Thus, suffering is the crucible where our love is purified of all the dross with which our sins sullied it, in order to become capable of being united to God Who is sanctity and love.

It is, also, the crucible where this union is forged, where our love is most solidly soldered on to divine love. The reparation which, even the pardoned sinner must accomplish, does not consist in purifying himself of his sins by forcing his sinful will to recant, in denying by means of acts of love, his failures to love. It consists, also, of purifying himself of self-love, of renouncing self in order to give himself completely to God. It is to renounce self, that is, not only of the evil and devious tendencies which are the source of sins, but, also, of this center of responsibility and of autonomy which is the human person. This renouncement is expressed practically by means of the free immolation to God of our will, not only in what it possesses that is bad, but, also, like Christ, in what it has that is good.

It is a question, then, of freeing our love of all egoism to be found there, of self-seeking, of self-complacency, in short, of disordered self-love whose subtle venom penetrates in all directions: "In our natural activity and in our inferior, as well as, our superior faculties, in our highest operations and in our supernatural activity." Now nothing purifies our love, of self-love, even in its most hidden recesses, as much as the fire of suffering because nothing strikes self-love as much as physical or moral, interior or exterior suffering, since, by consenting to suffering, we consent to what contradicts it, and what is the most repugnant to it. For that reason, it can be said that sufferng is the crucible where our love, in order to be soldered more and more solidly onto divine love, is proved like gold in the furnace, and thus furnishes the proof of its authenticity. When love remains faithful in the test, it proves that it is of good quality and authentic.

Suffering goes farther. It establishes our love in God's love. By killing self-love in us, it empties us of self, and opens us more and more to God's love. Suffering detaches us from self only in order for us to open unto God, in order to divinize us. Man, indeed, cannot complete himself except by attaining his end. This end, which he could possess only at birth, is God. Thus, man can be totally complete only by union with God. This communion with God is the work of obedience. Now acceptance of suffering is the greatest obedience.

Thus understood, suffering ceases to be detestable. From henceforth, we can love it, without this love being an unhealthy, unnatural feeling, physical grief. We can even desire it because it has become the generator and source of love. In this sense, we say that suffering is agreeable to God and that we offer Him our sufferings. It is not that God is a Moloch, the ancient Semitic deity, who is repaid by suffering, but that God is a heart which is nourished by love, and that love is drawn most and the best from suffering. One does not crush the grape for the pleasure of treading and crushing it, but to delight the heart with the wine that is squeezed out from it.

Thus, then, the failures and the humiliations, the illness and the sufferings of all kinds, as well as all the events of our life, but more and better than they, are destined, if we know how to understand them in the light of the cross and to accept them with Christ, to strengthen our consent to the will of God Who will realize our complete renunciation, and will complete our union with Him in Jesus Christ. "Suffering is an inroad, the penetration of God in us, and results in its joyful acceptance by those who understand it completely, by those who, at least in desire, put all their good in union with God. This love of suffering does not come from a pessimistic feeling and a hatred of life, on the contrary, it comes from a discerning love of the life which is established by means of it."[2]

It also comes from our love for our neighbor. Suffering, indeed, allows us "to complete," as St. Paul says, "what is lacking in Christ's passion for His Body which is the Church." From the moment that he suffers with the Head, each member is united to it, suffers like it, for the good of all members, thanks to the bond which unites them to the Head. Our sufferings make us participate in our brothers' redemption accomplished through Christ. "Evidently it is not in this sense that they would dispense themselves of suffering and would purify them in some way without it, but because they draw to themselves graces which cause them to walk in the way of purification."[3] That is not a new meaning given to suffering by means of Christ's cross, but the deepening of that which has already been revealed to us.

In the light of the Cross, suffering does not seem to us a punishment for sin nor a sign of abandonment by God, but the expression of our love for God and for our fellow men.

In the light of the Cross, the suffering of the innocent, also, finds its explanation and its meaning; a response is given to those who are scandalized that so many guilty persons are spared suffering while others, whose life is exemplary, are sadly stricken by it. Thanks to Christ's passion, having become a means of purification and of interior transformation, suffering leads to perfect love and to the most profound divine union.

Finally, I must add that Jesus Christ did not only free man from suffering by giving him, at the same time, the possibility and the ability to fight it, and to use it for his good during his life time; He, also, freed him from it by abolishing it forever in eternity. He destroyed it by His death and resurrection. Indeed, Christ's resurrection, as we have seen, was not a simple reanimation, a return of Christ to His original state, that of a "being of flesh and blood" to a "corruptible and mortal being," of a being with a body subjected to suffering as well as to death, but a birth to a new life, a life where His body having become spiritual is, from henceforth exempt from suffering, as well as from death. Such will be the state of our body on the day of our resurrection, thanks to Christ's. That day, says St. Paul, "the Lord Jesus will transfigure our miserable body into the image of His glorious body"(Ph 3:20-21) because, as he affirms elsewhere, "sown in the corruption of the body, he will rise incorruptible, sown in ignominy, he will arise in glory, sown in weakness, he will arise strong, sown as an animal body, he will rise a spiritual body"(1Cor 15:42-44).

Like men's liberation from death, their liberation from suffering through Jesus Christ will only be complete the day of the resurrection of the dead. Then only, as St. John says,

"God will dry every tear from their eyes, and death will be no longer; there will, no longer, be mourning, nor the cry of suffering, nor sorrow, because the first world has disappeared. Then, He who was on the throne said: 'Look, I make all things new' " (Rv 21:4).

Footnotes

1. Sess. 5, car. 2.
2. Y de Montcheuil, *Lecons sur le Christ*, Ed. l'Epi, Paris, 1947, p. 142.
3. *Ibid.* p. 143.

Chapter 13

LIBERATION OF TEMPORAL VALUES

When discussing the liberation of the human person in general, I had occasion to quote several passages from the talk that Paul VI gave December 7, 1965. I mentioned, in particular, the Pope's recalling the tremendous interest of the Council in human and temporal values.

We ought to be grateful to Vatican II and to Paul VI for having focused their attention on these values, for being concerned "with the multiple and extremely vast questions concerning human well-being." Indeed, there are, still, too many Christians, it seems, who, under the pretext of being only travelers here below enroute to heaven, believe themselves obliged to neglect, and even, to despise earthly things and temporal values, as if these were foreign, if not even harmful, to the spiritual life. They consider themselves, in any case, exempt from every temporal, political, social or other activity, and they escape towards eternity by being disinterested in the temporal, in the labors and the struggles undertaken by men of this world for a better organization of the earthly city, because they think that such activities are worldly ones, having no connection with their supernatural destiny and the true interests of the kingdom of God.

Those, among them, who refuse to renounce temporal values and to dissociate themselves from earthly matters, most often succeed only in having a bad conscience, or at the price of a sort of interior division, of a separation between their spiritual and their human life, persuaded as they are, that it is impossible to reconcile these two lives with each other.

Such is not, nor ought to be, the attitude of the "spiritual" man, that is, the man who lives according to the spirit, confronting the temporal order. The spiritual man has the right and the duty to love temporal values and to work for a better earthly city. In fact, the transformation that the Holy Spirit effects in the Christian does not occur without a radical transformation of the relationships of the Christian with all of humanity and with the world. This transformation does not consist in making him cut himself off, to withdraw as much as possible from the world, but, on the contrary, to make him communicate with it, with its values and its undertakings, by liberating this world of what St. Paul calls the "vanity" to which original sin had submitted it.

This liberation of the world is what remains for me to mention. I shall discuss here only the liberation of temporal values, leaving for the end that of earthly tasks. First of all, I shall define in what consists the slavery to which the values of the world have been subjected; then, how the Christian who lives according to the Spirit, far from opposing these values, communicates fully with them in order to expand his spiritual life by collaborating with the Holy Spirit to free them from their servitude.

Corruption of Temporal Values

Let us begin by defining what must be understood by the temporal values of the world. First of all, what world are we discussing here? We have seen, in fact, that the word "world" had several meanings. This one is not the world that Christ condemned or cursed, the evil that is found in it and which torments it. It is not the world of which St. Peter and St. John speak. The former says that "we have been snatched from the corruption rampant in the world through lust (2P 1:4). The latter says: "do not love the world nor what is in the world. If anyone loves the world, the Father's love is not in him, because all that is in the world: the lust of the flesh, the lust of the eyes and the pride of life, is not of the Father, but of the world" (1Jn 2:15). The world in question here is, according to the definition of Vatican II, "the entire human family with the universe the center in which it lives, works and struggles . . . ; the world fallen into the slavery of sin, but which Christ liberated, so that it might be transformed according to God's plan, and that it might arrive at its fulfillment";[1] the world about which Christ said: "God so loved the world that He gave His only Son so that every man who believes in Him may not perish, but that he might have eternal life. Thus, God did not send His Son into the world to condemn the world but so that the world might be saved by Him" (Jn 3:16-17); to be exact, it is the Universe in the heart of which this humanity "lives, works and struggles."

The world that I am describing here is, then, the creation, such as it is, that God made entirely good, according to His own statement reiterated seven times in the Book of Genesis (Gn 1:4-31). The Sacred writers repeated in emulation this affirmation: "You delight me, Lord, through the creation, sings the psalmist, and the works of your hands cause me to rejoice. How great are your works, O Lord! How profound are your thoughts!" Again: "How marvelous are your works, Lord! You have made them wisely; the earth is full of your gifts." "I want to recall now the Lord's works and to publicize what I have seen," says the author of the Book of Sirach. "By the Lord's words, his works have come into being, and creation obeys his will. He has disposed in order the marvels of his wisdom. . . . How good are all his works!" The author of the Book of Wisdom says, speaking to God: "You love all creatures, and are not dissatisfied with anything that you have made; for, if you had hated anything, you would not have formed it. How would anything have subsisted if you had not willed it. How would it have conserved its existence if you had not called it into being?

However, you spare everything because all is yours, Master, Friend of Life, you whose imperishable breath is in all things" (Ws 2:24-26). Echoing these words of the Old Testament, St. Paul affirms, in his turn: "All that God created is good" (1Tm 4:4).

Such is the world with whose values the spiritual life, far from constraining us to renounce, makes us communicate in all their plenitude.

What must be understood by these values? They are the values that are called temporal, and are distinguished from spiritual, religious and eternal ones. They are of two kinds: human and material.

Human values include those relative to the body: health, balance, strength, beauty, and values relative to the soul: its faculties and its activities. In preceding chapters, I have discussed all of these points.

Material values concern creation, that is, the whole of irrational creatures, the material elements of civilization: eating, drinking, dress, lodging, tools, means of transportation, comfort under all its forms, and, of course, money. These are the values that I have in mind here. Now these values are the fruits of a world which, according to Vatican II, has "fallen under the slavery of sin, but which Christ, through His death and resurrection . . . liberated so that it might be transformed according to God's plan; and that it might succeed in, thus, accomplishing it." Like this world, we will, also, see that these values have been corrupted and profaned in it, but, like the world, and in it, they have been freed from corruption and transformed by Christ's death and resurrection.

Humanity, as well as all creation, came forth injured by the fall of the first parents, not because they wanted it, not through their fault — how could creatures deprived of reason offend God? — but in spite of it and because of them. "Because you have eaten of the tree of which I enjoined you not to eat, cursed is the earth *because of you*" (Gn 3:17-18). St. Paul says that creation has been subjected to vanity — we will see, shortly, what needs to be understood by this word —

not freely, "but because of the one who has subjected it" (Rm 8:20). Creation having been made for man, it was logical that its downfall followed man's.

In what did this downfall consist. In my opinion, it did not consist, as is sometimes claimed, in a degeneration, in a perversion of the nature originally good, in a general decline of all the earth, in a disorder invading the world progressively, in a "regressive evolution," involving disorders of inanimate nature, in the transformation and disappearance of animal and vegetable species. I do not think that, before the fall, there were no brambles nor thrones, nor carnivorous animals, nor that lions, for example, rejected fruits and vegetables. Paleontological discoveries give truth to St. Thomas's writings concerning the state of creation before the fall:

"Some say that animals who now are ferocious and who kill other animals, would have been, in this initial state, completely gentle, not only toward man, but also toward other animals. That is something totally foolish. Man's sin, in fact, did not change the nature of animals, in such a way that those to whom it is now natural to eat the flesh of other animals would have lived on herbs in their original state, like lions and falcons."[2] On the contrary, I agree with Father Rideau, concerning the transition of the universe, "about an initial chaos," of a *tohubohu* (Gn 1:2) (a Hebrew word which means the formless and empty earth), and of a confusion of elements to a real order. I think "that with the constant help of its creator, but also through the act of a spontaneous force, nature evolved little by little — and continues to evolve — toward harmony; that, part of the extreme pluralism of a scattering of fragile and in-distinguishable structures, it tends toward a more perfect and more organic unity."[3]

Actually, we ought to set down as a principle that, in every way and in every hypothesis — whether Adam and Eve sinned or not — the imperfection of creation is a necessity because it holds together the ontological institution of the universe.

It remains, however, that by sinning, man has emphasized profoundly this essential imperfection of creation, more precisely, he has added to it another, such and so well that it can be said creation has truly suffered a fall.

How has it fallen? It has been, as St. Paul explains "subjected to vanity," reduced to slavery, "the slavery of corruption." What is there to say? Here vanity does not mean a perpetual change of things, but disorder, anomaly. Through Adam's sin, the world has been, as it were, turned upside down; creation has been turned inside out; it has been deflected from its right direction: it is no longer in order. In a word, it no longer realizes its finality: it no longer glorifies God, and it is no longer at the service of men.

Instead of serving the glory of the Creator by manifesting His invisible attributes and even His divinity, and by, thus, inviting man to glorify God, and to render Him thanks, (Cf. Rm 1:19-21) creation has been constrained to serve their vainglorious thoughts, their corrupt desires, their depraved gratifications and their vile passions. It has defamed its role; for them, it has lost a great deal of its end, of its initial vocation; it has been "emptied" of meaning: it no longer talks to them of God and His love, and it is no longer for them a means of attaining Him, a response of love to His love. Creation has become the end that they searched for, their supreme good, the end of their ultimate enjoyment and rest; in short, it has become an idol.

Indeed, having, thus, lost the meaning of creation, humanity succeeds very quickly in creating gods to its own liking. It is written in the Book of Wisdom: "Basically vain are all men who are unconscious of God, and who, by means of visible goods, have not been capable of knowing Him Who is, and have not recognized the Artist by considering His works. However, it is fire, wind, the moving air, the circle of the stars, the impetuous water, the stars in the heavens that they have regarded like gods governing the universe" (Ws 13:1-2). Humanity fell very early into idolatrous cults, such as fetishism, manism, anamism, astrology, magic, totemism, and then moved to the polytheism of the eatern religions, and finally to the classical cult of the gods of Greece and Rome: an aberration renewed in our days under other forms through materialistic atheism (Gn 1:26-28; 11:15; 9:2-7; Ws 9:1-4; Si 17:1-4). By making creation serve a purpose of which God disapproves, man makes creation participate, so to speak, in his disobedience and revolt: he turns it against its creator; he profanes and prostitutes it.

Creation, also, had as role to serve man. It was given to him, as we shall see more in depth in the following chapter, to use for the needs of his body and for the development of his faculties. To this end, man received the commission to dominate the elements of the universe, to manage the earth, the temporal milieu where he must spend his life and to work out his destiny. On this point, also, man turned creation away from its true meaning. By his fall, he reduced nature to an unstable state. Instead of using it as a means to realize his temporal and eternal vocation, he installed himself in it as a pleasure-seeker, without reference to his Creator. He even delivered it to "corruption"; he forced it to an activity contradictory to its being: thus it is, for example, that substances, made to contribute to the expansion of life, are forced to serve for criminal enterprises, for warlike and thus murderous ends by men, when they, no longer, like each other.

Thus violated and forced to serve, against its most profound impulse, the unreasonable thoughts and perverse desires of men, creation needs to be freed from this violence.

Now, if temporal realities have been profaned in this way, and subjected to men's corrupting vanity, if they have been injured and have become dangerous, it is not that they have been rendered bad in themselves, corrupted in their internal being by whatever poisons which would have made them corrupt, in their turn. On the contrary, the reason is that, from the day that man ceased to be directed toward God, he caused creation to deviate from its true order, by deterring it from its initial destiny. In themselves, creatures have remained innocent and always worthy of being loved because they have remained susceptible to being directed toward God. If they lost their first destiny, if they have been emptied of their meaning, the reason is that human intelligence has been struck, by reason of the first sin, by an injury which has deprived it of its supernatural light, weakened in its exercise, and rendered subject to ignorance and error. Likewise, the reason is that the human heart has been blinded by lusts which this fall had disordered and transformed into evil inclinations. Speaking of men who, no longer, knew how, according to the words of the Book of Wisdom, "by means of visible goods, to see Him who is, nor through consideration of His works, to recognize the Worker" (Ws 13:1). St. Paul writes: "They became vain in their thoughts, and their insensitive heart was enveloped in darkness. Boasting of being wise, they became foolish to the extent of attributing the glory of the incorruptible God — that is, the divinity — to the images of corruptible man, even birds, quadrupeds and reptiles. They adored and served creature instead of the Creator Who is blessed eternally. Amen." (Rm 1:21 ff.). Elsewhere: "They have darkened their intelligence and are separated from the divine life through their ignorance and the blindness of their heart" (Ep 4:18). Likewise, this darkening of the intelligence, by making them unaware of the laws of nature, prevents men from controlling the blind forces of the world, and places men under their domination. This blindness of heart, by leading humanity into egoism, hatred and pride, is the reason that men, instead of being content to utilize scientific discoveries with a view to making the world better than when they received it, use them to kill one another.

Thus, earthly values can create slavery for the Christian and harm his spiritual life. Cut off from God at the beginning and at the end, uprooted from their order, these values have been made disastrous. Isolated and shut in, they become, through their very riches, an immediate principle of temptation. Ceasing to give God to man and to orientate man towards God, they direct men toward themselves. So, from then on man is governed, no longer by his aspirations, but by his lusts which subject him to matter under all its forms, and plunge him into a materialism which leads him sooner or later to the denial of God and, thus, to the suppression of all spiritual life.

Purification of Temporal Values

However, this perversion ought not to lead the Christian to condemn temporal values purely and simply because it is possible to redirect this condemnable attitude. Plunged into this world which is a sinful one, but which Christ liberated from sin, into this world where temporal values no longer exist in a pure state, where they are often hidden and indistinguishable, sometimes even damaged or destroyed by evil, the Christian can and ought to love the real possibilities of existence, of trying to raise up, and to discover hidden values — the admirable work of purification and of liberation.

By offering himself to God in sacrifice, as an oblation of love, Jesus Christ made reparation for and renewed everything; He directed man's heart again toward divine love, and with and through Him, all creation.

Through His incarnation, Christ had already begun the renewal of all things and the reordering of the Universe toward God. By uniting Himself, indeed, to the most material elements of the Universe by the intermediary of the body that He took in Mary's womb and of which the Universe is the continuation, Christ took unto Himself, in some way, all creatures. By this assuming, He returned to them their original destiny by reorientating them to God in His person of the Word made flesh.

By triumphing, by means of His death, over sin and its consequences, Christ accomplished this reordering of the Universe for God; thanks to His resurrection and ascension, that His death merited for Him, Christ introduced, in reality, with His body, into the very bosom of God, the first fruits of creation. Let us add that Christ will only achieve this return in the glorious parousia, the day when all creation will be, as His body already is, a resurrected creation and when, as St. Paul says, "God will be all in everything" (1Cor 15:28).

Thanks to Christ, creatures have rediscovered for man their true meaning and their true role. However, that has not been done by submitting to changes in their nature, as one can deduce from what has just been said. What had to be changed was man not they. The reason which had made them ambiguous by confusing their meaning and by altering their role was not in them but in fallen man: this blindness of his heart and mind, as a result of sin. Sincerely, the reason that a blind person is unable to see is found not in the sun, but in the blind person himself: it is his blindness.

Christ, then, gave back to creation its meaning and its role, not by changing something in it, but by freeing man of the blindness of his mind and heart, or more precisely, by giving him the possibility and the means of freeing himself. Consequently, creatures, in fact, do not discover their true meaning and their true destiny unless they try to enlighten their mind and purify their heart; unless they shut their eyes to the "disordered seduction of creation in order to reopen them, purified, enlightened and discerning."[4] Those who do not, remain inexplicable tempters. They hide God from others, and they are a disturbing invitation to disordered pleasure and carnal love.

Because, even after the redemptive Incarnation of the Word, creatures, also, surrender their divine meaning only to those who regard them with a new mind and heart, with interior eyes that see and that enlighten what they see, man can discover their meaning only by means of a liberation accomplished, thanks to an act of his mind and heart under the action of the Holy Spirit.

To live in the Spirit, to be spiritual man, we are not forced to renounce all use of this world's goods, nor to reject all kinds of comfort, but to let the Holy Spirit, thanks especially to the gift of knowledge, enlighten our intelligence and purify our hearts in order to let us discover the meaning of creatures and of earthly values. Creation, I reiterate, has as role to serve man, as well as to speak to him of God and to lead him to God. In order to be able to use creatures and to understand temporal values, we must, on the one hand, instead of our being subject to creation by adoring it as an idol or by using it as egotistical pleasure seekers and as independent masters or even worse, as criminals, to repeat, we must use it as a means of realizing our temporal and eternal vocation, because "temporal realities if they do not condition Christ's parousia, they condition, in part, the present Christian existence. Certain human conditions are useful to the Christian life." On this point, St. Paul gives the right formula: "All is yours, but you are Christ's and Christ is God's." Utilized in this spirit, earthly values (money, comfort, technical progress, the goods of this world in general), from bad masters become good servants, especially if we are always ready to sacrifice them when they become an obstacle. "Cut off your hand and pull out your eye," says the Lord, "if necessary, in order to enter into life."

Thus, the spiritual man loves Jesus Christ, and the God of Jesus Christ with all his strength; he will be able to welcome into his purified heart, all of creation because his love of creatures will then be a detached and rescued love, because it will turn first of all to God and the eternal. He should rely on Him, at the moment when he uses created good; thus, he remains free without his equilibrium being affected. Again, it is St. Paul who formulates best this truth: "It is necessary that those who buy, be as if they did not possess, and that those who use this world as if they were not using it" (1Cor 7:29).

On the other hand, creation has as its mission to give God to man and to give man to God. The spiritual man ought, then, not only to regard creation with a purified heart and to use it with a rectified will, but also to restore it completely to God by adoring and glorifying God through it. What is demanded of the Christian who lives according to the Spirit, is not, as one sometimes thinks, to destroy or to depreciate creation, still less to despise or to hate it, but, to take it, to sanctify it, in order to offer it in homage to God. This restitution and consecration of the Universe to God, inaugurated by Christ in the Incarnation, accomplished, in principle, through the Redemption, is followed by the risen Christ through His Spirit, in His Church, thanks to the Christian sacramentalism, especially the Sacramentals and the Sacrament of the Eucharist.

In order to help discover the true meaning of creatures, the Church has made it the object of what are called sacramentals. Indeed, in prayers where God is asked to bless and consecrate them, the Church tells us in what spirit we ought to use material things, like, for example, the home, the dining room, the kitchen, the pantry, the bread, fruits, fields, instruments of work, music, water, fire, railroads, automobiles, the telegraph and the list could be lengthened because all of nature and all works of art and of science can be blessed, as indicated by the numerous prayers provided for this purpose by the Ritual (the name of the official collection of sacramental rites and blessings) and to which besides, the Church can always add others, as she has done in recent years for the blessing of planes, radio-stations, and as she will soon, no doubt, do it for T.V., radar and satellites. The Ritual can be described as: "an unfinished book, an open book which awaits other pages insofar as the exploration, through thought, handcraft, tools, and liberated energy, will add new things to those that the priest's hands already bless."[5]

The following is an example of the formulas for blessing the dining room, kitchen and refrigerator.

"All powerful and merciful God, Who nourishes your servants in this place, by renewing the strength of their bodies: Grant them, we pray, to receive gratefully nourishment and drink, blessed by you, and may they merit to be saved by you now and forever. Through Christ our Lord."

"God, all powerful and merciful, who is present everywhere, we pray beseechingly: may your grace deign to be present in this kitchen, in order to keep far from it all difficulties and to increase in it abundantly the fullness of your blessings through Christ our Lord."

"O God, you who give mercifully to those who serve you in mind and body what is necessary for their life, may, we beg of you, the goods placed here through your goodness, for the use and bodily needs of your servant, be in abundance and preserved, so that, by using them now, in an exterior manner, and being interiorly cloaked with the garment of justice we merit to show ourselves always consecrated to you. Through Christ Our Lord."

Consecration of Temporal Values

Do not let this practice of the Church shock or surprise us. It is not necessary to see in it a kind of magic. Magic consists in wanting to capture supernatural forces in order to use them for purely material things—natural, artificial or fabricated—the means of teaching us how to use them in order, and the means of directing them to God. There is no magic nor concession here, made to the ordinary mind of the rank and file, but a profound intelligence and an exact vision of the Universe, at the same time, a perfect knowledge of human nature and a true conception of the world of sin.

Creation, "subject to vanity, the slave of corruption" (Rm 8:20-21), a "return to grace," a reconciliation, a benediction, a consecration. Without a doubt, this consecration of the Universe was inagurated by the Incarnation of the Son of God who, by becoming man, wanted, as the Roman Martyrology tells us, to consecrate the world through His completely merciful coming: *"Mundum volens adventu suo piissimo consecrare."*[6] "At the moment when the Word became flesh," writes Msgr. Journet, "divine virtue was carried, in some way, to the bosom of the material universe in order to restore, transform and sanctify it. Not only Christ's bodily nature, but also, all of material nature, was invited to participate in a dignity unheard of up to that time."[7]

However, the sacraments, and above all the sacramentals realize practically this consecration of the universe in a progressive way, by starting with the humblest realities.

The universal consecration of the created, thanks to Christian sacramentalism seems to us, thus, like the fulfillment in time of this, "impatient waiting for Creation," as St. Paul says, "which sighs for the manifestation of the sons of God" (Rm 8:19), that is, their integration into the new order of things established by Christ.

Thus understood, the sacramentals, far from being obsolete and out-of-date practices of a backward religion, seem to us more contemporaty than ever. We live in a world where so many men look on matter as an absolute, where as many men have lost, or have not yet found the meaning of things; or rather, having rediscovered that visible realities have a hidden meaning, do not yet know how to decipher this meaning. To these men who live in anguish for having emptied the universe of God, Christianity brings the most soothing response. By means of its sacramentalism, it is the most contemporary response to their anxieties and needs. It says to them, on the one hand, that matter is not an absolute. Yet, by saying to them, on the other hand, that material realities have tremendous meaning, that they are at the same time signs which reveal God and a way which leads to Him, Christianity, far from condemning matter and values stemming from it, as well as the advances of science and technology, as contrary to the spiritual, life, is a consecration, a divinization of the material world.

This consecration of the world to God is realized, above all, by the Eucharist. This affirmation does not date with Teilhard de Chardin and his *Messe sur le monde*. It is a traditional truth. Already in the second century, St. Ireneaus expressed it by presenting the Eucharist as the sacrifice of the first fruits by which is effected the return of creation to God. Here are some extracts from this text: "Christ ordained His disciples to offer to God the first fruits of His creatures, not that He needed them, but so that they themselves might be fruitful and productive. He took bread which was part of creation, and He gave thanks saying: 'This is my Body.' Likewise, for the chalice which is part of our created world, He affirmed that it was His Blood, teaching that it was the new offering of the New Testament which Malachy had announced. . . . The Lord is the son of the Creator of the world, that is, His word by which trees bear fruit, streams flow, the land gives, first, the plant, then the ear, and finally the full wheat of the corn. . . . We offer them to God, not as to someone who is in need, but by thanking Him for His power, and by sanctifying His creation."[8]

We can develop this theme in the following way. Material creation, which man turned from God by turning himself from Him, returns to God, entirely, through the eucharistic sacrifice. The bread amd wine which constitute the matter of this sacrifice, are in fact, the two most important elements, in any case, the most common of our nourishment. They are, thus, the most apt to represent and to signify not only all creation, all the material world which has slowly prepared them, but also man's work and life, and man himself. "Just as all material creation, in its secular evolutions and in its slow germinations, prepared the wheat and the fruit of the vine, so it was necessary for men to transform this grape and this wheat through their work into this bread and into this wine which they can consume in their everyday meals," and from which the priest draws the matter for the Eucharist. It can, then, be stated that all human work is, thus, found summarized in this sacrament, if one thinks, above all, of the sum of the relationships and of the exchanges that, in our modern economical diets, one single host and the very small quantity of wine which form the matter of the eucharistic sacrifice imply. That is what the new liturgy of the Mass expresses so felicitously in the words which the priest presents to God bread and wine:

> Blessed are you, God of the Universe,
> You who give us this bread,
> Fruit of the earth and of men's work,
> We present it to you:

It will become the bread of life. . .

Blessed are you, God of the universe,
You who give us this wine,
Fruit of the vine and of men's work,
We present it to you:
It will become the wine of the eternal Kingdom.

So then, all creation, all men's work and efforts—and, consequently, science and technology—are represented through the bread and wine which become the Body and the Blood of the Son of God and are in this body and in this blood, consecrated and offered in thanksgiving and in glory to God.

Moreover, because the bread and wine become Christ's body and blood, they are not only sanctified, but sanctifying. They communicate to us the very source of all life and of all sanctity. Far from being contrary to the material world and the values that it incites, the spiritual life frees them not only by giving them back to their first destiny, but, also, by using them to nourish themselves and to grow. Thanks to the Eucharist, the heavy, opaque and dangerous matter is spiritualized; it changes into the substance of its Creator; it goes to God and, thus, definitively, we also, go to the Father in the Son through the Holy Spirit.

Footnotes

1. *Gaudium et Spes*, no. 2, par. 2.
2. St. Thomas, Ia, q. 96, a. 1 ad. 2.
3 Rideau, *Consécration*, Desclée de Brouwer, Paris, 1945, p. 14.
4. Carré.
5. Cardinal Suhard, *Lettre Pastorale*, Lent of 1949, p. 64.
6. Rom. Martyrology, Dec. 25.
7. Journet, *L'Eglise du Verbe incarné*, 2 vol., Desclée de Brouwer, Paris, 1941, vol. 1: "La hiérarchie apostolique," p. 121.
8. Cf. *Adversus Haer.* IV, 17 nos. 4 and 18, nos. 4-6.

Chapter 14

LIBERATION OF EARTHLY TASKS

As I said in the preceding chapter, there are still too many
Christians who, in order to live according to the Spirit,
believe themselves obliged to neglect all temporal, political,
social, or other activity, and who escape towards eternity by
being disinterested in the works and struggles undertaken by
men of this world for a better organization of the earthly city.
They think that such activities are worldly, foreign, even
detrimental, to their spiritual life.[1] Likewise, modern man
considers Christians as enemies of the temporal life. From
whence this remark of Canon J. Leclercq: "The contemporary world dismisses any preoccupation with the
hereafter; it is like a challenging answer to Christians who
want to save themselves by a kind of preservation of grace,
separated from earthly action, that is, without concern about
working for a better civilized world. The modern mind
responds to it through action in the earthly world, to the
exclusion of orientation toward celestial life. Two ex-
clusives, thus, confront one another to no purpose.
Christianity ought, then, to rehabilitate itself by showing
that preoccupation with the hereafter involves a transforming action on earth since one is Christ's disciple to the
extent that one is united to His love for mankind, and that
this love is manifested by works here below."[2]

Participation of Christians in Earthly Tasks

In fact, the disinterestedness with regard to earthly tasks is not in conformity with the spirit of Christianity. Vatican II spoke of it forcefully in the Constitution on the Church in the world today. It says, "The Council exhorts Christians, citizens of both kingdoms, to fulfill zealously and faithfully their earthly tasks, by letting themselves be led by the spirit of the Gospel. They separate themselves from the truth, those who, knowing that we do not have a lasting city but that we are marching toward the future city, believe to be able because of that, to neglect their human tasks, without noticing that faith itself, taking into account each one's vocation, makes it a very exacting obligation for them (Cf. 2Th 4:6-13; Ep 4:28). They are, no less mistaken, those who, in the opposite direction, believe to be able to give themselves over entirely to earthly activities by acting as if they were complete strangers to their religious life, limiting themselves to the practice of a cult and to some determined moral obligations. The separation between the faith which they claim for themselves and the daily conduct of a great number is to be counted among the most serious errors of our time. Even in the Old Testament, the prophets denounced this scandal vehemently (Cf. Is 58:1-12), and in the New Testament, more forcefully yet, Jesus Christ, Himself, threatened it with serious punishments (Cf. Mt 23:3-23; Mk 7:10-13). Let no one create the artificial opposition between professional and social activities, on the one hand, and religious life, on the other. By failing in his earthly obligations, the Christian fails in his obligations toward his neighbor, even more, toward God Himself, and he places in danger his eternal salvation. Like Christ Who led the life of a worker, let Christians rejoice rather in being able to manage all of their earthly activities by uniting in a vital synthesis all human, domestic, professional, scientific, and technological efforts with religious values under the sovereign order in which everything is coordinated to God's glory."[3]

Good in themselves because desired by God, earthly tasks

have been deviated from their meaning through man's sin which has forced them to direct the world toward man and not toward his Creator. Christ liberated them from this constraint, and abolished, thanks to this liberation, all opposition between religious life and earthly activities, by uniting the spiritual and human life into a vital synthesis.

If, as I have tried to show in preceding chapters, human and temporal values have strict ties with the spiritual life, we ought to conclude that those who wish to live according to the Spirit are not less anxious than other men to try to possess and to care for the world. The spiritual man ought not to be inclined toward possessing God by despising the natural development of humanity in time, as if this development had no value from God's point of view, as if it were something completely unimportant and, perhaps, harmful. "There would be, therein, a serious deviation, a kind of pseudomysticism, which is not in conformity with the Christian idea. . . . To leave men in ignorance, with a lack of culture, in disorder or in an inhuman order, in subjection to the forces of matter, is not compatible with the pursuit of the transcendent end. One can do it in very good faith, but it is still wrong."[4]

Likewise, God has given creation to men so that they can use it to nourish, to clothe, and to shelter themselves, as well as to develop their senses, through their intelligence and all other faculties. They ought to fashion this world which He has created for them. They ought to explore and to improve it, and to put their stamp upon it, to humanize it by integrating it into their life, and to make it, in the very eyes of its Creator, more beautiful than the day they received it from Him. To act thus, is not to retouch or to correct the divine work, it is to lead it to its completion. It proceeds, actually, from many passages of Holy Scripture that the Universe was given to men in a sketchy state with the mission to make it succeed, as is said today: to bring it to its ulitmate destiny. Is not that the meaning of these words of Genesis: "Then God said: 'Let us make man to our image and likeness, and let him dominate the fishes of the sea, the birds of the air, domestic animals and everything on the earth, and all reptiles that crawl on the earth.' And God created the human being to His image; He created him to God's image; man and woman He created him. And God, blessed them and He said to them: 'Increase and multiply, fill the earth and subject it, and dominate the fishes of the sea, the birds of the air, and all animals that move on the earth'?'' (Gn 1:26-28). Is not that, likewise, the meaning of that other statement from the same book: "Yahweh God took man and placed him in the garden. of Eden to cultivate and preserve it?" (Gn 2:15). To this mission confided to humanity in the person of its first representatives—even before their fall, let us note—Sacred Scripture alludes several times. We read, for example, in the Book of Wisdom: "God of our Fathers, Lord of Mercy, who made the Universe by your word and who, by your wisdom, established man to dominate all creatures whom you have made, in order to rule the world in sanctity and justice, and to exercise control in the uprightness of his heart, give me the Wisdom which is seated near your throne" (Ws 9:1-4; cf. Gn 9:2-7; Si 17:1-4).

The following lines of Pius XII, taken from his radio message on Christmas, 1953, attest that that is, indeed, the meaning of the passages of the Bible just quoted: "The believer will find . . . natural to place, alongside of gold, incense, and myrth, offered by the magi to the Infant God, the modern conquests of technology. . . . Furthermore, this offering is like a presentation of the work that He himself commanded once upon a time and which is now fortunately in the process, although not yet completed. People the earth and dominate it, God said to man by confiding to him creation as his temporary allotment. What a long and difficult route from that time to the present when men can, in a certain way, say that they have accomplished God's command!" The liturgy of the mass echoes this teaching of Holy Scripture in the fourth eucharistic prayer: "All Holy Father, we proclaim that you are great and that you created all things with wisdom and through love: you made man to your image and you entrusted to him the universe so that by serving you, his Creator, he reigns over creation."

Now, if man received the mission to dominate the elements of the universe, to till the earth, to perfect the world, it is because the cosmos is the temporal milieu in which he lives and in which he works out his eternal destiny, and it is in order to use it with the intention of developing his imperishable being and to help his brothers to do the same. He was to use this universe in a spirit of gratitude and adoration. We know how, since the first sin, humanity has discharged this mission for his own benefit and for that of him who has conquered it. Man turned creation away from its true meaning. Instead of using it as a means of realizing his temporal and eternal vocation, he installed himself in it as a pleasure seeker with no reference to his Creator. Temporal tasks, too, found themselves, thus, turned away from their final end, and they needed to be liberated from the violence which was thus done to them.

Through His redemptive incarnation, Christ brought about this liberation. By becoming a part of humanity in order to snatch it from egoism and to lead it toward its Creator, Christ, indeed, made him rediscover the meaning of temporal activities and the spirit in which humanity must perform them. Men must work toward the completion of creation, and must consecrate it to God by offering it to him as a sign of adoration and thanksgiving.

Humanity is as much entrusted with this mission as if original sin is not, as we have shown, the cause of the physical evil in the universe; original sin is however responsible in part. In fact, although indirectly, it exposed man to suffering and death, and, by striking his intelligence with ignorance and making his inclinations uncontrolled, led him into error, the cause of so many mishaps and maladies, as well as into the disorders of sensuality and intemperance, the source of so many evils. Now Christ inaugurated by means of His sacrifice the liberation of humanity from all of those consequences of original sin. So men are invited to make this liberation their own by fighting against these consequences, united to the resurrected Christ whose liberating activity is continuous and always present, thanks to "the Spirit that He sent in the service (of the Father) and who follows His work in the world" (fourth eucharistic prayer).

If then the cataclysms and mishaps which are at the root of evil and of suffering are due to the voluntary or involuntary ignorance of laws which regulate the order of physical and moral nature, it is a question of man's defending himself against them by conforming himself to these laws—"one only rules nature by obeying it"—through a better knowledge that he will strive to have of them, because it is necessary "to know in order to foresee, and to foresee in order to act." It is clear indeed that, as Pius XII has remarked, "knowledge of natural laws makes it possible for man to dominate the forces of nature and to put them to his own use in modern technology that is progressing so much."[5]

These advances ought not only to be limited to the field of medicine. It is not sufficient, in fact, for man to work towards fighting misfortunes, sickness, suffering, death; it is also necessary for him to try to better the ordinary conditions of his existence here below, for, temporal values, by procuring good conditions for earthly existence, can favor the spiritual life.

It is a question, then, of causing all sciences to progress so that man can make himself, more and more master of creation, and can master the forces of nature. Likewise, "the great adventure of science," as an eminent Catholic intellectual has said, "is that of the discovery of the laws of the Universe and of the domination of the world. Today this adventure interests the best minds and the most organized heads. Never, at any stage in the evolution of humanity, has an ideal united so many resolute men; never has an ideal subjected to the same asceticism so much genius, so much courage, so much obstinancy, and I think, also that no other adventure has equaled it."[6]

So it is necessary to conquer the Universe, to deliver the soil from its thorns and prickles, to dominate all animals. "It is necessary to come to the aid of the forest, and of the thorn which asks to become a rose. It is necessary to come to the aid of this great stream which asks us to prevent its overflowing, to aid the bird, the brute beast, and all animals according to their kind."[7] It is necessary to fashion matter "created by God" as Pius XII said, "at the beginning of the world and shaped by him through the centuries, in the depths and on the surface of the earth, by means of cataclysms, fermentations, erosions and transformations."[8] It is necessary to prepare the earth by tilling it: "Hail, powerful and subjugated earth!"[9] subjugated by means of the organization which adapts it to human enterprises, by means of the work of transformation which captures all the forces of nature: water power, hertzian waves, nuclear energy. Creation is, as St. Paul says, in childbirth: it carries in its womb "the new heavens and the new earth" of which Scripture speaks. Like an obstetrician, man ought to help it in this gigantic task about which the theory of evolution procures for us such a grandiose vision. It is an exciting and fascinating task for man, which gives him an eminent dignity since it associates him with the creative act by making him complete God's work, and by making it more beautiful than before.

The management of the land ought not to stop there. The domination of the forces of nature is not an end in itself; it ought to serve the construction of the best possible earthly city.

Without a doubt, the true end of earthly life is the preparation of human beings for another life through their participation, in faith in Christ, in the life of God, and not the establishment in this world of the best society possible. However, the supernatural end of man does not come from his natural life. It is necessary, indeed, for him to continue to provide for the immediate needs of this life, and for him to remain capable of looking for cultural wealth and to create a civilization. Now, all that forms part of the divine plan. "God," writes Father de Montcheuil, "created a world which, from the natural, as well as the supernatural point of view, is incomplete, and which comprises possibilities of development in all the levels of the body and of the spirit. On the natural plane, humanity is developed through its own effort, thanks to its work. There are, then, indeed two distinct orders, that can be called the temporal and religious: man and the Christian, the natural and supernatural life do not conceal themselves adequately. It is the same person who is, at the same time, man and Christian. It is not possible to make a complete break between one and the other. There is a perpetual interaction between one and the other."[10] For that reason, if "humanity must tend toward God, it succeeds after this present life, which fact obliges it to lift itself always above the purely temporal plane and to refuse to be content with human values, as with a restrictive absolute. . . . Humanity, in order to attain its end, ought to pursue its natural development in all domains: it ought to be only an ordered, hierarchical development, in harmony with the search for the ultimate end in the hereafter."[11]

Consequently, the spiritual life, far from preventing Christians to collaborate in the construction of a more human world, makes it a pressing duty for them, so much the more pressing that, as I have just remarked, this betterment of human living conditions can create more favorable conditions for this spiritual life itself.

The spiritual man ought then to try to exercise indefatigable zeal on the political, economic and social level. He even ought to become involved in the struggle for the liberation of his brothers from all the oppressions which weigh on them at all levels. Furthermore, by his collaboration in the establishment of an always better world, he will be able to infuse into the public and private structures and institutions, the evangelical ideal of charity, justice, respect for the human person, his dignity, rights, liberties so indispensable for the construction of such a world.

To be sure, the liberation provided by Christ and entrusted to his Church and to the faithful is neither of the political, economic or social order. It is, first of all, of the spiritual order. As Msgr. Ancel has written: "to affirm that Jesus' mission is oriented, above all, to the service of a purely human liberation would constitute a serious error on the level of evangelical interpretation. On the contrary, Jesus says: 'seek, first of all, the kingdom of God and His justice, and the rest will be given to you in addition' " (Mt 6:33).[12] Yet this spiritual liberation ought to be if not preceded at least, accompanied, in any case to be followed, by a temporal liberation. Indeed, this spiritual liberation, as we have seen, implies the liberation of the human person. Now, it could happen that this person finds himself in some conditions of life which oppress and alienate him, and which thus impede his human and spiritual development: oppressions and estrangements precisely in the political, economic and social realms, as well as on the individual and collective level. A work for the earthly liberation of man is then indispensable. It imposed itself on the Church, as the 1971 Synod of Bishops affirmed: "The struggle for justice and the participation in the transformation of the world appear to us clearly as a constitutive dimension of the preaching of the Gospel, which is the mission of the Church for the redemption of humanity and its liberation from every oppressive situation."[13]

This liberating action is imposed, likewise, on every Christian. Jesus Christ, it is true, did not speak of a political involvement as it is understood today. However, he placed men to face squarely their responsibilities, by ordering them to treat each other with justice and love. Now, this commandment demands that all the reasons for injustice, misery, violence, oppression, division, disagreement, discord, revolt and hatred disappear. That is what the French bishops recalled to mind at the time of their plenary session in 1972: "Created to God's image, the most insignificant among men is called to fulfill himself and to accomplish it by participating in the march of humanity. No Christian man nor woman can be at rest as long as one of his brothers is, somewhere, a victim of injustice, oppression or degradation."[14]

That statement does not mean Christianity is only one factor in man's temporal liberation. It is, on the contrary, the indispensable factor. We know, indeed, that the source of all oppressions and alienations is sin understood in its personal and, at the same time collective sense. Sin runs the risk, even, of invalidating the struggle for earthly liberation because this struggle can then be accompanied by violence and hatred. Earthly liberation cannot be accomplished truly and efficaciously except by faith in Jesus Christ Who alone frees man from sin and its consequences.

The above does not mean that temporal liberation is the condition *sine qua non* of spiritual liberation by means of faith in Jesus Christ and of the development of the life of union with Him. It is always possible, in reality, for Christians to lead an authentically Christian life, whatever the conditions of existence are, because he who is animated by a true faith, hope and love uses obstacles, themselves, in order to believe, to hope and to love more. Yet, average men, even sincere Christians, are not always capable of such heroism, and it is not always through heroism that one can begin and persevere in the Christian life. For that reason, the absence, on the part of Christians, of an activity liberating all earthly alienations "constitutes an obstacle to evangelization, either because, overwhelmed by misery, men run the risk of blaspheming God or forgetting him, or because this absence of justice and of fraternity becomes, at times, a counter-witness, especially when the Church seems bound to the powerful and to the rich, who oppress their fellow men."[15]

Collaboration in the Divine Work

Thus, what justifies, in the eyes of the Christians, their participation in earthly tasks, is the fact that these tasks, even those which are the most ordinary, are, in themselves, in conformity with God's plan: they are willed by the Creator for the accomplishment of his Creation; they make men collaborate in the divine work. Vatican II recalled this truth in *Gaudium et Spes*. "For believers," it declared, "one thing is certain: considered in itself, individual and collective human activity, this gigantic effort by which men, all through the ages, work at bettering their living conditions corresponds to God's plan. Man, created in God's image, has, indeed, received the mission to subject the earth and all that it contains, to govern the world in sanctity and justice (Gn 1:26-27; 9:2-3; Ws 9:2-3) and, by recognizing God as Creator of all things, to refer to Him his being as well as the Universe: thus, everything being subject to man, the very name of God is glorified by all the earth (Ps 8:7, 10). This teaching is applicable, also, to the most ordinary activities. Because these men and women who, while earning a living for themselves and for their family, conduct their activities in such a way as to serve society well, they are justified in seeing in their work a continuation of the work of their Creator, a service to their fellow men, a personal contribution to the realization of the plan of providence in history."[16]

This teaching is applicable, also, to another activity which devolves, likewise, upon men, and which corresponds, also, to God's plan, namely: the temporal unification of humanity.

Without a doubt, God's plan is the spiritual unification, in the religious and moral order, of men in Jesus Christ. "God" writes St. Paul, "revealed to us the mystery of his will . . . namely: to reunite all things in Christ." According to St. John, "Jesus had to die . . . in order to bring together in unity all the dispersed children of God." However, alongside of this spiritual unity of men, given freely by God, and supported continuously by Christ and by His Spirit among His members and with their collaboration, there exists a temporal unity in the world, at least, in principle, and as a means of realization.

There is, indeed, in the depth of every human soul, an aspiration towards a great fraternal community which would bring together all men. As far back as one can go in the history of philosophies and of religions, it is stated that the idea of an all as a means of formation has always fascinated the greatest minds and the most beautiful souls. "The world is one family," wrote Confucius, "on this side of the four seas, all are brothers." "We are of the one same family," says a Malgache proverb, "Excavate the earth, it is the same root: Gather everything: it is the same basket." Seneca's famous remark is well-known: "We are members of a large body. Nature has produced us from the same root: nature has placed in us a mutual love; she has formed us sociable. . . . Thus, may this verse of Terence be in our heart and on our lips: 'I am a man, and I think that nothing human is a stranger to me.' "

Human unity flows, then, from the fact that all men have a common origin and an equality of nature.

In our day, this aspiration of human nature is expressed in the very current ideas of fraternity, of community, of syndicalism, socialism, communism, of a Society of nations, of united states, of united nations, of internationalism, of federalism, etc.

So, then, if we examine the tendencies of men's minds and hearts at the present time, as in the past, we discover, through the multiplicity of concepts and the divergence of systems in which they are expressed, the desire and the search for a certain union, truly, of a certain unity. Indeed, such was the order that God wanted to establish in humanity, an order where men were invited to unite themselves by loving each other with a love analogous to that which is in the bosom of the Blessed Trinity where the three Persons are all love, each one for the other two, and they are, thus, blended, without being confused, into the indivisible unity of the divine nature. Will not Christ say, when speaking of men: "Father, that they may be one, as you and I are one." If this unity of love, which was willed by God for men, has been compromised by the sin of the first man, even destroyed, so to speak, in its beginnings by the germs of disaggregation that this sin placed there, humanity does not continue, as we just saw, to work less, consciously or not—and whatever appearances lead one sometimes, and even often, to believe—prompted by this desire and this need for unity. The incurable nostalgia for the original order overcomes!

Men tried to satisfy this longing—rooted in human nature and the human will—for a great fraternal community which would gather together mankind. The undertaking of the tower of Babel is a typical attempt of these efforts. As we know, when men became sufficiently numerous, they attempted to establish the world's unity: they constructed the famous tower of Babel whose meaning was that it could serve to bring humanity together from then on. Having wanted to achieve this unity by themselves and without reference to God, their attempt failed miserably, and was settled by the division of peoples and the confusion of tongues.

Our contemporaries hope to realize one day this fraternal community by rational and scientific means. Now this task, which has become more urgent in our days because of the development of sciences and technology, can not leave Christians indifferent, who want to live according to the Spirit, under the pretext that this task has no relationship to the spiritual life. Indeed, even if "the unity of the Church is not, of itself, linked to the unity of the world," they have the obligation, as sons of the Church, and under the jurisdiction of man's world, to aspire resolutely to the encounter of this unity which is sought with the divine unity which awaits it."[17]

Undoubtedly, the Church would remain one and complete, even if humanity remained dispersed, and a unification of the world without God could not, in any way, destroy the unity of the Church in her divine consistency. However, he who sees, on the one hand, only such a unification, could hinder and, even, prevent the establishment of the religious and moral unity in humanity. On the other hand, if it is possible to organize the world without God and without Christ, and thus, without the Church, man can only, after all, organize it against himself, and such an organization is doomed fatally to the same failure as the tower of Babel. For that reason, the Church, as Pope Pius XII stated, rejects "this false and narrow conception of her spirituality and of her interior life, which would want to confine it, blind and mute, in the retreat of the sanctuary. The Church cannot lock herself inert in the secret of her Churches, and, thus, forsake the mission which divine Providence had confided to her, to form the whole man, and, thus, to collaborate unceasingly in establishing the foundation of society and to build the powerful framework of the human community."[18]

Now, if it belongs to the hierarchy to play the role which comes back to it by teaching the essential conditions and the necessary foundations for the temporal unification of the world, it belongs to the faithful to realize these conditions and to establish these foundations, practically.

However, it is a unity by the construction of which they ought to begin, that they are, furthermore, forced to realize, in every respect, and which will help them to build, with their fellow men, the other unity. This is the unity of Catholics of all nations, the supranational unity.

Of course, this unity ought not to be limited only to Catholics; it ought to be open to our separated Christian brothers and to our unbelieving brothers; it ought to be eucumenical and missionary.

The spiritual man ought to do more: to bring to the temporal unification of the world a direct participation. He ought to do it so that the universal unification, for which his fellow men work, is a unification in Jesus Christ, by giving to the unity of the world a meaning, a value, a soul, all the while knowing well, I repeat, that the unity of the Church is not, of itself, linked to this unity.

The two most important factors of this unification are, it seems to me, the economic linking, or unification, and technical progress.

The economic unification causes people's destinies to be in a reciprocal dependence to a degree which exceeded, by far, all that had been seen up to that time. Thus dependence imposes upon these peoples, as an indispensable condition for their survival, association, federalism. Likewise, countless are the structures of economic collaboration which have been and continue to be created a little in all directions. From such undertakings, reconciliations among men are brought about; they, thus, collaborate in the temporal unification of humanity.

For its part, the development of technology has introduced, so to speak, a narrowing of the planet by bringing together equally, in time and space, all peoples and continents, favoring, thus this same unification.

So, the economic link and technical progress result in activities which correspond well to the design of God Who desires men's spiritual unity. Now, I repeat, men's spiritual unification can be facilited by their temporal unity.

If it is so, Christians ought not, under the pretext of being spiritual men, to scorn, nor even, to abandon—to speak only of it—technical activity and its productions. On the contrary, they ought to be the first to promote new conditions of work and of life created by the technicians. Furthermore, these conditions, in addition to their favoring greatly the world's unity, bring to millions of human beings a true freedom by liberating them from an onerous servitude which deprives them of all existence, proper to their professional task.

As I have already said, it is true that these new conditions can seriously harm man and humanity. For that reason, I have, likewise, said, by quoting Bergson, that the modern world needs a "supplement of the soul." "It is the duty," writes Louis de Broglie, "of those who have the mission to be spiritual or intellectual guides of humanity to work to awaken in humanity this supplement of the soul." These are the conditions demanded of Christians under which they can welcome and favor technical civilization, if they wish to be spiritual men: to acquire a supplement of the soul, in order to avoid, by means of a theoretical and practical affirmation of man's primacy over the machine, and of the spiritual over matter, so that man is not dehumanized, or that his spirit is not psychologically extrapolated or materialized by technology.

technology.

Here is, also, the obligation that is demanded of Christians: that they become involved resolutely in the progress of science and in the development of its technical application, because, if it is necessary and urgent to work to awaken in man and in humanity a supplement of the soul, this mission is incumbent, above all, upon those who have, as master and model, Him Who created the highest spiritual and moral values, He Who has pledged to man and to humanity the truest and the most profound respect, by giving witness to them of the most disinterested and most complete love. Love! That is, indeed, the only force that can bring about the unity of the world, whose technical realizations are a mysterious and providential instrument. Love is "the energy, powerful enough to unite without depersonalizing."[19]

Now, this love which, alone, is capable of surmounting all the obstacles of races and of cultures, can only be charity or to speak as St. Paul, "divine love poured into hearts through the Holy Spirit." It is, then necessary that those who live by this Spirit are present to the world alongside other men in order to tell them that, if they really wish to realize the unity of mankind, they must turn to the Spirit who, on Pentecost, began to help rediscover in men the unity lost by the sin of Babel. They must, also, tell them that the Holy Spirit, the Spirit of love can only bring about this unity by means of the Cross. It is only by placing Christ's cross in the heart of humanity, that is, by freeing men from their egoisms, their hatreds, their chauvinisms, their sectarisms, their individualisms, their particularities, their closed nationalities, their imperialisms, that the Holy Spirit can open the only way possible for the world's unity and the communion of all men in love, by means of their union with Jesus Christ, our Lord.

Thus, the spiritual life is not incompatible with earthly tasks; it ought not to make Christians fugitives of the present time, men of another world. Christians can become involved in temporal activities without harming their religious life.

Better still: it flows from what I have just said that they ought to, in the very name of this life and in continuance with it.

No Opposition between the Spiritual Life and Earthly Activities

Even better still: thanks to their liberation by Christ's Spirit, Who has reintegrated them, as we have seen, into God's redemptive plan, earthly tasks can be accomplished by Christians without its being at the price of a kind of interior division, of a dichotomy between their spiritual and their professional life. On the contrary, Christians can unite them in a vital synthesis because, by working for the betterment of the world, they work for the completion of the Kingdom of God.

Indeed, as a result of fundamental ideas of the Bible, creation has been effected by the Word of God, Jesus Christ, and as a function of Him. Jesus Christ is its principle and end. "All has been made by Him," affirms St. John, by identifying with Christ, "the Word" pre-existing eternally in God, the Word (or the Wisdom) of God that the Old Testament shows us as being the action of God, His creative energy, Who from the beginning of time, has made creation from nothing, Who has organized it progressively, and Who continues to exert Himself in order to move it from within toward its perfection.

St. Paul develops this concept of the world to its completion. Christ, he says "is the image of the invisible God, the first born of all creation; it is in Him that all has been created in heaven as on earth, things visible as well as invisible. . . . All has been created by and for Him. He was before everything and each thing subsists in Him" (Col 1:15-17). A bit farther on, he says that God's plan is "to restore all in Christ, whatever is in heaven as well as on earth" (Col 1:20). Furthermore, he states that, if Christ ascended into heaven and is seated at the right hand of the Father, it is "in order to fill up all things" (Ep 4:10), and that, at the end of the world, "when all things will have been submitted to Him, then the Son Himself will submit to Him who will have everything submitted to Him, so that God may be all in all" (1 Cor 15:28). While waiting, "all creation aspires to this end, groaning until that day, in the pains of childbirth" (Rm 8:19-22), the birth of "the new heavens and the new earth," the "Kingdom of God" finally universally established forever, the "Body of Christ" arrived at the fullness of His age and of His stature (Cf. Ep 4:13-16).

This Christian vision of the world, contained in revealed doctrine, but whose study has not been sufficiently probed in depth up to the present time because of extremely limited and imperfect ideas of the universe, has just increased in value through the results of contemporary science, which results have given it a remarkable comfirmation, as Teilhard de Chardin has shown so well. In this vision, in fact, is found remarkably reconciled the new concept that the present perspectives of science have substituted for the ancient ptolemaic and static concept of our ancestors. Doesn't the idea of a universe in expansion fit in with the Pauline idea of creation in childbirth? Of the Kingdom in the process of being established? The evolution of the universe, its progressive ascent from matter and by passing through life, towards conscience and towards spirit, and the ascent of the latter towards an individual universal spirit which would assume, by completing them, all the particular individual spirits, doesn't it coincide with the building of Christ's Body, of the Christ of St. Paul, principle and end of all things, the "head" who ought to sum up everything in him? Are we not allowed "to see, in this Universe where the bodies of the elect immerse their roots, the matter from which is formed Christ's Body, whose members they are, and which develops to the fullness of His age?" This Universe in progressive formation, this Cosmogenesis, in Teilhard de Chardin's words, which is realized before our eyes, after having been discovered, following its principal axis, Biogenesis, then, Noogenesis, would culminate in Christogenesis.

In this perspective, there is no opposition nor separation

between God and the world, nor tension among earthly occupations which absorb the largest part of the day and rare moments when man turns himself truly in adoration and with love toward God. The Christians' earthly tasks acquire a new value. They are valuable only because of the intention which animates them and and makes them meritorious: their value does not come solely from the fact that they are accomplished for the love of God and through obedience to His will. Their value comes, also, from the fact that they cooperate in the completion of the world, which is the support on which is built Christ's Body, thus, from the fact that they are really finalized through Christ and through God. Consequently, Christians can be interested in earthly tasks for themselves; they can be devoted to scientific research, to the conquest of natural energies, as well as politics, economic and social progress, to everything that contributes to bettering the world, since, by that very fact, these different activities are finally oriented toward the realization of the total Christ, the coming of the Kingdom. Wildiers has expressed the idea very well in his work devoted to Teilhard de Chardin. Let us quote two passages: "Aspiration to union with God and faith in our divine destiny no longer turn us away from our earthly tasks; they do not separate us from the work that we must accomplish in this world. Quite the contrary! Christ's love becomes the great source of inspiration of our activity, even on the temporal level, because we know that this work is necessary and directed interiorly toward Christ. . . . Far from distracting us from the earthly task or favoring indifference with regard to men's work, Christianity, well-understood, will, indeed, mean, on the contrary, an unequaled and unsurpassed stimulant for accomplishing fittingly our earthly tasks, and will bestow on every human effort its most lofty consecration."[20]

". . . In this light, then, the life of the Christian acquires a profound and organic unity in its earthly dimension, as well as, in its heavenly. In this perspective, it becomes possible for him to be oriented entirely toward God, and at the same time, to be devoted with all his strength to the progress of the world. From this angle, it becomes possible to love the earth without betraying our heavenly vocation. Formerly, there seemed to be only two geometrically possible attitudes for man: to love heaven or earth. Now, in the new space, a third way is discovered: to attain heaven by means of earth: There is a (true) communion with God by means of the World."[21]

The Christian who wishes to live according to the Spirit must not, then, be afraid to be present to the world and its tasks. This presence ought, even, to become for him an obligation, since to be present to the world, is to work with God for the completion of creation, but, also, for the coming of His kingdom, and this task accomplished with love will cause his personal spiritual life to grow.

May this magnificent Christian concept of earthly activity, by allowing Christians to unite "in a vital synthesis all their human, family, professional, scientific and technical efforts, with religious values under the sovereign ordinance by which values all is coordinated to God's glory," appease their conscience up to that time torn between the call to a profound spiritual life and the service of the earthly city! May it also incite them to become more resolutely and more fully involved in the unselfish service of the world! Such is what we ought to repeat, above all, to the young who are beginning.

From what I have just said, we ought to conclude that one should not place in opposition spiritual men and men of action. It is known that Bergson was struck vividly by the exceptional efficaciousness in the activity of those spiritual men, par excellence, the mystics. If Bergson saw correctly, if the mystics, as history proves, are the most lucid and the most efficient men of action while their vocation is to work in the temporal domain, nothing is more desirable than, in the world of today and in all the sectors of activity of this world (cultural, political, civic, juridical, economic, social, scientific, technical, industrial, agricultural, journalistic) there arise men and women who, becoming involved in living an authentic spiritual life, live in the intimacy of God, and allow themselves to be moved by His Spirit. They perform these activities not so much as Christians, but as Christians with competence and loyalty, with a genuine incorruptibility, a great taste for life, action, creation, risk, adventure, not as a game, but in the way of redemption, with the virtue of justice and of indignation, if necessary, the virtue of munificence, a just optimism which causes one to love the temporal while being aware of the presence of sin in the world.

Vatican II's Constitution on the Church in the world today contains a page which illustrates admirably what I wanted to express in this chapter: "The Word of God, by whom all has been made, became Himself flesh and came to dwell on men's earth. The perfect Man, He entered into the history of the world, assuming it and recapitulating it in Him. . . . Become Savior by His resurrection, Christ, to Whom all power has been given in heaven and on earth (Mt 28:18), acts from then on in men's hearts through the power of His Spirit. He arouses not only the desire of future ages, but, also, animates, purifies and fortifies those generous aspirations which drive the human family to better his living conditions, and to submit to this end the entire world. Of course, the gifts of the Spirit are diverse: while He calls some to give witness openly to the desire for the heavenly kingdom and to guard vividly this witness in the human family, He calls others to dedicate themselves to the earthly service of men, preparing by this ministry the matter of the kingdom of heaven. However, in all, He makes men free so that, renouncing self-love and gathering together all earthly energies for human life, they march toward the future, towards that time when humanity, itself, will become a pleasing offering to God. We do not know the time of the end of the world and of humanity (Ac 1:7); we do not know the mode of transformation of the Cosmos. Certainly, the face of this world, deformed by sin (1Cor 7:31),[22] vanishes, but, as we have learned, God is preparing for us a new dwelling and a new earth where justice (2Cor 2:9; 2P3:13) will reign and whose blessedness will fulfill and surpass all the desires for peace, which fill man's heart (1Cor 2:9; Rv 21:4-5). Thus, death having been conquered, the sons of God will arise in Christ, and what was sown in weakness and corruption will put on incorruptibility (1Cor 15:42, 53). Charity and its deeds will remain (1Cor 13:8; 3:14), and all this creation that God has made for man will be delivered from the slavery of vanity (Rm 8:19-21). Indeed, we know well that it serves man for nothing to win the universe if he ends up by losing himself (Lk 9:25). Yet, the expectation of the new earth, far from weakening in us the concern for cultivating this earth, ought, rather, to awaken it: the body of the new human family grows there, which body offers already some rough draft of the time to come. For that reason, it is necessary to distinguish carefully the earthly progress of the growth of Christ's kingdom. This progress has a great deal of importance for God's kingdom, to the degree that it can contribute to a better organization of human society.[23] Those values of dignity, of fraternal union and of liberty, all excellent fruits of our nature and of our efforts, that we will have propagated on earth, according to the Lord's commandment and in His Spirit, will be rediscovered by us later; they will be purified of all stain, illuminated, transfigured, while Christ will restore to His Father 'an eternal and universal kingdom: the kingdom of truth and of life, the kingdom of sanctity and of grace, the kingdom of justice, of love and of peace.'[24] Mysteriously, the kingdom is already present on this earth; it will attain its perfection when the Lord comes.''[25]

I shall conclude by responding to an objection that I cannot avoid. I belong to a state of life obviously opposed to the openmindedness that Vatican II wishes Christians to take with regard to the world of today. Isn't the monastic state a kind of life deliberately separated from the world? It seems, then, that it is outmoded, out-of-date, that it is, at any rate, hardly compatible, if not contradictory, to the directions given by the Council especially in the Constitution *Gaudium et Spes*. Not at all. The passage from this Constitution, which I quoted last, contains a short sentence which is brief, and runs the risk of being overlooked. Nevertheless, it is a solemn affirmation of the usefulness, indeed, of the constant and, now, more than ever, importance of the monastic life. The conciliar text declares that the Holy Spirit "calls certain ones to witness openly to the desire for the heavenly kingdom, and to keep alive this witness in the human family." This witness is given precisely by religious, especially by contemplatives, and even more so, by monks who have as their particular role to do so. In the midst of today's world, the monks are witnesses of the future world. Indeed, for those who are busy completing creation by means of the conquest of the universe and the disposition of the earthly City, the danger is to obtain so much satisfaction from it that they run the risk of forgetting the heavenly Kingdom for which the earthly one ought to prepare, and towards which they ought to conduct themselves. Monks remind men that, as St. Paul says, "we have not here a lasting city, but we search for the one to come." They help those who work for the construction of the earthly Kingdom in order to maintain its orientation toward the heavenly one which is its end; to prepare, by the completion of creation, "the matter of the kingdom of the heavens." This is what the same Council had already affirmed solemnly in its most important document, the Constitution on the Church, *Lumen Gentium*: "No one ought to think that, by their consecration, religious become strangers to men or useless in the earthly Kingdom. If they are not always directly present alongside of their contemporaries (and that is especially the case of monks, by definition, separated from the world), they are present more profoundly to them in the heart of Christ, cooperating spiritually with them so that the construction of the earthly Kingdom might always have its foundation in the Lord, and might be oriented towards Him."

Footnotes

1. In a speech given November 1, 1966, on "the role of the Christian in political life," his Eminence Cardinal Zoungrana, Archbishop of Ouagadougou, quoted, without stating the author, these words: "Because they have been put on their guard against political passions which destroy, or compromises which await men in authority, certain Catholics have, for a long time, been unaware of, disparaged or ran away from political involvements, and have not become involved under the pretext of keeping themselves evangelical. It is as if Christ had not stipulated to "render to Caesar what belongs to Caesar!" (In *Documentation Catholique*, Dec. 18, 1966, co. 2.167).
2. J. Leclercq, *Penser chrétiennement notre temps*, Téqui, Paris, 1951, p. 77.
3. *Gaudium et Spes*, no. 43, par. 1.
4. Y. de Montcheuil, *Aspect de l'Eglise*, Cerf. Paris, 1949, p. 142.
5. Pius XII, talk to the Pontifical Academy of Science, Feb. 8, 1948.
6. Leprince-Ringuet, "L'Aventure existe-t-elle encore?", *Elites francaises*, June 1949, p. 3.
7. Claudel, *L'Annonce faite a Marie*, Gallimard, Paris, 1949.
8. Discours aux travailleurs italiens, Pentecost, 1943.
9. Claudel, *L'Annonce faite a Marie*, Act IV, sc. 2.
10. Y. de Montcheuil, *Aspects de l'Eglise*, p. 141.
11. *Ibid*, p. 142.
12. "Libération de l'homme et salut par la foi en Jesus-Christ," *Doc. Cath.*, June 3, 1973, no. 1633, p. 534.
13. *Doc. Cath.* Jan. 2, 1972, no. 1600, p. 12.
14. *Doc. Cath.* Nov. 19, 1972, no. 1620, p. 1011.
15. Msgr. Ancel, *op. cit.*, p. 536.
16. John XXIII, *Pacem in Terris*, p. 297, no. 34, par. 1 and 2.
17. Cardinal Feltin, "L'Unité dans l'Eglise," *Lettre pastorale*, 1952 Lahure, Paris, 1952, p. 11.
18. Pius XII, Address at the Consistory, Feb. 20, 1946.
19. Teilhard de Chardin.
20. N.M. Wildiers, *Teilhard de Chardin*, Ed Universitaires, Paris, 1961, p. 113.
21. Teilhard de Chardin, *Christologie et Evolution*, p. 12, in *op. cit.*, p. 114.
22. St. Ireneaus, *Adversus haereses*, V, 36, P.G., VIII, 1221.
23. Pius XI, encycl. *Quadragesimo anno*: A.A.S., XXIII (1031), p. 207.
24. Preface of the feast of Christ the King.
25. *Gaudium et Spes*, no. 38, par. 1; 39, par. 1-3.